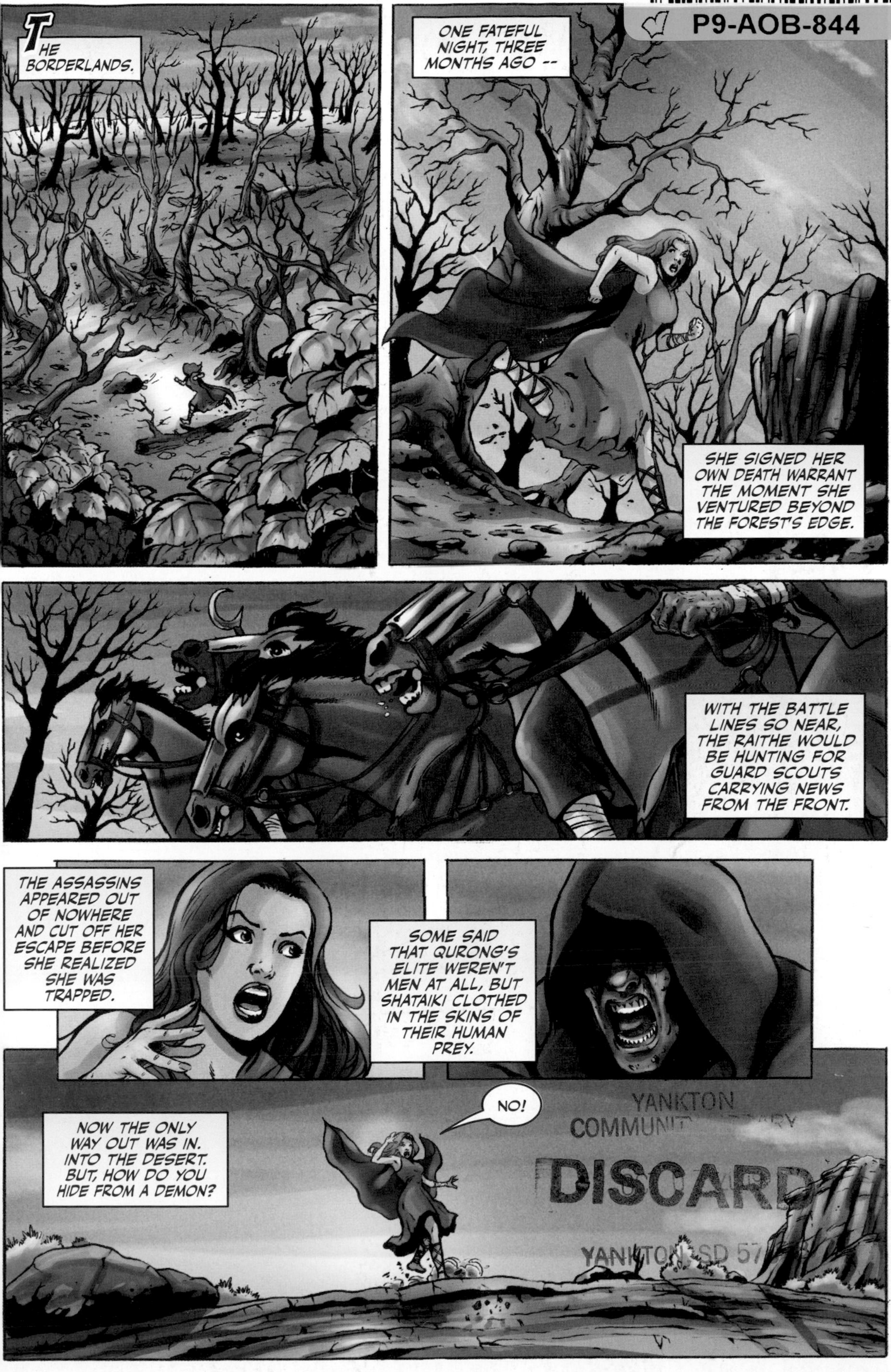
THE BORDERLANDS.
ONE FATEFUL NIGHT, THREE MONTHS AGO --
SHE SIGNED HER OWN DEATH WARRANT THE MOMENT SHE VENTURED BEYOND THE FOREST'S EDGE.
WITH THE BATTLE LINES SO NEAR, THE RAITHE WOULD BE HUNTING FOR GUARD SCOUTS CARRYING NEWS FROM THE FRONT.
THE ASSASSINS APPEARED OUT OF NOWHERE AND CUT OFF HER ESCAPE BEFORE SHE REALIZED SHE WAS TRAPPED.
SOME SAID THAT QURONG'S ELITE WEREN'T MEN AT ALL, BUT SHATAIKI CLOTHED IN THE SKINS OF THEIR HUMAN PREY.
NOW THE ONLY WAY OUT WAS IN. INTO THE DESERT. BUT, HOW DO YOU HIDE FROM A DEMON?
NO!

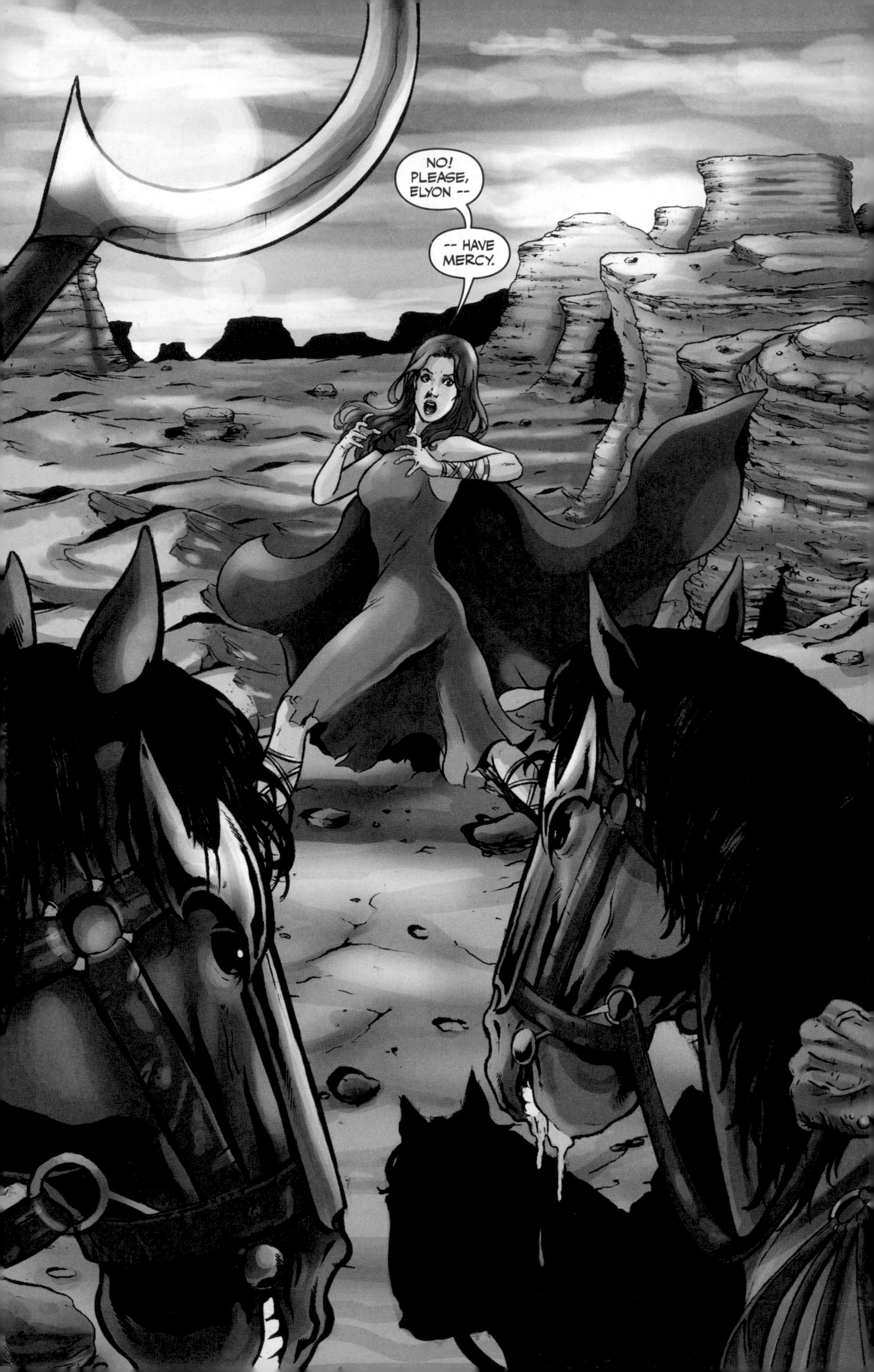
NO! PLEASE, ELYON --
-- HAVE MERCY.

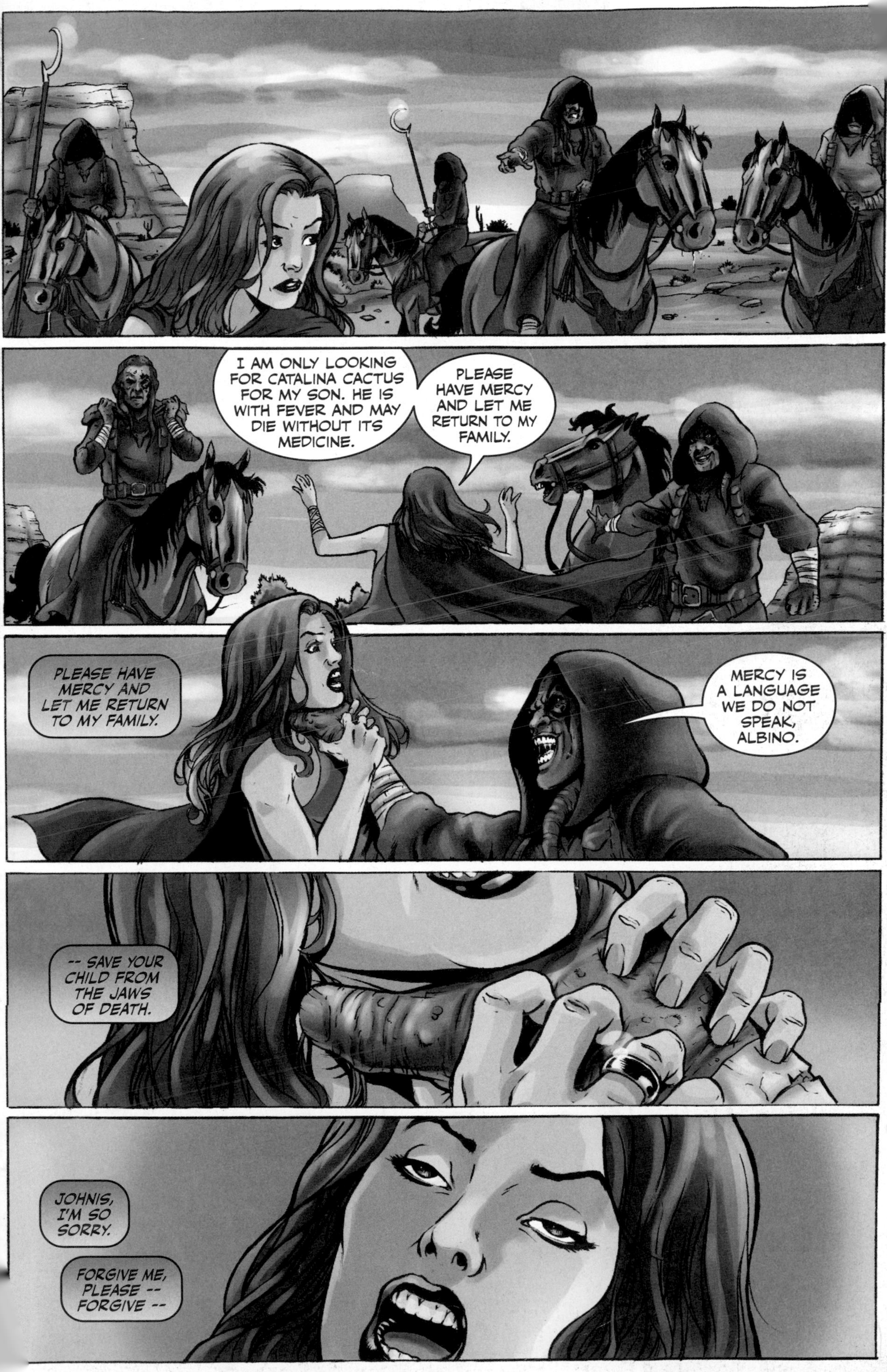
I AM ONLY LOOKING FOR CATALINA CACTUS FOR MY SON. HE IS WITH FEVER AND MAY DIE WITHOUT ITS MEDICINE.
PLEASE HAVE MERCY AND LET ME RETURN TO MY FAMILY.
PLEASE HAVE MERCY AND LET ME RETURN TO MY FAMILY.
MERCY IS A LANGUAGE WE DO NOT SPEAK, ALBINO.
-- SAVE YOUR CHILD FROM THE JAWS OF DEATH.
JOHNIS, I'M SO SORRY.
FORGIVE ME, PLEASE -- FORGIVE --

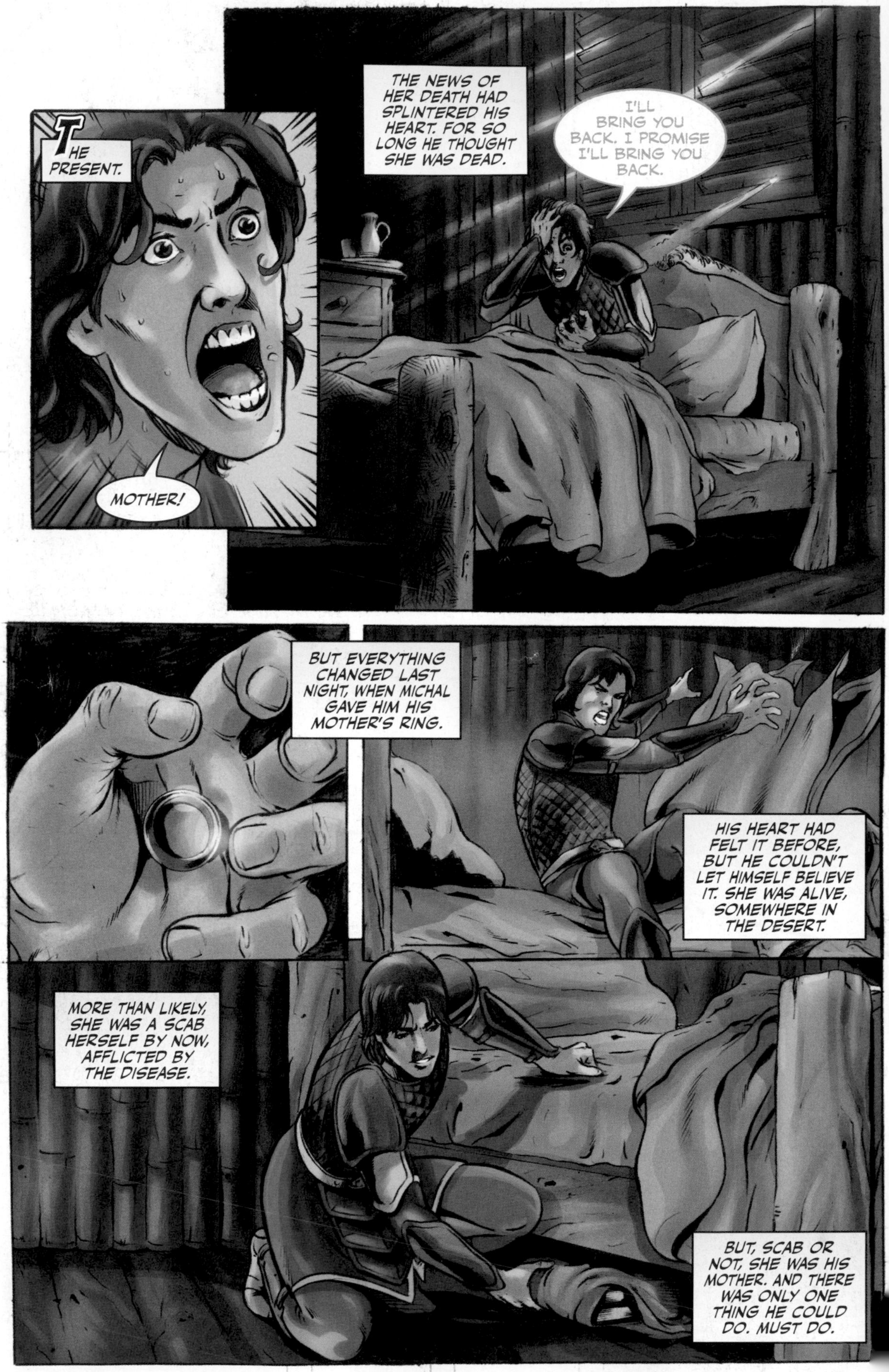
THE PRESENT.
MOTHER!
THE NEWS OF HER DEATH HAD SPLINTERED HIS HEART. FOR SO LONG HE THOUGHT SHE WAS DEAD.
I'LL BRING YOU BACK. I PROMISE I'LL BRING YOU BACK.
BUT EVERYTHING CHANGED LAST NIGHT, WHEN MICHAL GAVE HIM HIS MOTHER'S RING.
HIS HEART HAD FELT IT BEFORE, BUT HE COULDN'T LET HIMSELF BELIEVE IT. SHE WAS ALIVE, SOMEWHERE IN THE DESERT.
MORE THAN LIKELY, SHE WAS A SCAB HERSELF BY NOW, AFFLICTED BY THE DISEASE.
BUT, SCAB OR NOT, SHE WAS HIS MOTHER. AND THERE WAS ONLY ONE THING HE COULD DO. MUST DO.

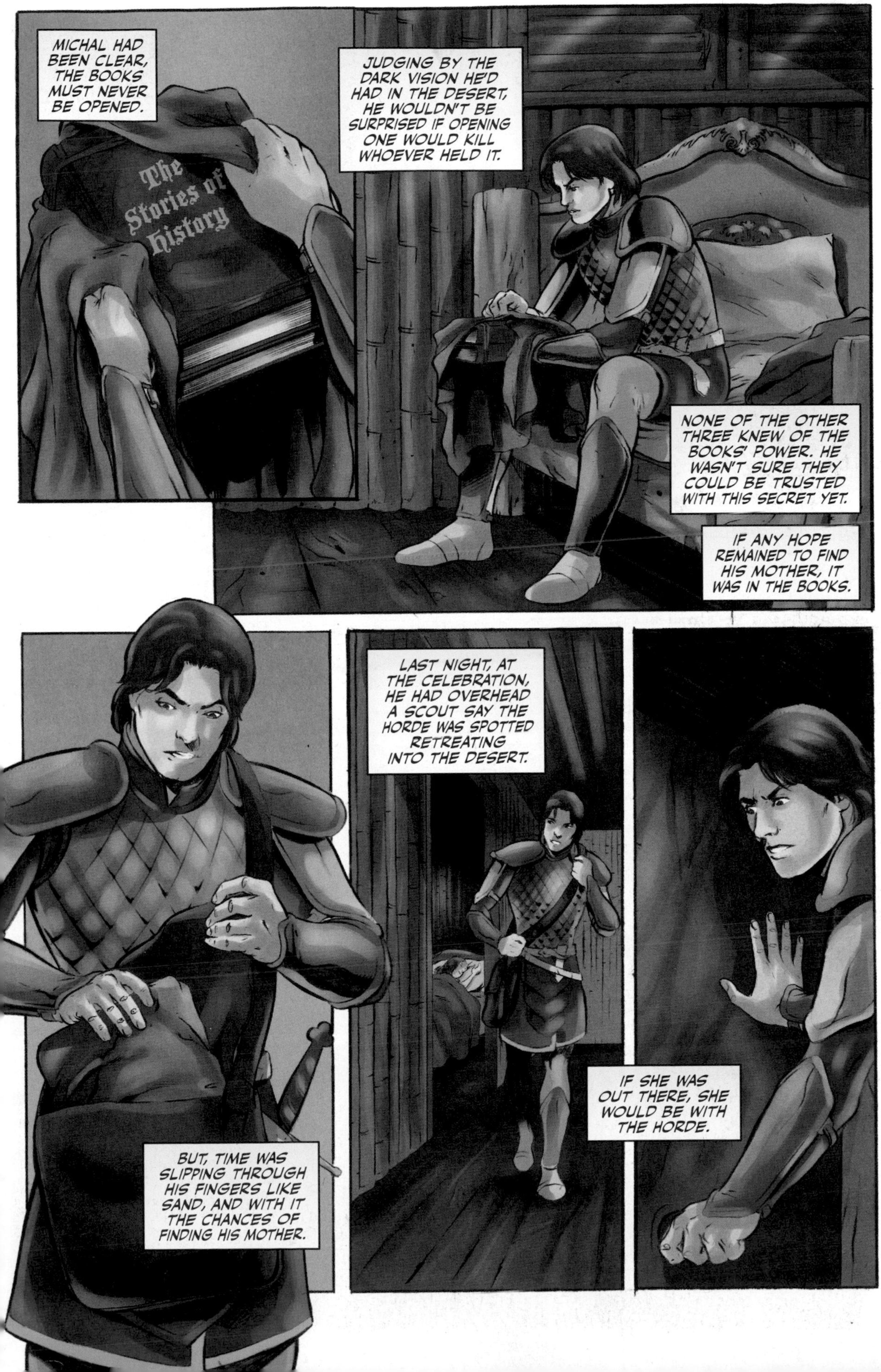
MICHAL HAD BEEN CLEAR, THE BOOKS MUST NEVER BE OPENED.
The Stories of History
JUDGING BY THE DARK VISION HE'D HAD IN THE DESERT, HE WOULDN'T BE SURPRISED IF OPENING ONE WOULD KILL WHOEVER HELD IT.
NONE OF THE OTHER THREE KNEW OF THE BOOKS' POWER. HE WASN'T SURE THEY COULD BE TRUSTED WITH THIS SECRET YET.
IF ANY HOPE REMAINED TO FIND HIS MOTHER, IT WAS IN THE BOOKS.
BUT, TIME WAS SLIPPING THROUGH HIS FINGERS LIKE SAND, AND WITH IT THE CHANCES OF FINDING HIS MOTHER.
LAST NIGHT, AT THE CELEBRATION, HE HAD OVERHEAD A SCOUT SAY THE HORDE WAS SPOTTED RETREATING INTO THE DESERT.
IF SHE WAS OUT THERE, SHE WOULD BE WITH THE HORDE.

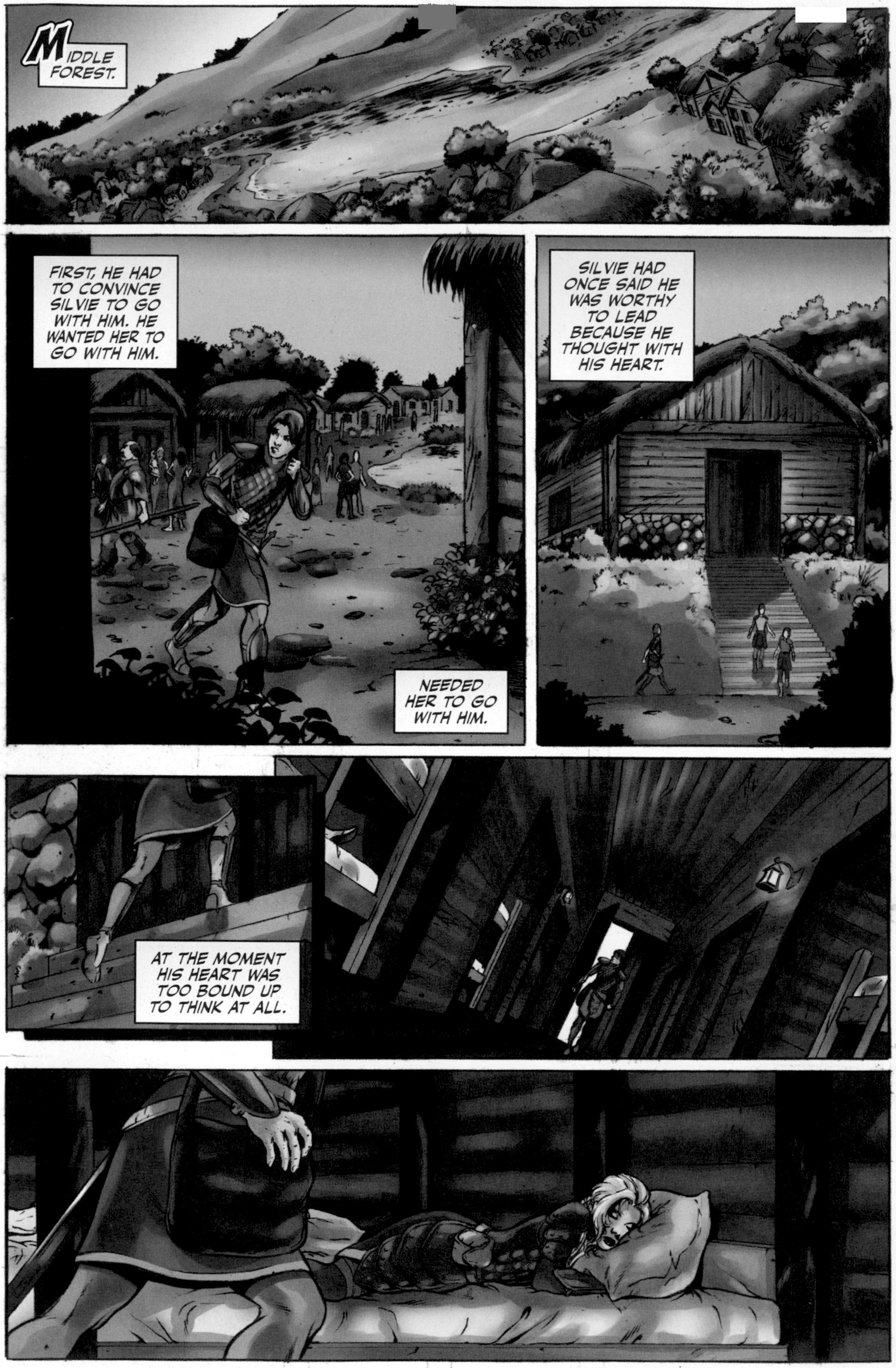
MIDDLE FOREST.
FIRST, HE HAD TO CONVINCE SILVIE TO GO WITH HIM. HE WANTED HER TO GO WITH HIM.
NEEDED HER TO GO WITH HIM.
SILVIE HAD ONCE SAID HE WAS WORTHY TO LEAD BECAUSE HE THOUGHT WITH HIS HEART.
AT THE MOMENT HIS HEART WAS TOO BOUND UP TO THINK AT ALL.

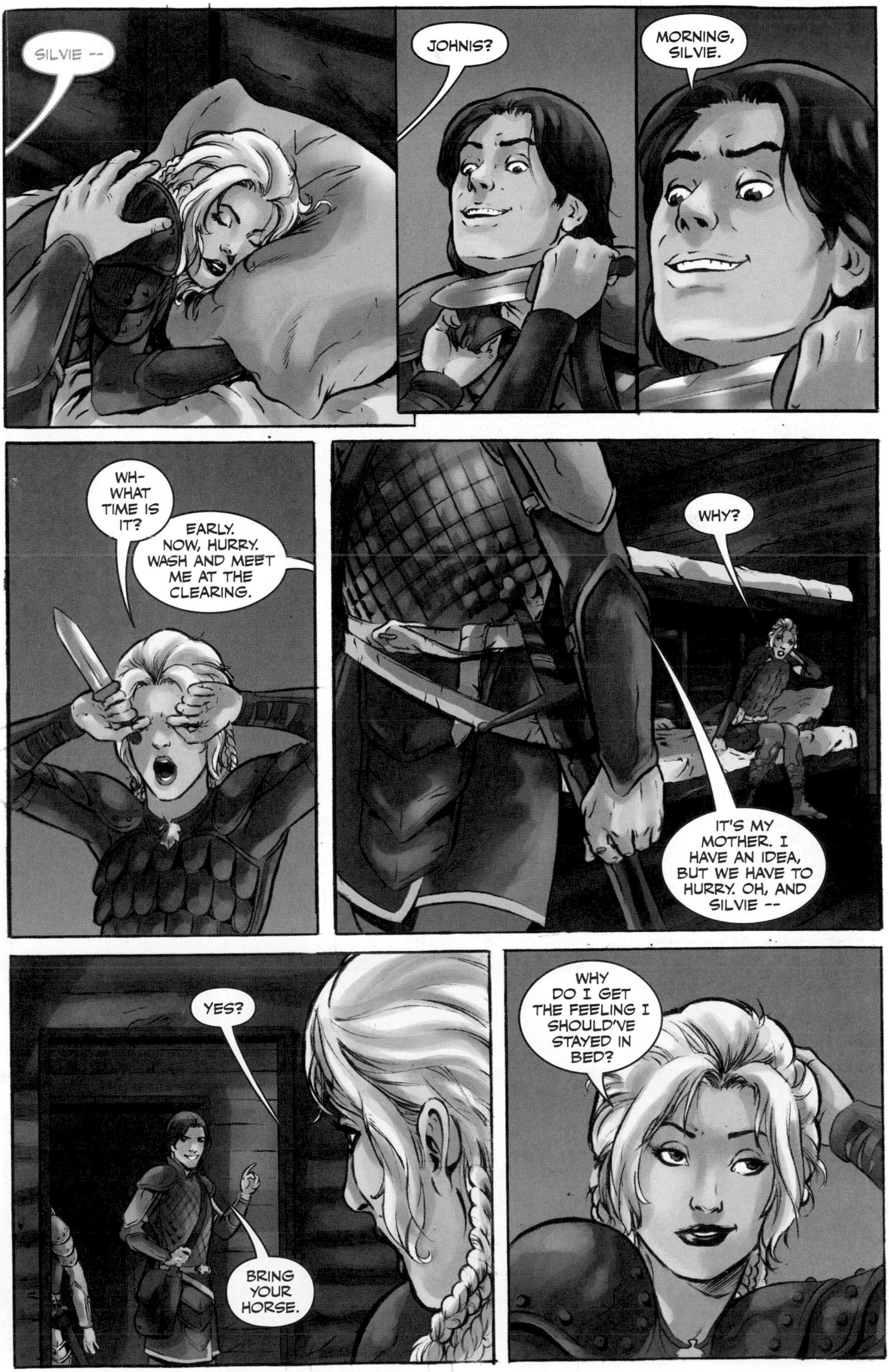
SILVIE --
JOHNIS?
MORNING, SILVIE.
WH- WHAT TIME IS IT?
EARLY. NOW, HURRY. WASH AND MEET ME AT THE CLEARING.
WHY?
IT'S MY MOTHER. I HAVE AN IDEA, BUT WE HAVE TO HURRY. OH, AND SILVIE --
YES?
BRING YOUR HORSE.
WHY DO I GET THE FEELING I SHOULD'VE STAYED IN BED?

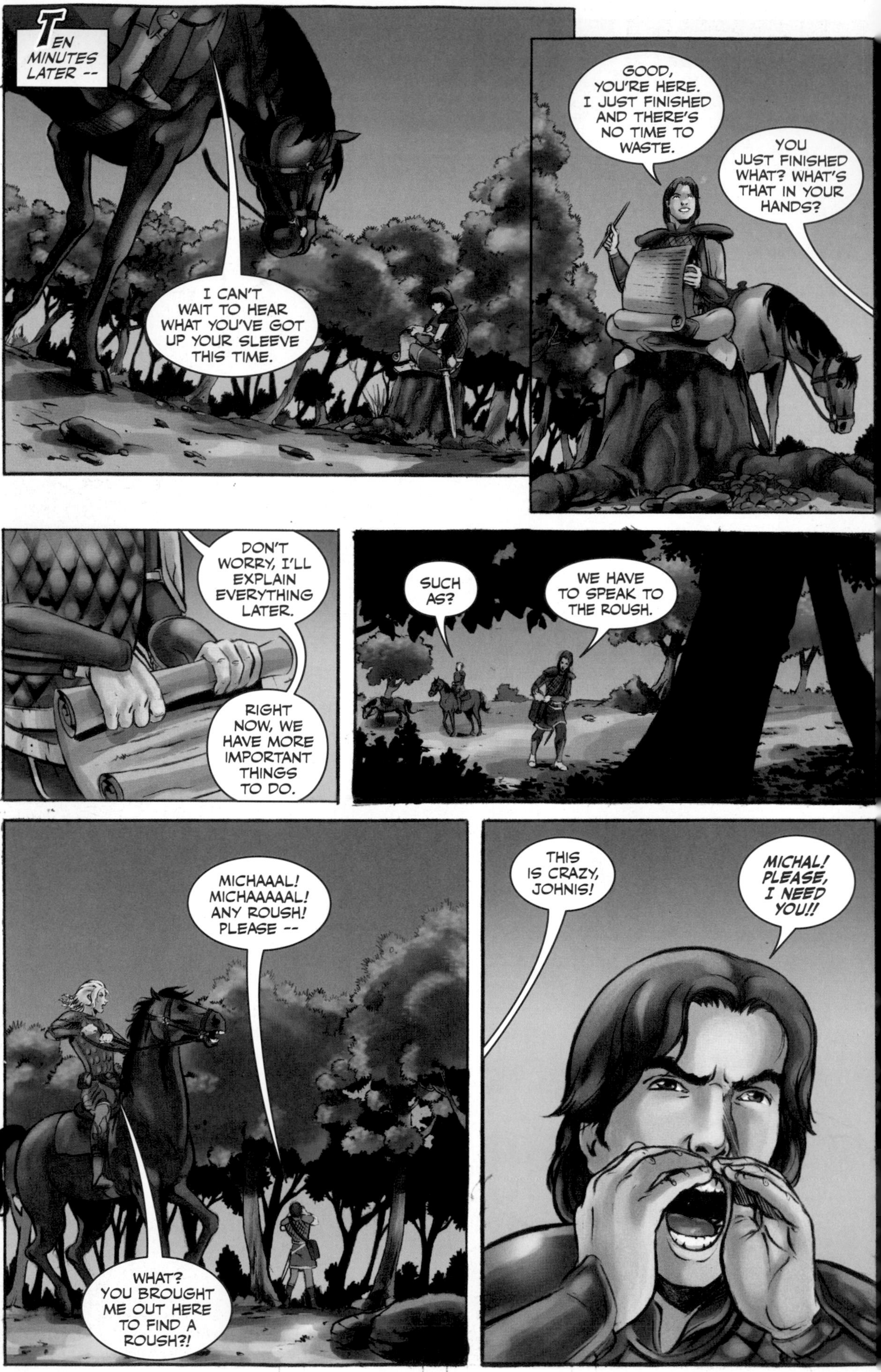
TEN MINUTES LATER --
I CAN'T WAIT TO HEAR WHAT YOU'VE GOT UP YOUR SLEEVE THIS TIME.
GOOD, YOU'RE HERE. I JUST FINISHED AND THERE'S NO TIME TO WASTE.
YOU JUST FINISHED WHAT? WHAT'S THAT IN YOUR HANDS?
DON'T WORRY, I'LL EXPLAIN EVERYTHING LATER.
RIGHT NOW, WE HAVE MORE IMPORTANT THINGS TO DO.
SUCH AS?
WE HAVE TO SPEAK TO THE ROUSH.
MICHAAAL! MICHAAAAAL! ANY ROUSH! PLEASE --
WHAT? YOU BROUGHT ME OUT HERE TO FIND A ROUSH?!
THIS IS CRAZY, JOHNIS!
MICHAL! PLEASE, I NEED YOU!!

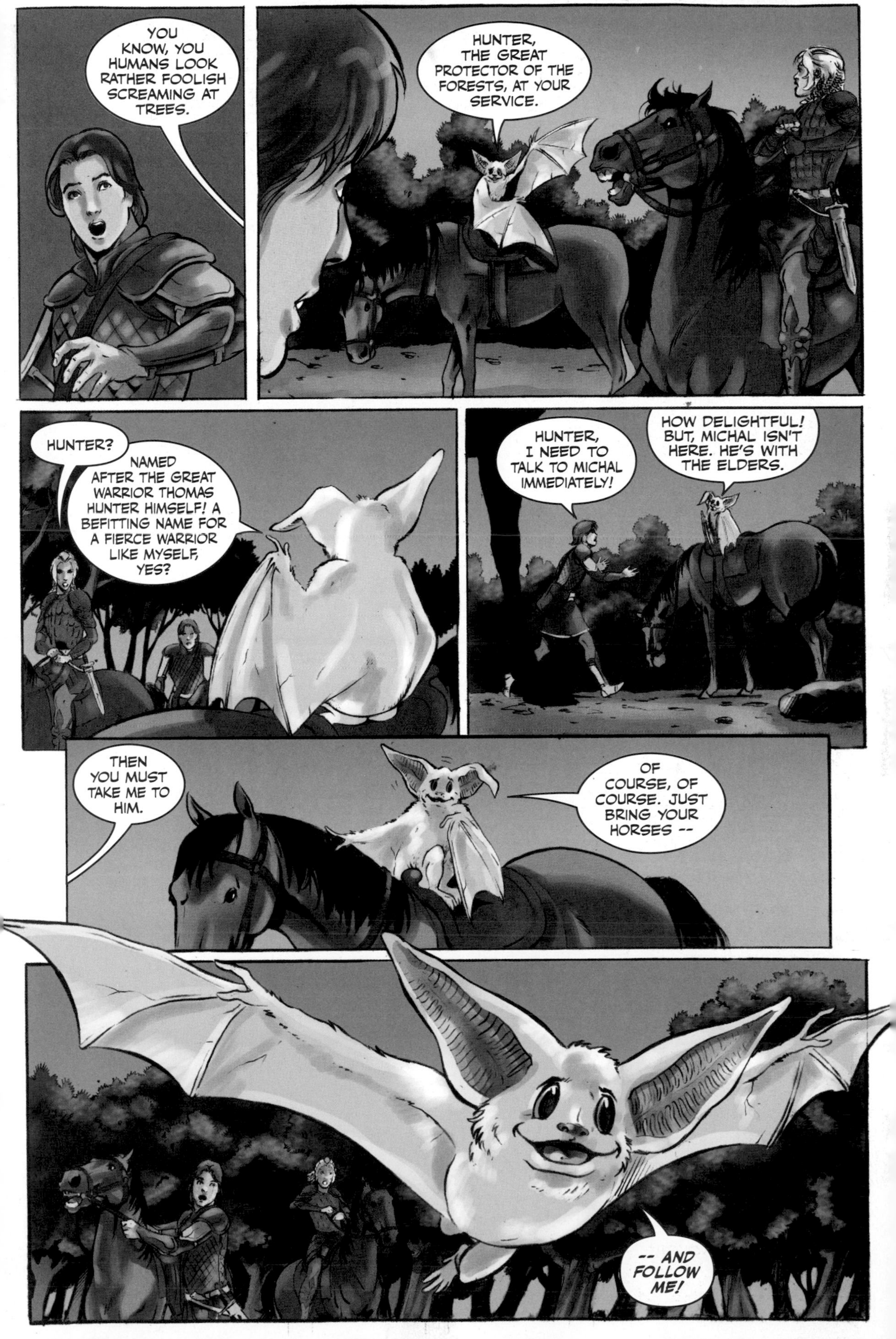
YOU KNOW, YOU HUMANS LOOK RATHER FOOLISH SCREAMING AT TREES.
HUNTER, THE GREAT PROTECTOR OF THE FORESTS, AT YOUR SERVICE.
HUNTER?
NAMED AFTER THE GREAT WARRIOR THOMAS HUNTER HIMSELF! A BEFITTING NAME FOR A FIERCE WARRIOR LIKE MYSELF, YES?
HUNTER, I NEED TO TALK TO MICHAL IMMEDIATELY!
HOW DELIGHTFUL! BUT, MICHAL ISN'T HERE. HE'S WITH THE ELDERS.
THEN YOU MUST TAKE ME TO HIM.
OF COURSE, OF COURSE. JUST BRING YOUR HORSES --
-- AND FOLLOW ME!

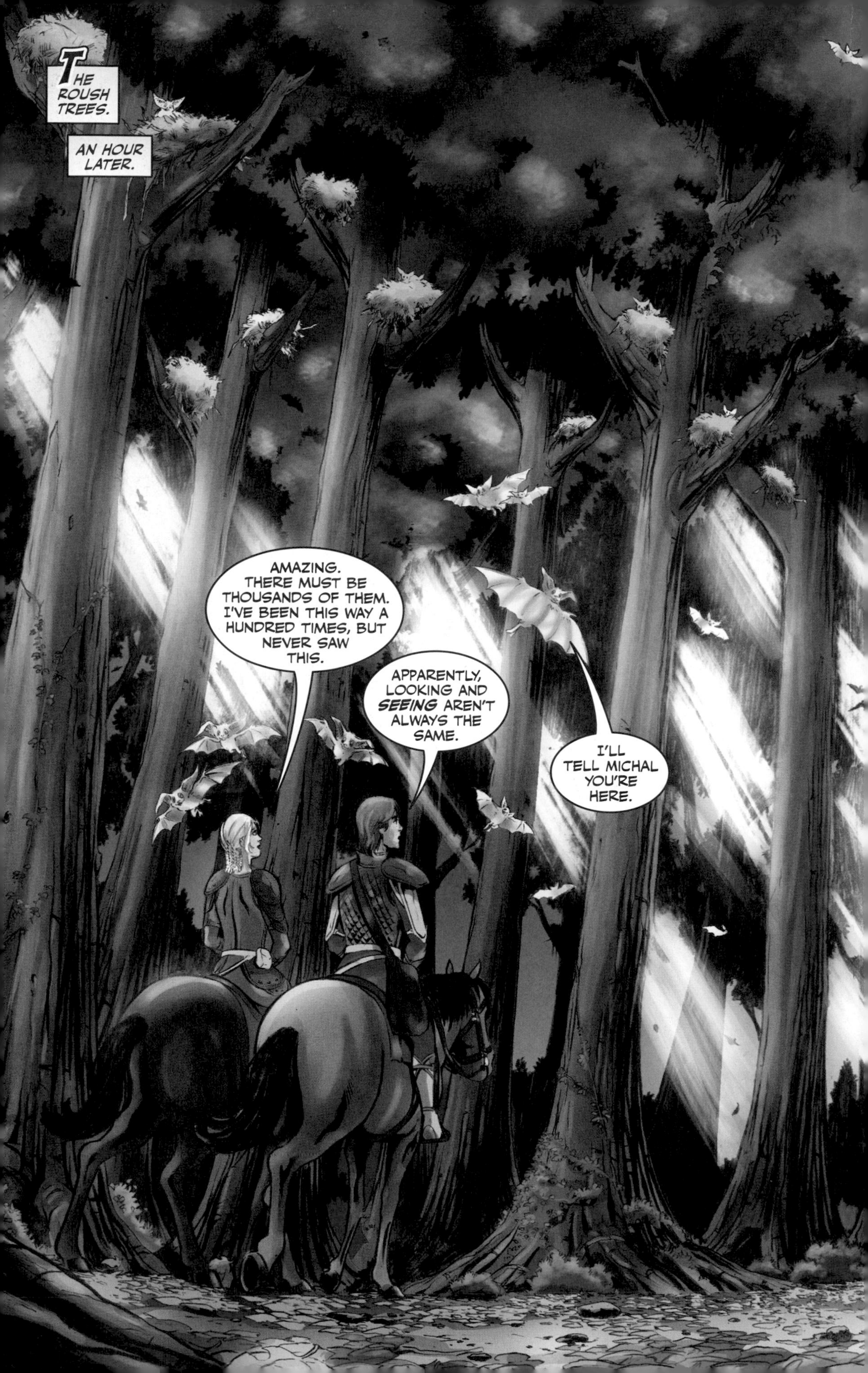
THE ROUSH TREES.
AN HOUR LATER.
AMAZING. THERE MUST BE THOUSANDS OF THEM. I'VE BEEN THIS WAY A HUNDRED TIMES, BUT NEVER SAW THIS.
APPARENTLY, LOOKING AND SEEING AREN'T ALWAYS THE SAME.
I'LL TELL MICHAL YOU'RE HERE.

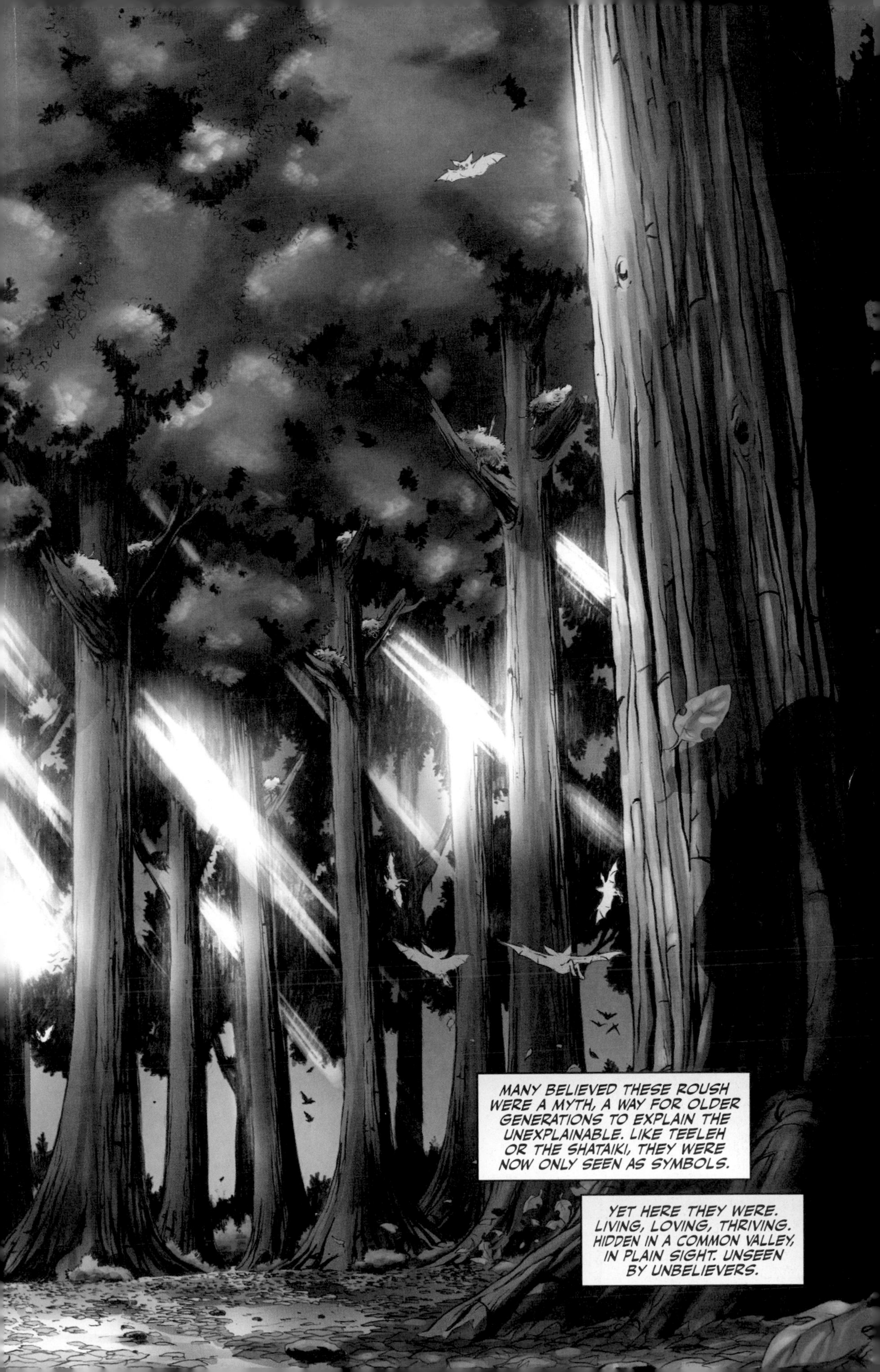
MANY BELIEVED THESE ROUSH WERE A MYTH, A WAY FOR OLDER GENERATIONS TO EXPLAIN THE UNEXPLAINABLE. LIKE TEELEH OR THE SHATAIKI, THEY WERE NOW ONLY SEEN AS SYMBOLS.
YET HERE THEY WERE. LIVING, LOVING, THRIVING. HIDDEN IN A COMMON VALLEY, IN PLAIN SIGHT. UNSEEN BY UNBELIEVERS.

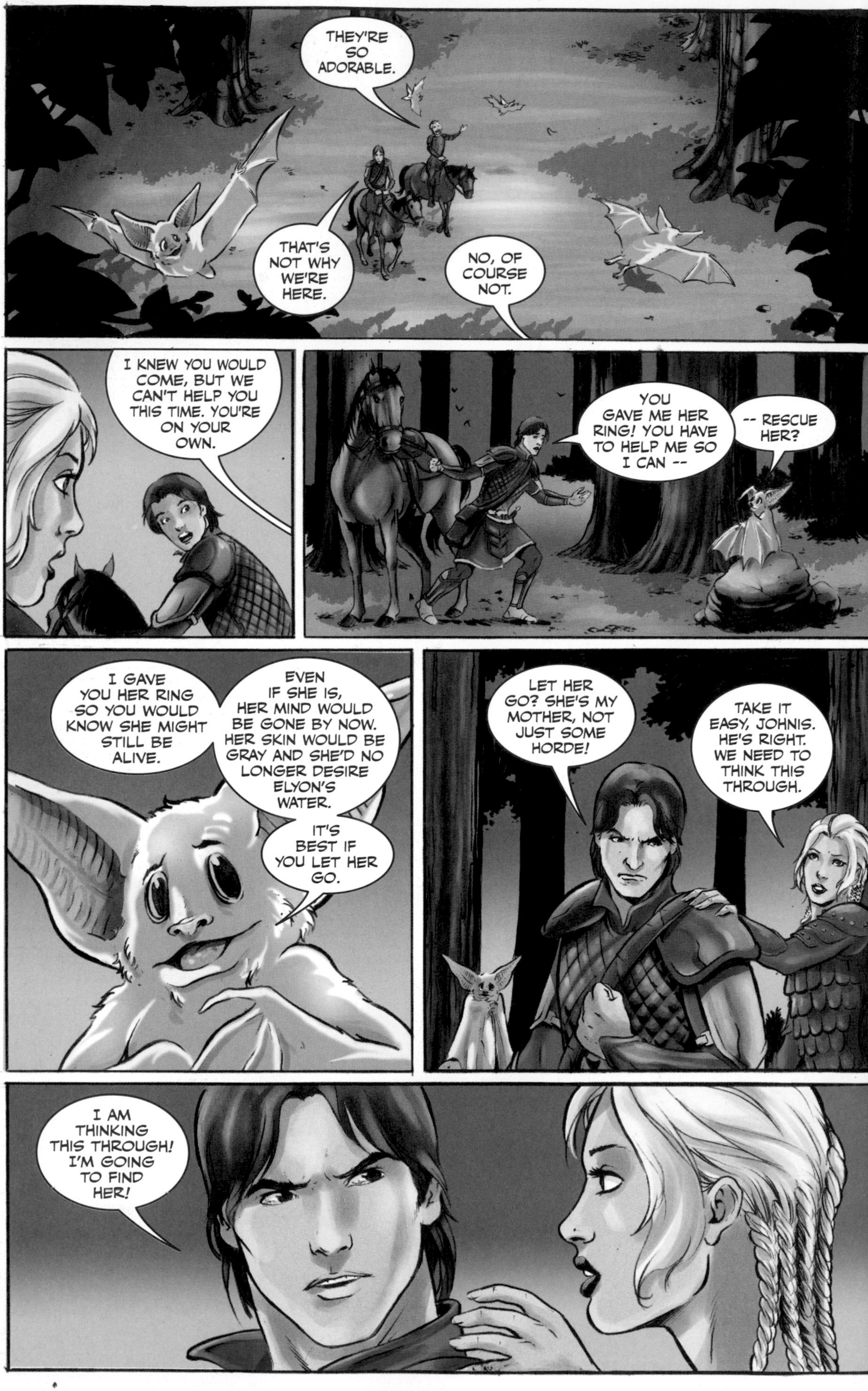
THEY'RE SO ADORABLE.
THAT'S NOT WHY WE'RE HERE.
NO, OF COURSE NOT.
I KNEW YOU WOULD COME, BUT WE CAN'T HELP YOU THIS TIME. YOU'RE ON YOUR OWN.
YOU GAVE ME HER RING! YOU HAVE TO HELP ME SO I CAN --
-- RESCUE HER?
I GAVE YOU HER RING SO YOU WOULD KNOW SHE MIGHT STILL BE ALIVE.
EVEN IF SHE IS, HER MIND WOULD BE GONE BY NOW. HER SKIN WOULD BE GRAY AND SHE'D NO LONGER DESIRE ELYON'S WATER.
IT'S BEST IF YOU LET HER GO.
LET HER GO? SHE'S MY MOTHER, NOT JUST SOME HORDE!
TAKE IT EASY, JOHNIS. HE'S RIGHT. WE NEED TO THINK THIS THROUGH.
I AM THINKING THIS THROUGH! I'M GOING TO FIND HER!

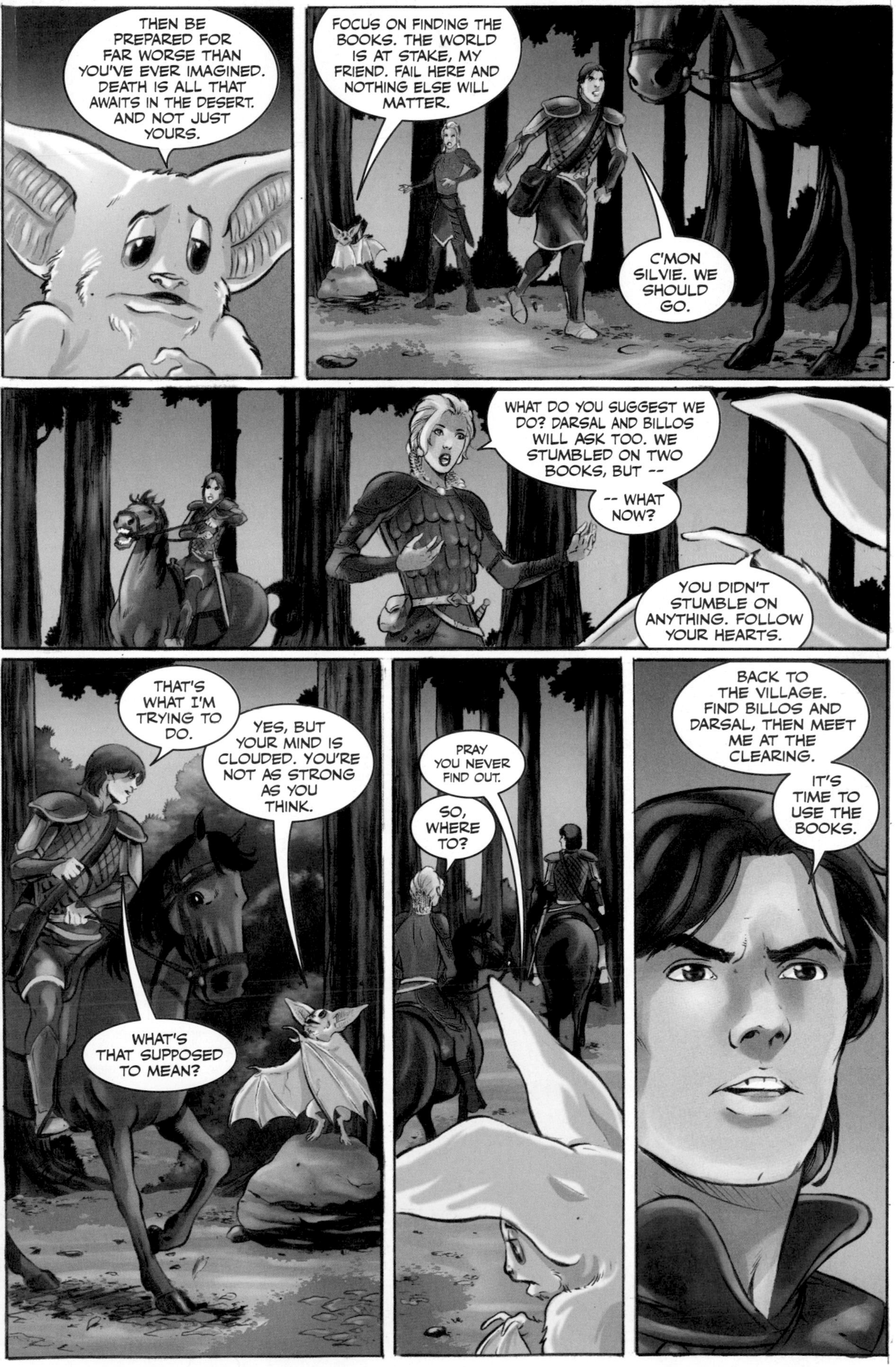
THEN BE PREPARED FOR FAR WORSE THAN YOU'VE EVER IMAGINED. DEATH IS ALL THAT AWAITS IN THE DESERT. AND NOT JUST YOURS.
FOCUS ON FINDING THE BOOKS. THE WORLD IS AT STAKE, MY FRIEND. FAIL HERE AND NOTHING ELSE WILL MATTER.
C'MON SILVIE. WE SHOULD GO.
WHAT DO YOU SUGGEST WE DO? DARSAL AND BILLOS WILL ASK TOO. WE STUMBLED ON TWO BOOKS, BUT --
-- WHAT NOW?
YOU DIDN'T STUMBLE ON ANYTHING. FOLLOW YOUR HEARTS.
THAT'S WHAT I'M TRYING TO DO.
YES, BUT YOUR MIND IS CLOUDED. YOU'RE NOT AS STRONG AS YOU THINK.
WHAT'S THAT SUPPOSED TO MEAN?
PRAY YOU NEVER FIND OUT.
SO, WHERE TO?
BACK TO THE VILLAGE. FIND BILLOS AND DARSAL, THEN MEET ME AT THE CLEARING.
IT'S TIME TO USE THE BOOKS.

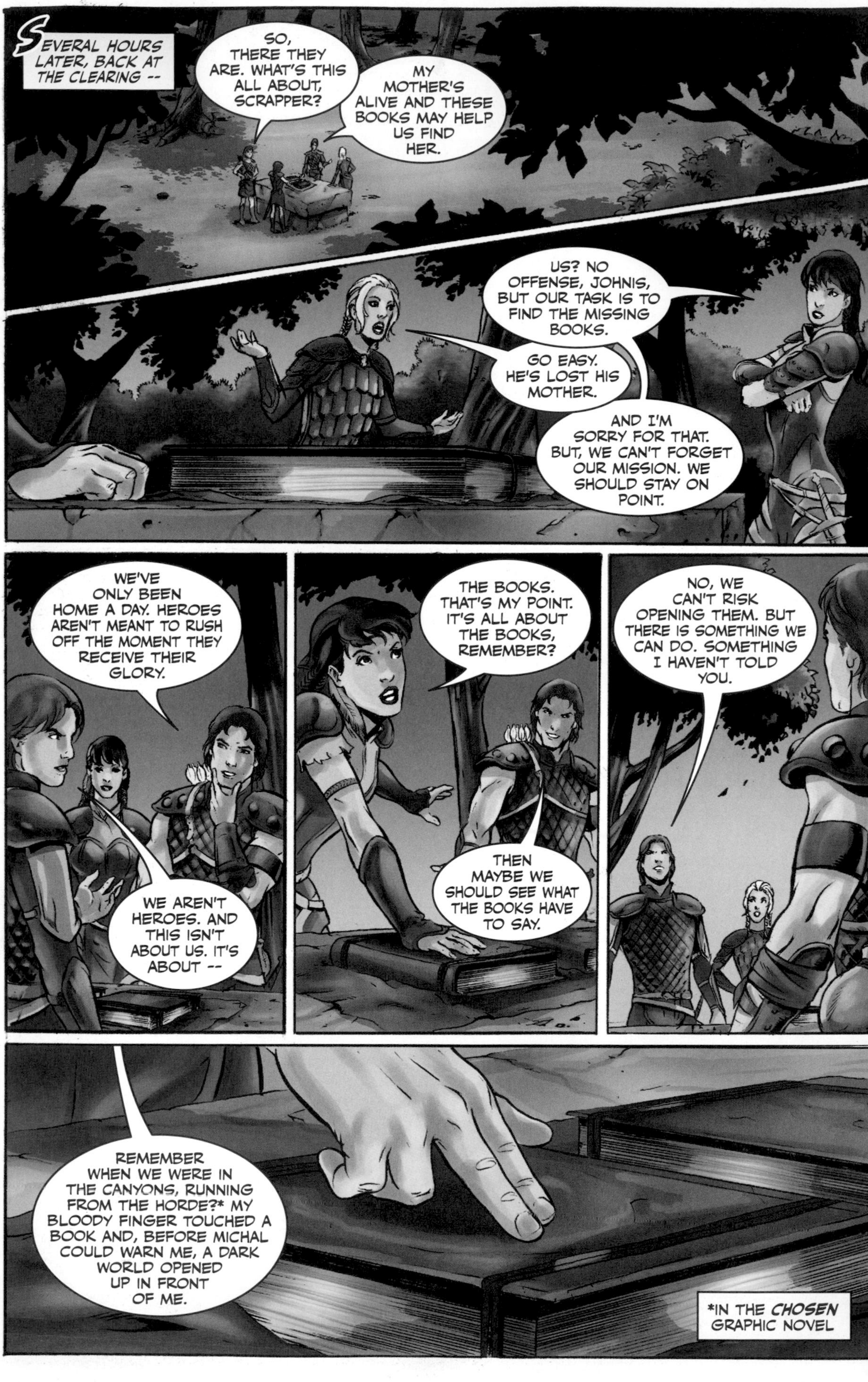
SEVERAL HOURS LATER, BACK AT THE CLEARING --
SO, THERE THEY ARE. WHAT'S THIS ALL ABOUT, SCRAPPER?
MY MOTHER'S ALIVE AND THESE BOOKS MAY HELP US FIND HER.
US? NO OFFENSE, JOHNIS, BUT OUR TASK IS TO FIND THE MISSING BOOKS.
GO EASY. HE'S LOST HIS MOTHER.
AND I'M SORRY FOR THAT. BUT, WE CAN'T FORGET OUR MISSION. WE SHOULD STAY ON POINT.
WE'VE ONLY BEEN HOME A DAY. HEROES AREN'T MEANT TO RUSH OFF THE MOMENT THEY RECEIVE THEIR GLORY.
WE AREN'T HEROES. AND THIS ISN'T ABOUT US. IT'S ABOUT --
THE BOOKS. THAT'S MY POINT. IT'S ALL ABOUT THE BOOKS, REMEMBER?
THEN MAYBE WE SHOULD SEE WHAT THE BOOKS HAVE TO SAY.
NO, WE CAN'T RISK OPENING THEM. BUT THERE IS SOMETHING WE CAN DO. SOMETHING I HAVEN'T TOLD YOU.
REMEMBER WHEN WE WERE IN THE CANYONS, RUNNING FROM THE HORDE?* MY BLOODY FINGER TOUCHED A BOOK AND, BEFORE MICHAL COULD WARN ME, A DARK WORLD OPENED UP IN FRONT OF ME.
*IN THE *CHOSEN* GRAPHIC NOVEL

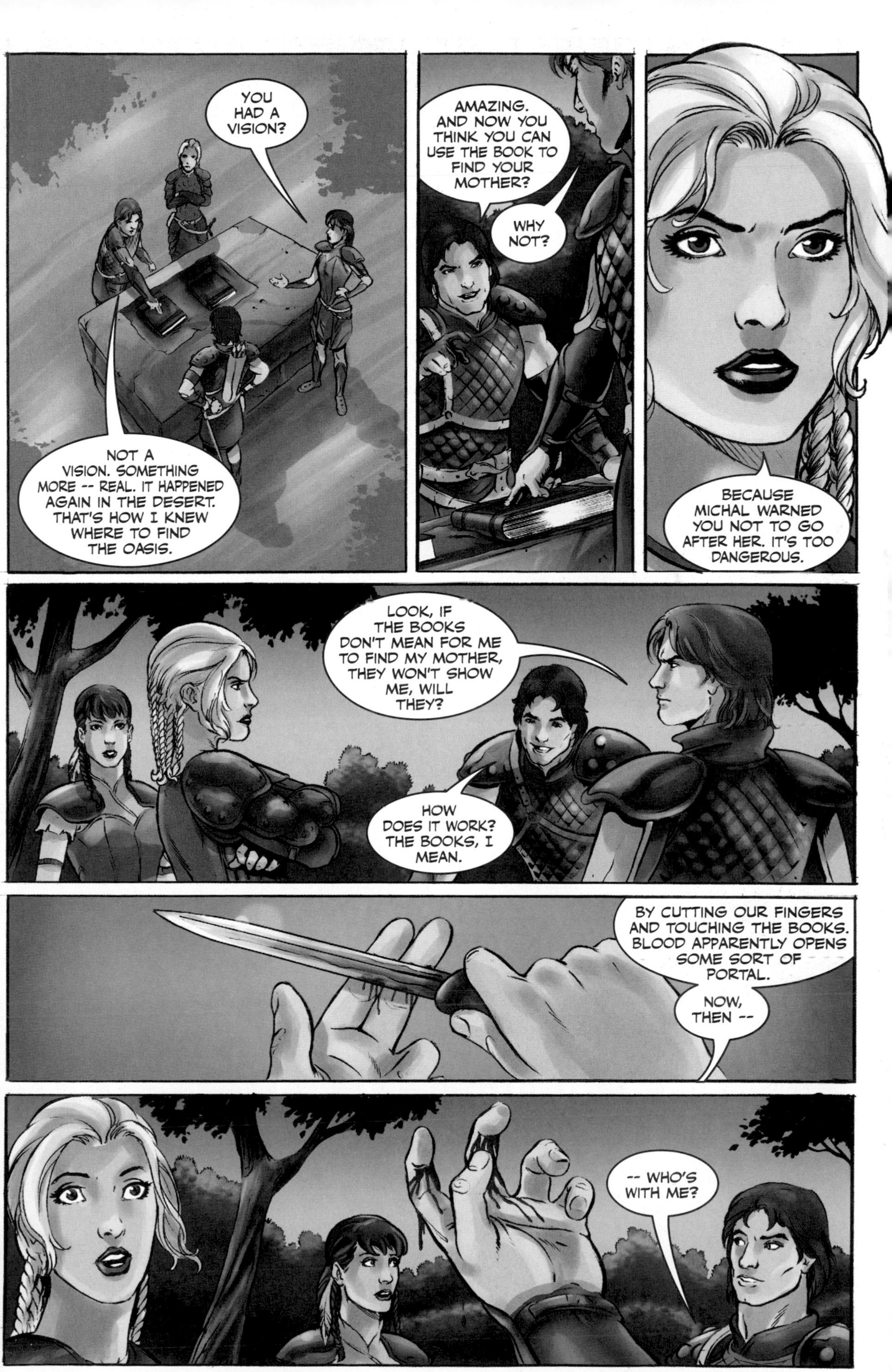
YOU HAD A VISION?
NOT A VISION. SOMETHING MORE -- REAL. IT HAPPENED AGAIN IN THE DESERT. THAT'S HOW I KNEW WHERE TO FIND THE OASIS.
AMAZING. AND NOW YOU THINK YOU CAN USE THE BOOK TO FIND YOUR MOTHER?
WHY NOT?
BECAUSE MICHAL WARNED YOU NOT TO GO AFTER HER. IT'S TOO DANGEROUS.
LOOK, IF THE BOOKS DON'T MEAN FOR ME TO FIND MY MOTHER, THEY WON'T SHOW ME, WILL THEY?
HOW DOES IT WORK? THE BOOKS, I MEAN.
BY CUTTING OUR FINGERS AND TOUCHING THE BOOKS. BLOOD APPARENTLY OPENS SOME SORT OF PORTAL.
NOW, THEN --
-- WHO'S WITH ME?

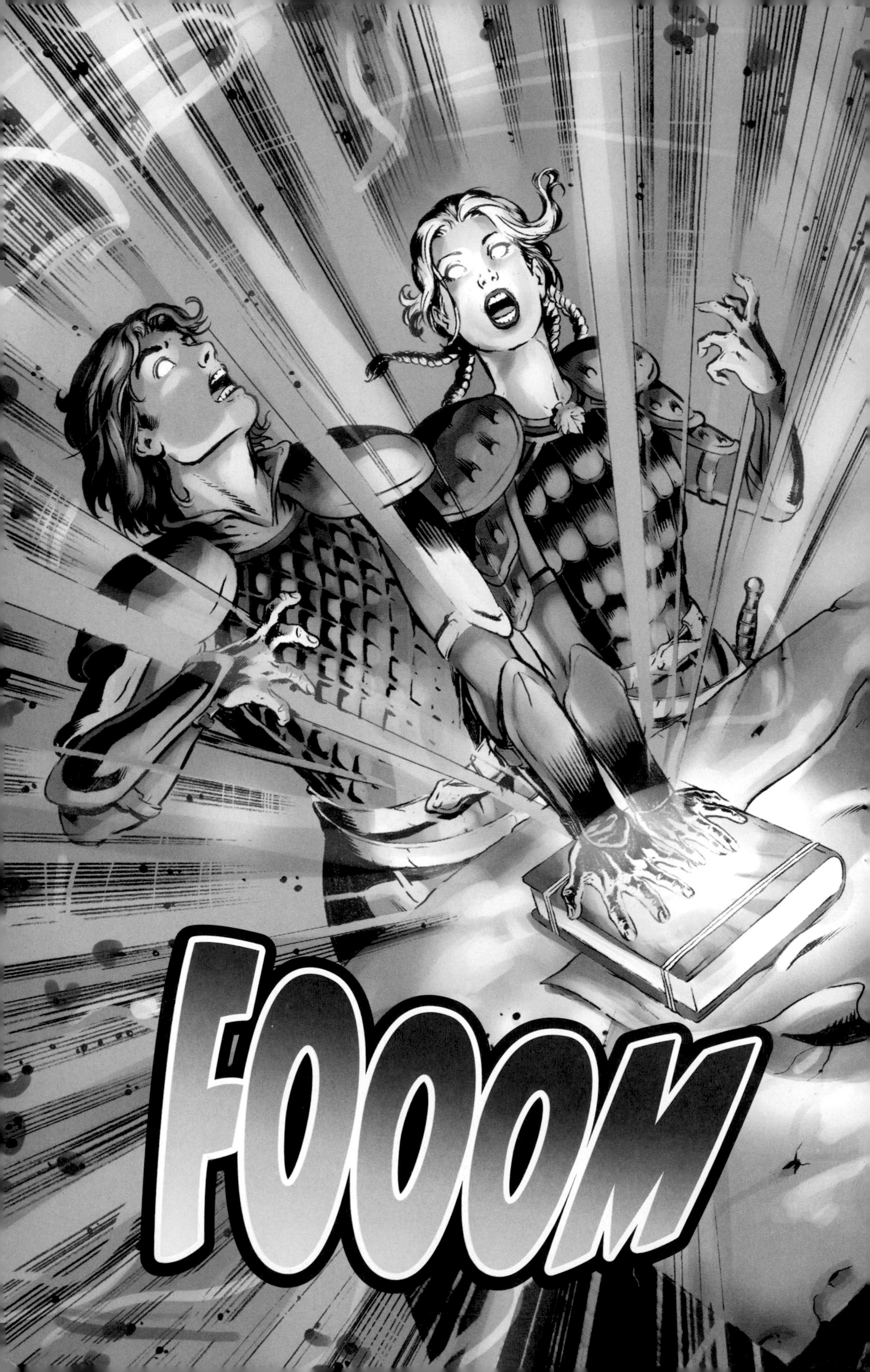
FOOOM

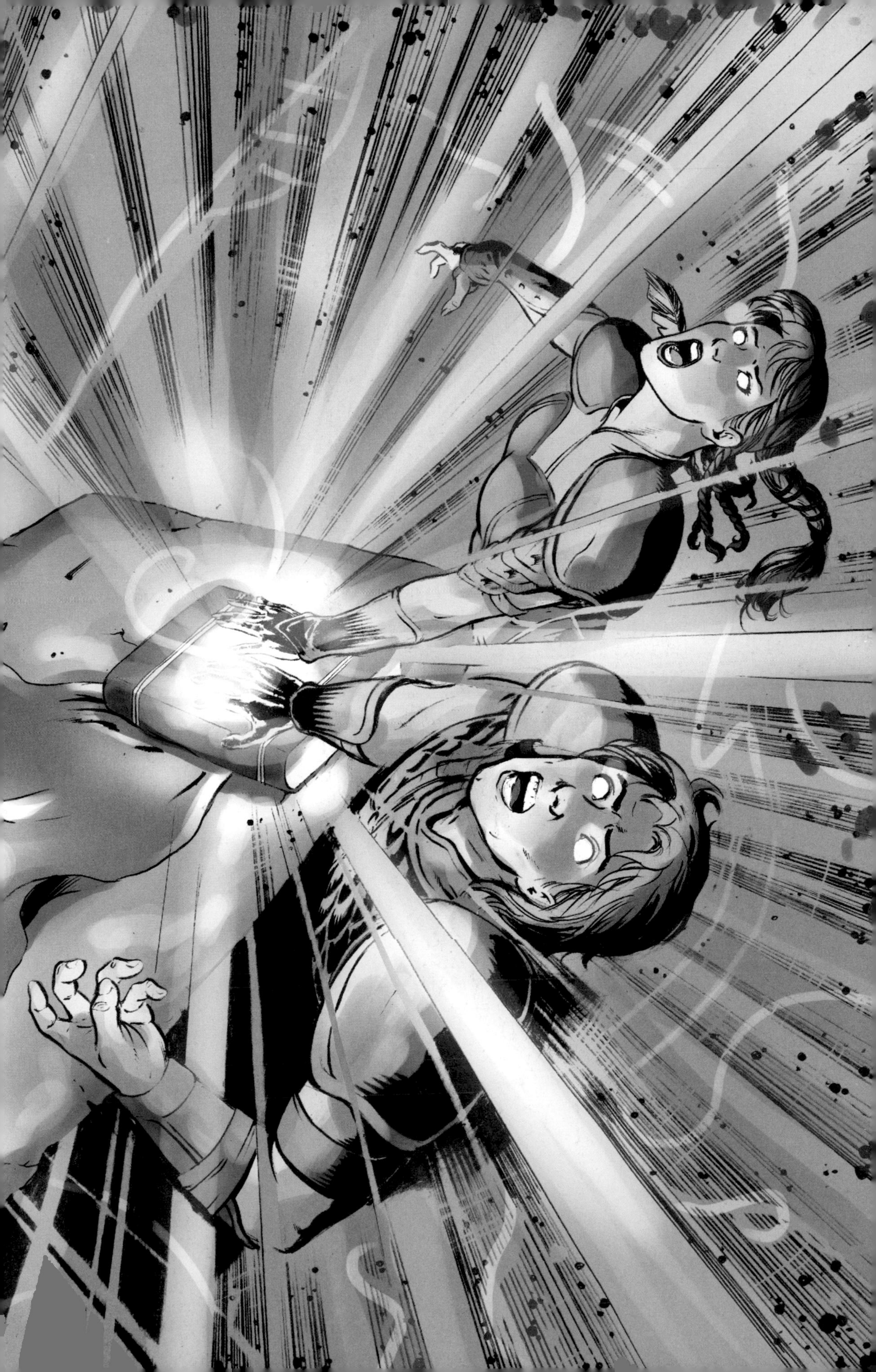

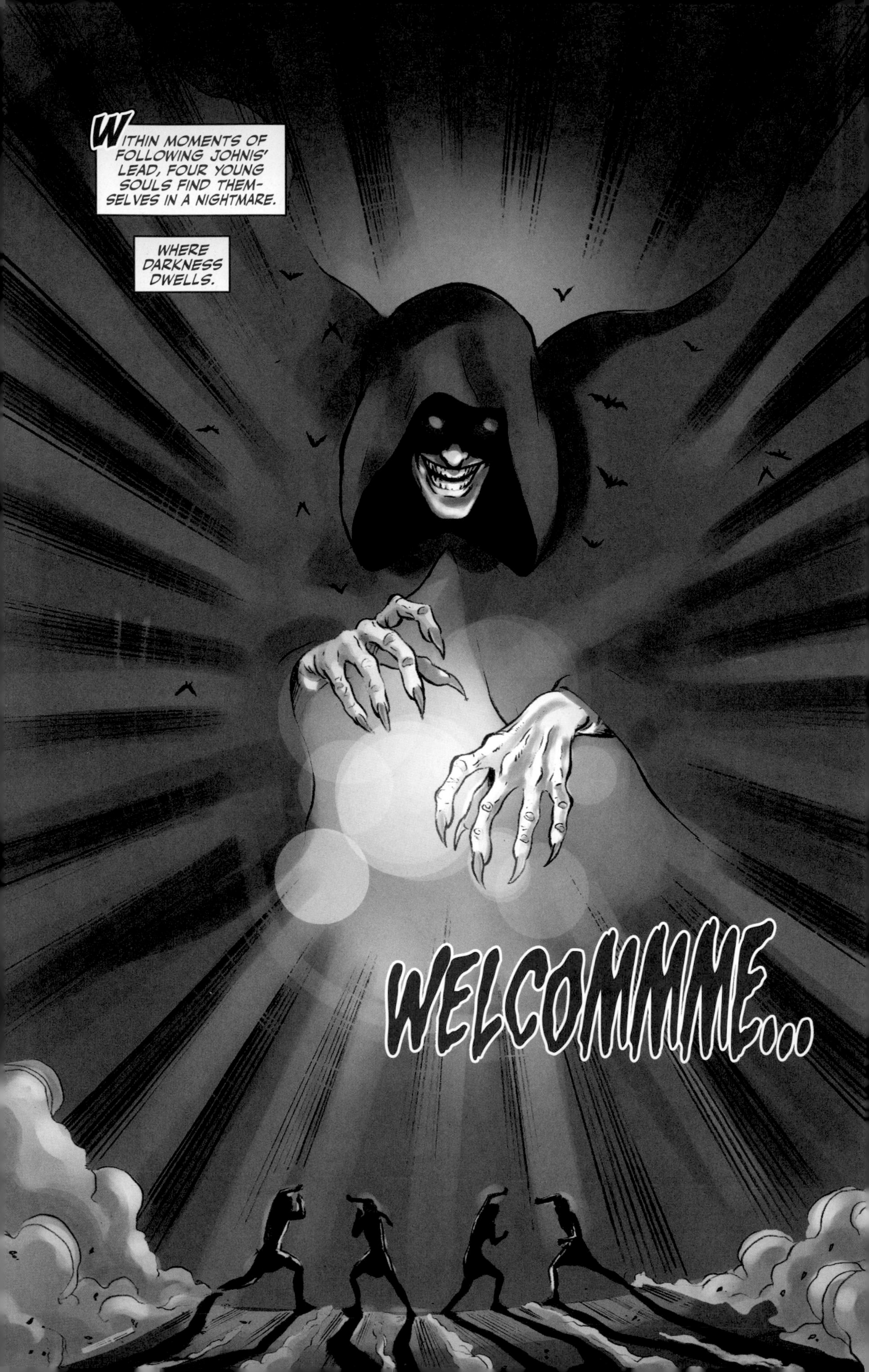
WITHIN MOMENTS OF FOLLOWING JOHNIS' LEAD, FOUR YOUNG SOULS FIND THEMSELVES IN A NIGHTMARE.
WHERE DARKNESS DWELLS.
WELCOMMME...

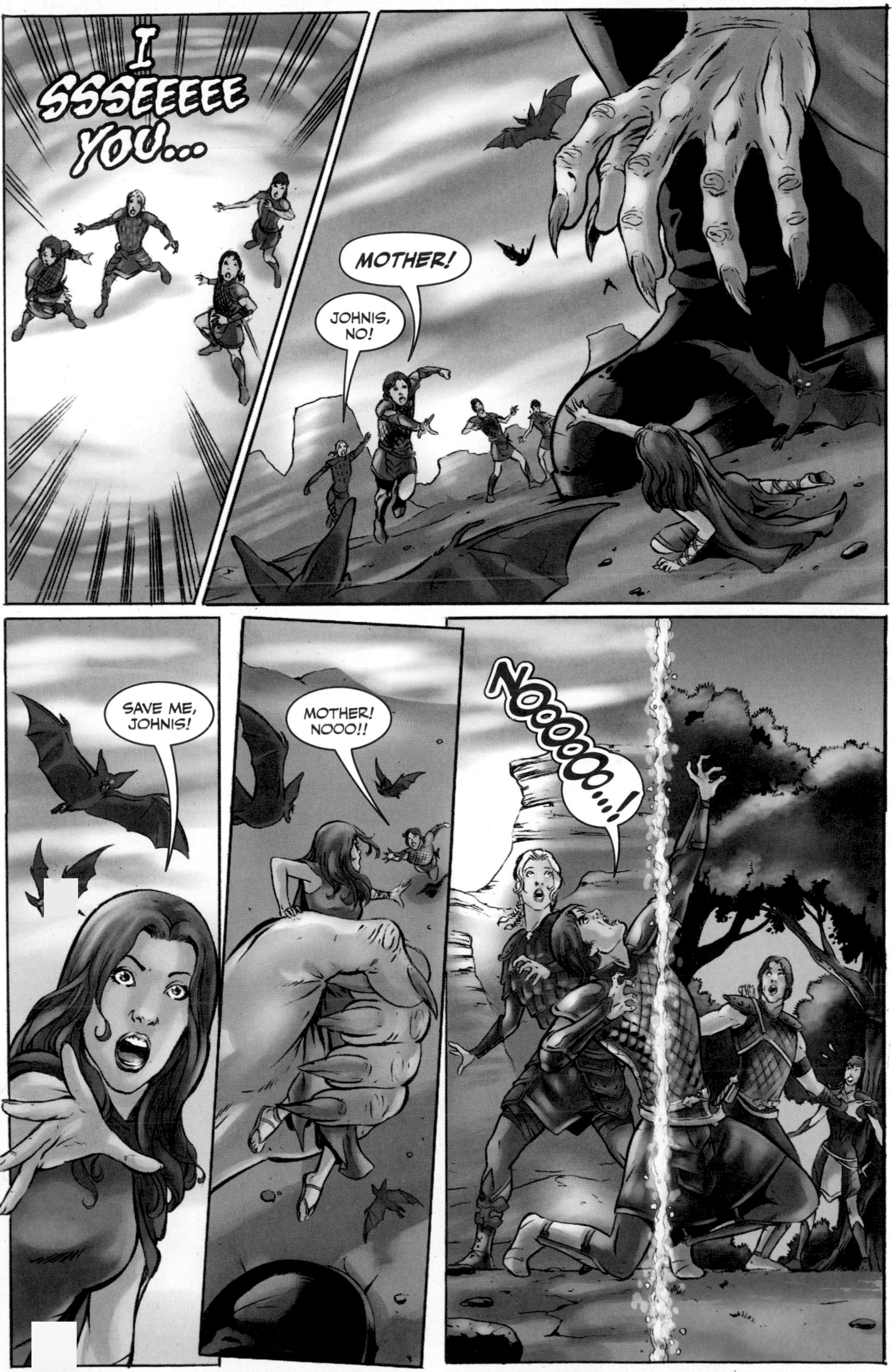
I SSSEEEEEE YOU...
MOTHER!
JOHNIS, NO!
SAVE ME, JOHNIS!
MOTHER! NOOO!!
NOOOOOO...!

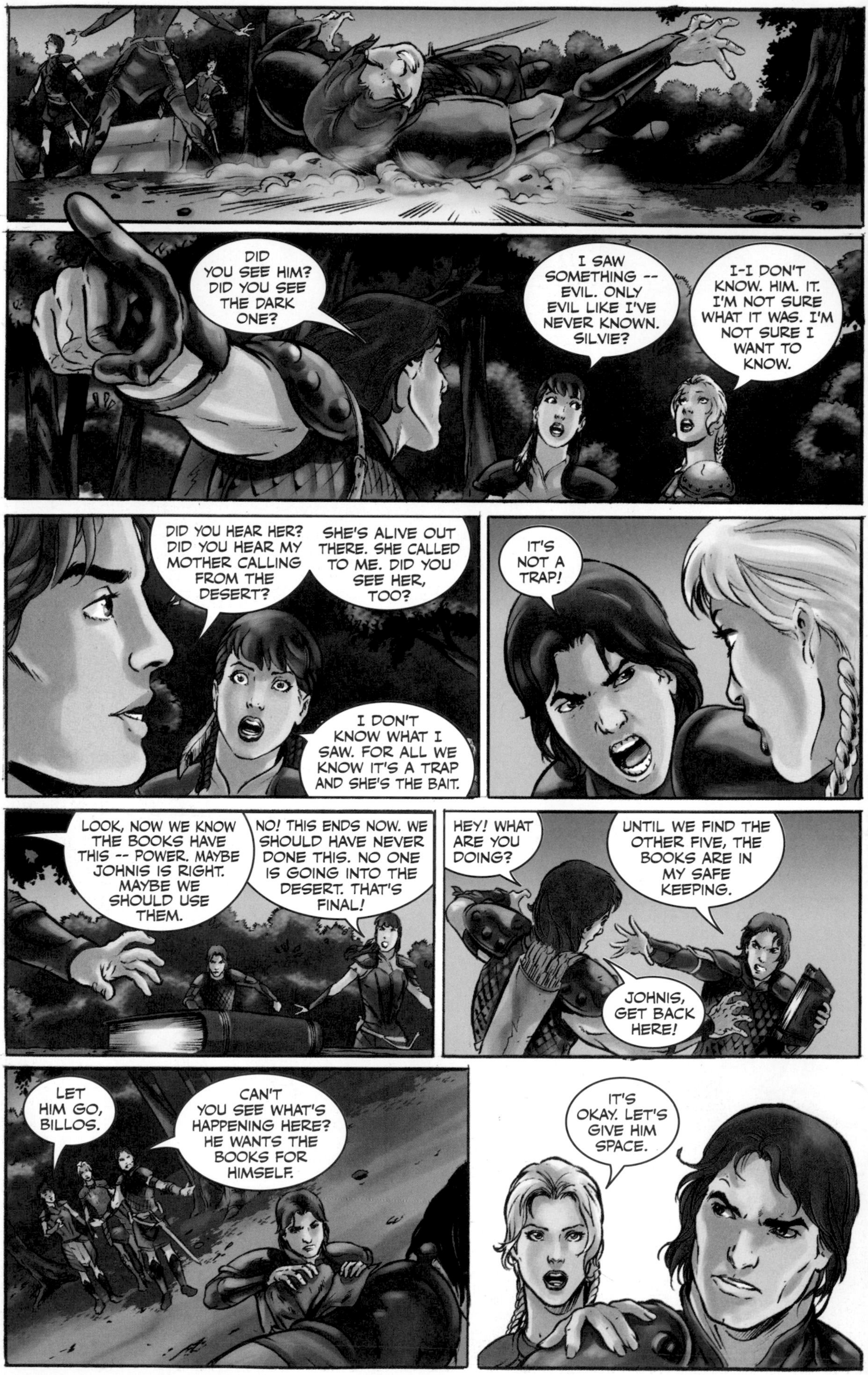
DID YOU SEE HIM? DID YOU SEE THE DARK ONE?
I SAW SOMETHING -- EVIL. ONLY EVIL LIKE I'VE NEVER KNOWN. SILVIE?
I-I DON'T KNOW. HIM. IT. I'M NOT SURE WHAT IT WAS. I'M NOT SURE I WANT TO KNOW.
DID YOU HEAR HER? DID YOU HEAR MY MOTHER CALLING FROM THE DESERT?
SHE'S ALIVE OUT THERE. SHE CALLED TO ME. DID YOU SEE HER, TOO?
I DON'T KNOW WHAT I SAW. FOR ALL WE KNOW IT'S A TRAP AND SHE'S THE BAIT.
IT'S NOT A TRAP!
LOOK, NOW WE KNOW THE BOOKS HAVE THIS -- POWER. MAYBE JOHNIS IS RIGHT. MAYBE WE SHOULD USE THEM.
NO! THIS ENDS NOW. WE SHOULD HAVE NEVER DONE THIS. NO ONE IS GOING INTO THE DESERT. THAT'S FINAL!
HEY! WHAT ARE YOU DOING?
UNTIL WE FIND THE OTHER FIVE, THE BOOKS ARE IN MY SAFE KEEPING.
JOHNIS, GET BACK HERE!
LET HIM GO, BILLOS.
CAN'T YOU SEE WHAT'S HAPPENING HERE? HE WANTS THE BOOKS FOR HIMSELF.
IT'S OKAY. LET'S GIVE HIM SPACE.

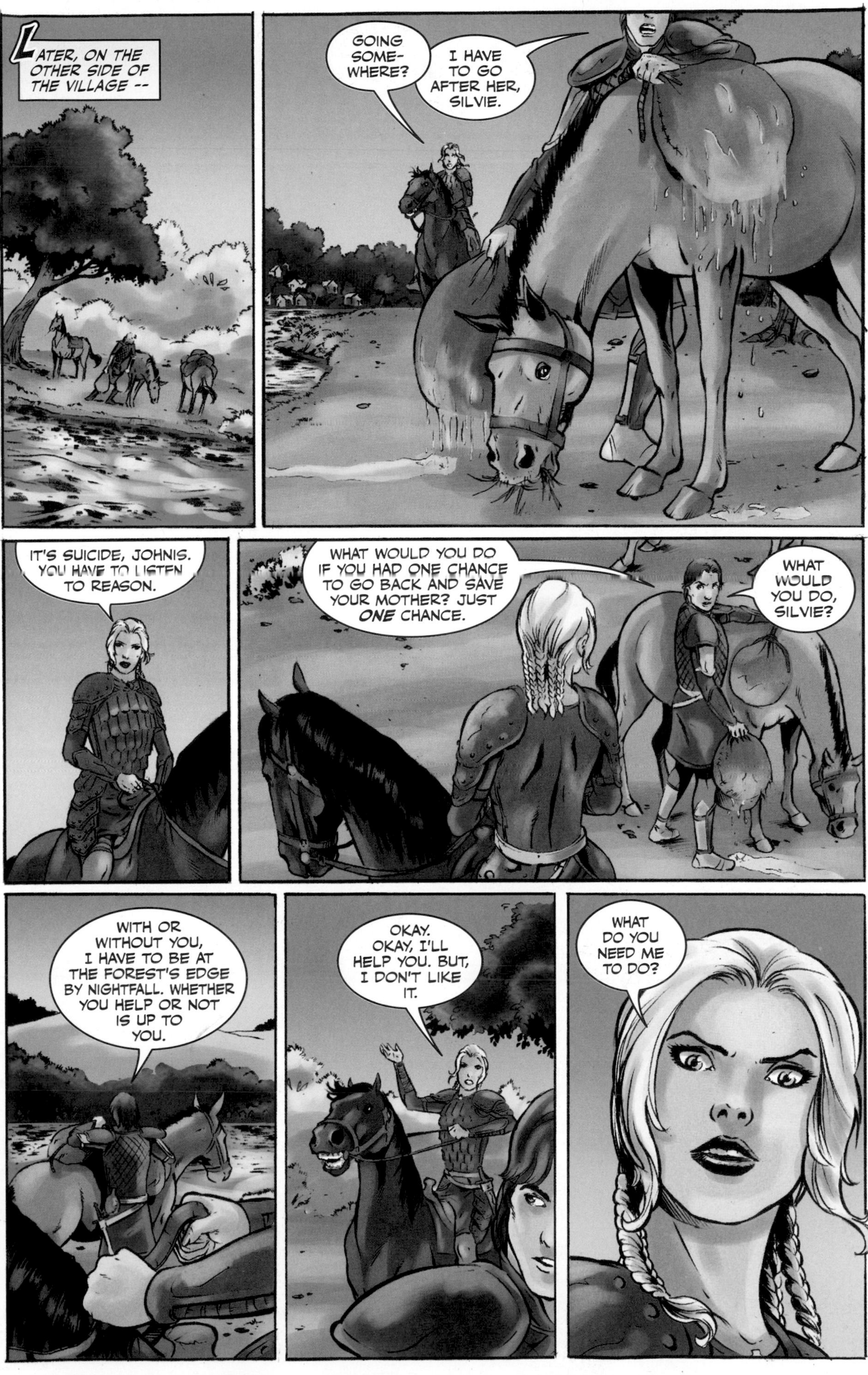
LATER, ON THE OTHER SIDE OF THE VILLAGE --
GOING SOME-WHERE?
I HAVE TO GO AFTER HER, SILVIE.
IT'S SUICIDE, JOHNIS. YOU HAVE TO LISTEN TO REASON.
WHAT WOULD YOU DO IF YOU HAD ONE CHANCE TO GO BACK AND SAVE YOUR MOTHER? JUST ONE CHANCE.
WHAT WOULD YOU DO, SILVIE?
WITH OR WITHOUT YOU, I HAVE TO BE AT THE FOREST'S EDGE BY NIGHTFALL. WHETHER YOU HELP OR NOT IS UP TO YOU.
OKAY. OKAY, I'LL HELP YOU. BUT, I DON'T LIKE IT.
WHAT DO YOU NEED ME TO DO?

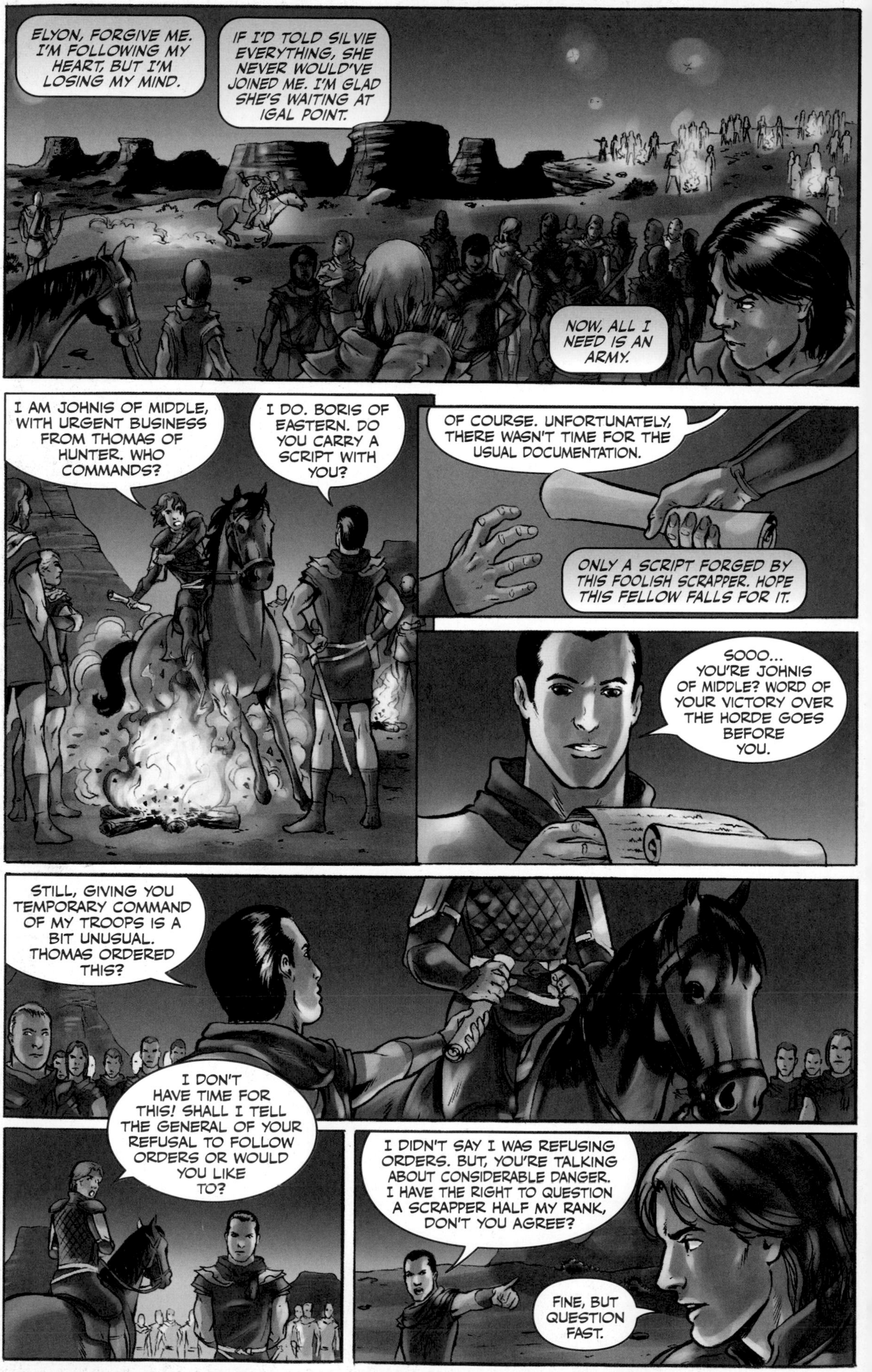
ELYON, FORGIVE ME. I'M FOLLOWING MY HEART, BUT I'M LOSING MY MIND.
IF I'D TOLD SILVIE EVERYTHING, SHE NEVER WOULD'VE JOINED ME. I'M GLAD SHE'S WAITING AT IGAL POINT.
NOW, ALL I NEED IS AN ARMY.
I AM JOHNIS OF MIDDLE, WITH URGENT BUSINESS FROM THOMAS OF HUNTER. WHO COMMANDS?
I DO. BORIS OF EASTERN. DO YOU CARRY A SCRIPT WITH YOU?
OF COURSE. UNFORTUNATELY, THERE WASN'T TIME FOR THE USUAL DOCUMENTATION.
ONLY A SCRIPT FORGED BY THIS FOOLISH SCRAPPER. HOPE THIS FELLOW FALLS FOR IT.
SOOO... YOU'RE JOHNIS OF MIDDLE? WORD OF YOUR VICTORY OVER THE HORDE GOES BEFORE YOU.
STILL, GIVING YOU TEMPORARY COMMAND OF MY TROOPS IS A BIT UNUSUAL. THOMAS ORDERED THIS?
I DON'T HAVE TIME FOR THIS! SHALL I TELL THE GENERAL OF YOUR REFUSAL TO FOLLOW ORDERS OR WOULD YOU LIKE TO?
I DIDN'T SAY I WAS REFUSING ORDERS. BUT, YOU'RE TALKING ABOUT CONSIDERABLE DANGER. I HAVE THE RIGHT TO QUESTION A SCRAPPER HALF MY RANK, DON'T YOU AGREE?
FINE, BUT QUESTION FAST.

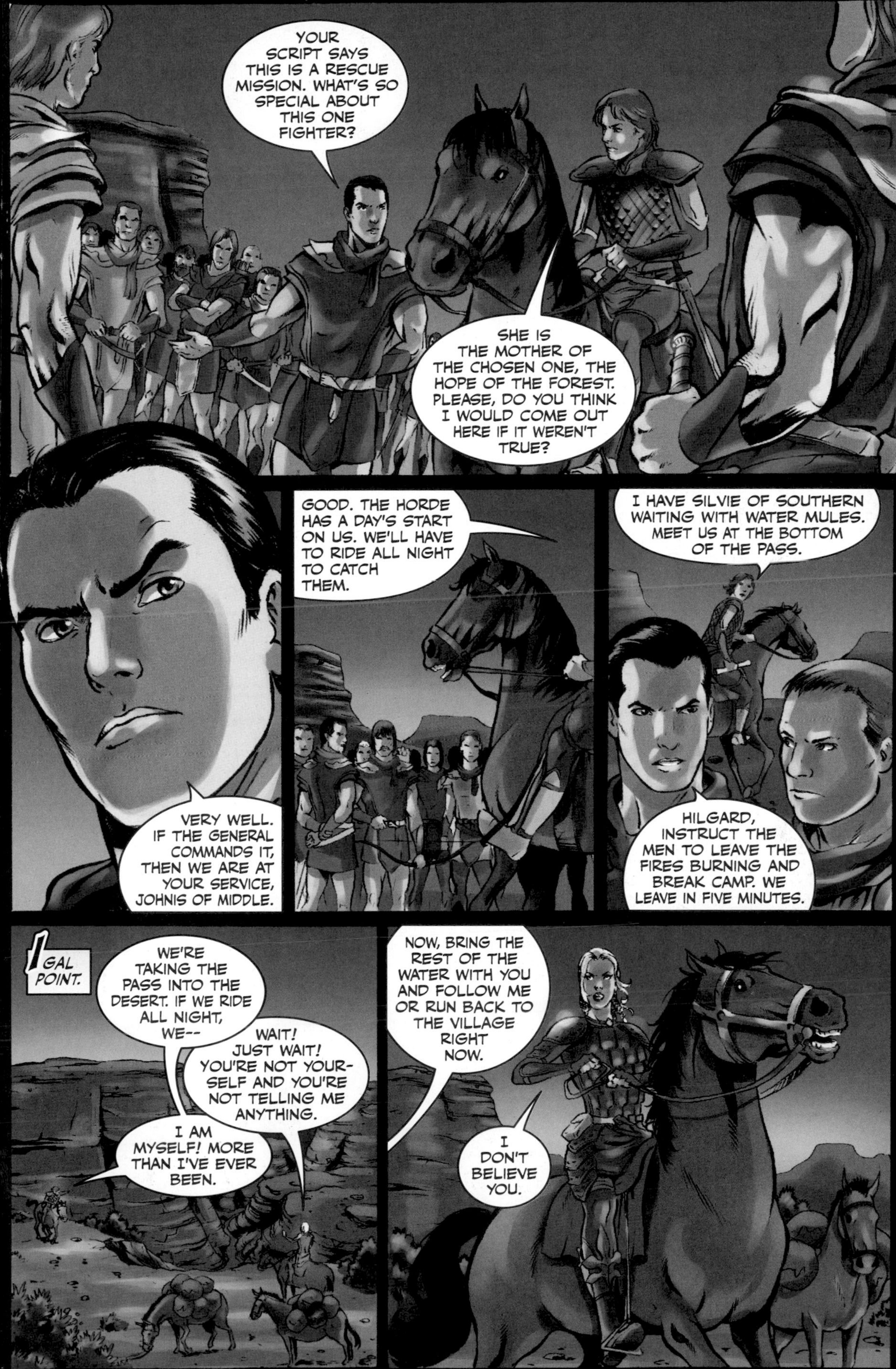
YOUR SCRIPT SAYS THIS IS A RESCUE MISSION. WHAT'S SO SPECIAL ABOUT THIS ONE FIGHTER?
SHE IS THE MOTHER OF THE CHOSEN ONE, THE HOPE OF THE FOREST. PLEASE, DO YOU THINK I WOULD COME OUT HERE IF IT WEREN'T TRUE?
VERY WELL. IF THE GENERAL COMMANDS IT, THEN WE ARE AT YOUR SERVICE, JOHNIS OF MIDDLE.
GOOD. THE HORDE HAS A DAY'S START ON US. WE'LL HAVE TO RIDE ALL NIGHT TO CATCH THEM.
I HAVE SILVIE OF SOUTHERN WAITING WITH WATER MULES. MEET US AT THE BOTTOM OF THE PASS.
HILGARD, INSTRUCT THE MEN TO LEAVE THE FIRES BURNING AND BREAK CAMP. WE LEAVE IN FIVE MINUTES.
GAL POINT.
WE'RE TAKING THE PASS INTO THE DESERT. IF WE RIDE ALL NIGHT, WE--
WAIT! JUST WAIT! YOU'RE NOT YOURSELF AND YOU'RE NOT TELLING ME ANYTHING.
I AM MYSELF! MORE THAN I'VE EVER BEEN.
NOW, BRING THE REST OF THE WATER WITH YOU AND FOLLOW ME OR RUN BACK TO THE VILLAGE RIGHT NOW.
I DON'T BELIEVE YOU.

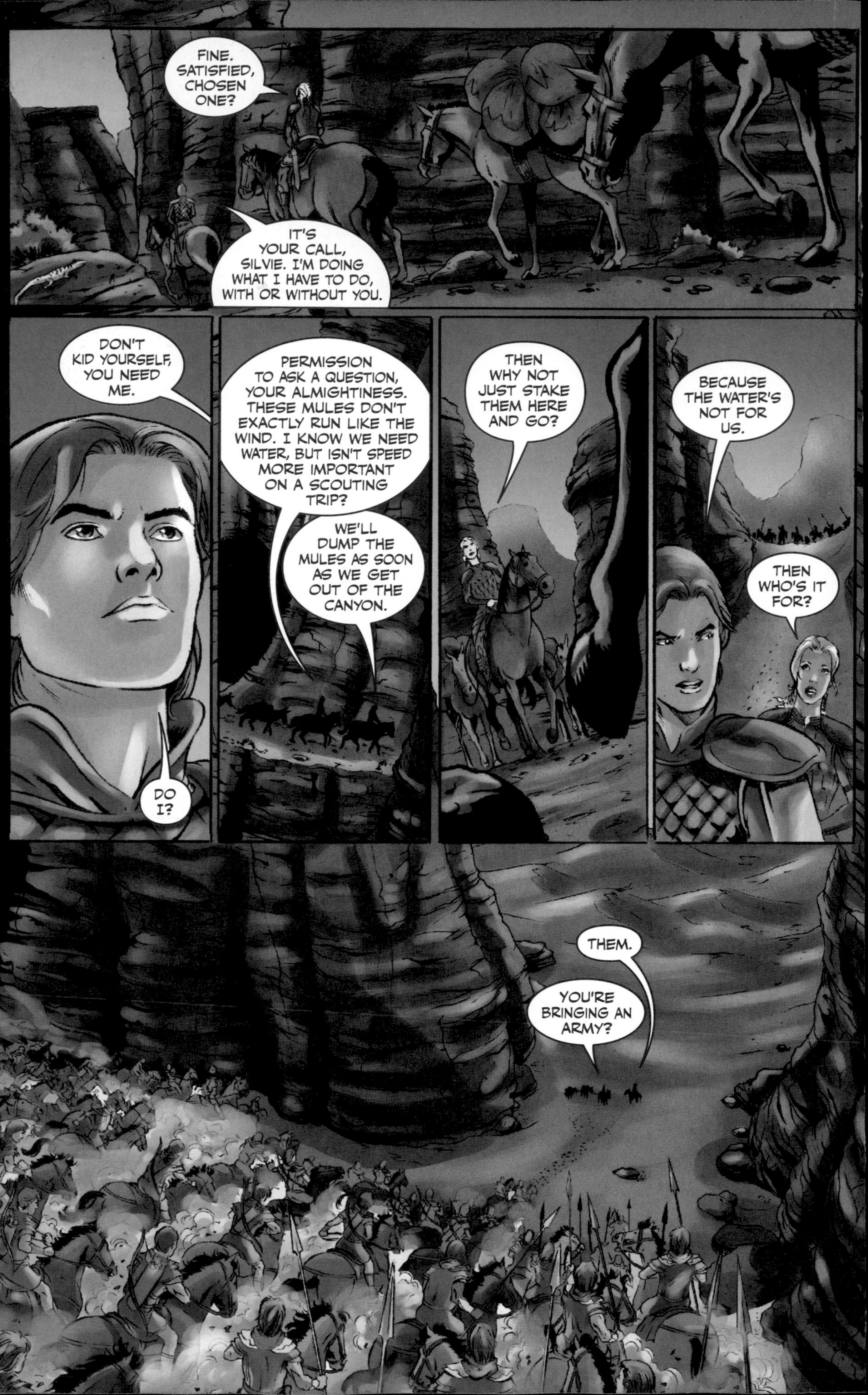
FINE. SATISFIED, CHOSEN ONE?
IT'S YOUR CALL, SILVIE. I'M DOING WHAT I HAVE TO DO, WITH OR WITHOUT YOU.
DON'T KID YOURSELF, YOU NEED ME.
DO I?
PERMISSION TO ASK A QUESTION, YOUR ALMIGHTINESS. THESE MULES DON'T EXACTLY RUN LIKE THE WIND. I KNOW WE NEED WATER, BUT ISN'T SPEED MORE IMPORTANT ON A SCOUTING TRIP?
WE'LL DUMP THE MULES AS SOON AS WE GET OUT OF THE CANYON.
THEN WHY NOT JUST STAKE THEM HERE AND GO?
BECAUSE THE WATER'S NOT FOR US.
THEN WHO'S IT FOR?
THEM.
YOU'RE BRINGING AN ARMY?

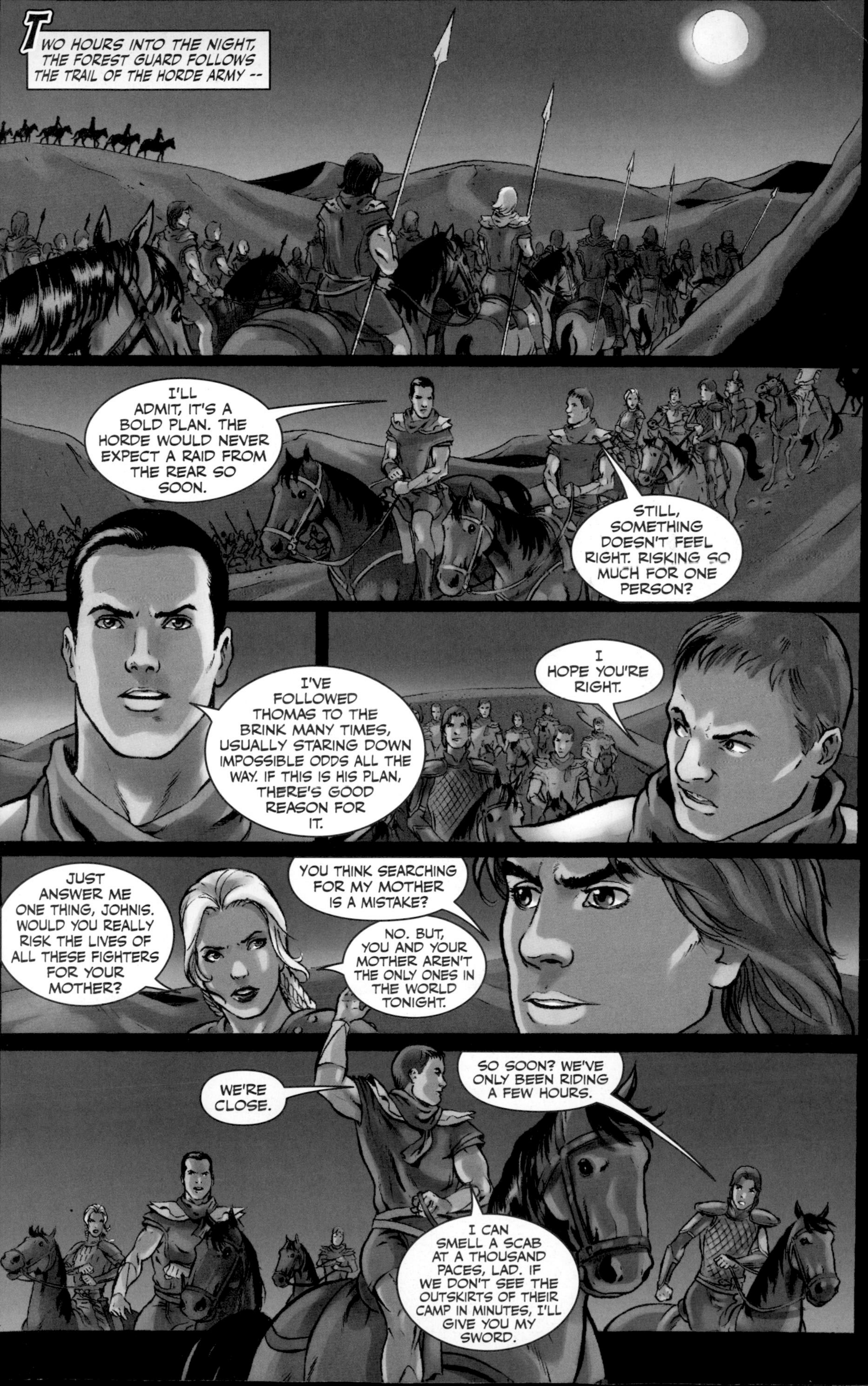
TWO HOURS INTO THE NIGHT, THE FOREST GUARD FOLLOWS THE TRAIL OF THE HORDE ARMY --
I'LL ADMIT, IT'S A BOLD PLAN. THE HORDE WOULD NEVER EXPECT A RAID FROM THE REAR SO SOON.
STILL, SOMETHING DOESN'T FEEL RIGHT. RISKING SO MUCH FOR ONE PERSON?
I'VE FOLLOWED THOMAS TO THE BRINK MANY TIMES, USUALLY STARING DOWN IMPOSSIBLE ODDS ALL THE WAY. IF THIS IS HIS PLAN, THERE'S GOOD REASON FOR IT.
I HOPE YOU'RE RIGHT.
JUST ANSWER ME ONE THING, JOHNIS. WOULD YOU REALLY RISK THE LIVES OF ALL THESE FIGHTERS FOR YOUR MOTHER?
YOU THINK SEARCHING FOR MY MOTHER IS A MISTAKE?
NO. BUT, YOU AND YOUR MOTHER AREN'T THE ONLY ONES IN THE WORLD TONIGHT.
WE'RE CLOSE.
SO SOON? WE'VE ONLY BEEN RIDING A FEW HOURS.
I CAN SMELL A SCAB AT A THOUSAND PACES, LAD. IF WE DON'T SEE THE OUTSKIRTS OF THEIR CAMP IN MINUTES, I'LL GIVE YOU MY SWORD.

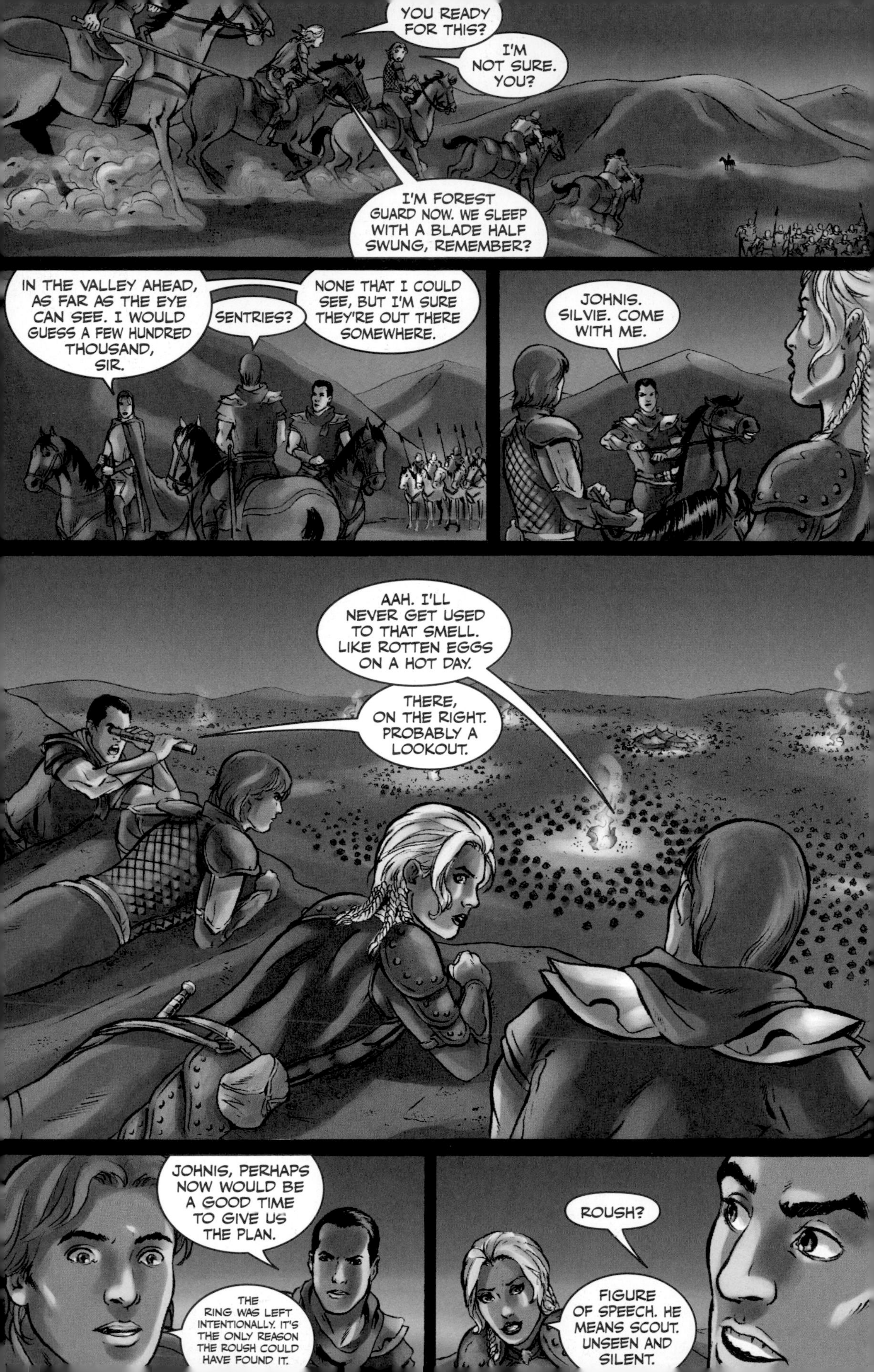

YOU READY FOR THIS?
I'M NOT SURE. YOU?
I'M FOREST GUARD NOW. WE SLEEP WITH A BLADE HALF SWUNG, REMEMBER?
IN THE VALLEY AHEAD, AS FAR AS THE EYE CAN SEE. I WOULD GUESS A FEW HUNDRED THOUSAND, SIR.
SENTRIES?
NONE THAT I COULD SEE, BUT I'M SURE THEY'RE OUT THERE SOMEWHERE.
JOHNIS. SILVIE. COME WITH ME.
AAH. I'LL NEVER GET USED TO THAT SMELL. LIKE ROTTEN EGGS ON A HOT DAY.
THERE, ON THE RIGHT. PROBABLY A LOOKOUT.
JOHNIS, PERHAPS NOW WOULD BE A GOOD TIME TO GIVE US THE PLAN.
THE RING WAS LEFT INTENTIONALLY. IT'S THE ONLY REASON THE ROUSH COULD HAVE FOUND IT.
ROUSH?
FIGURE OF SPEECH. HE MEANS SCOUT. UNSEEN AND SILENT.

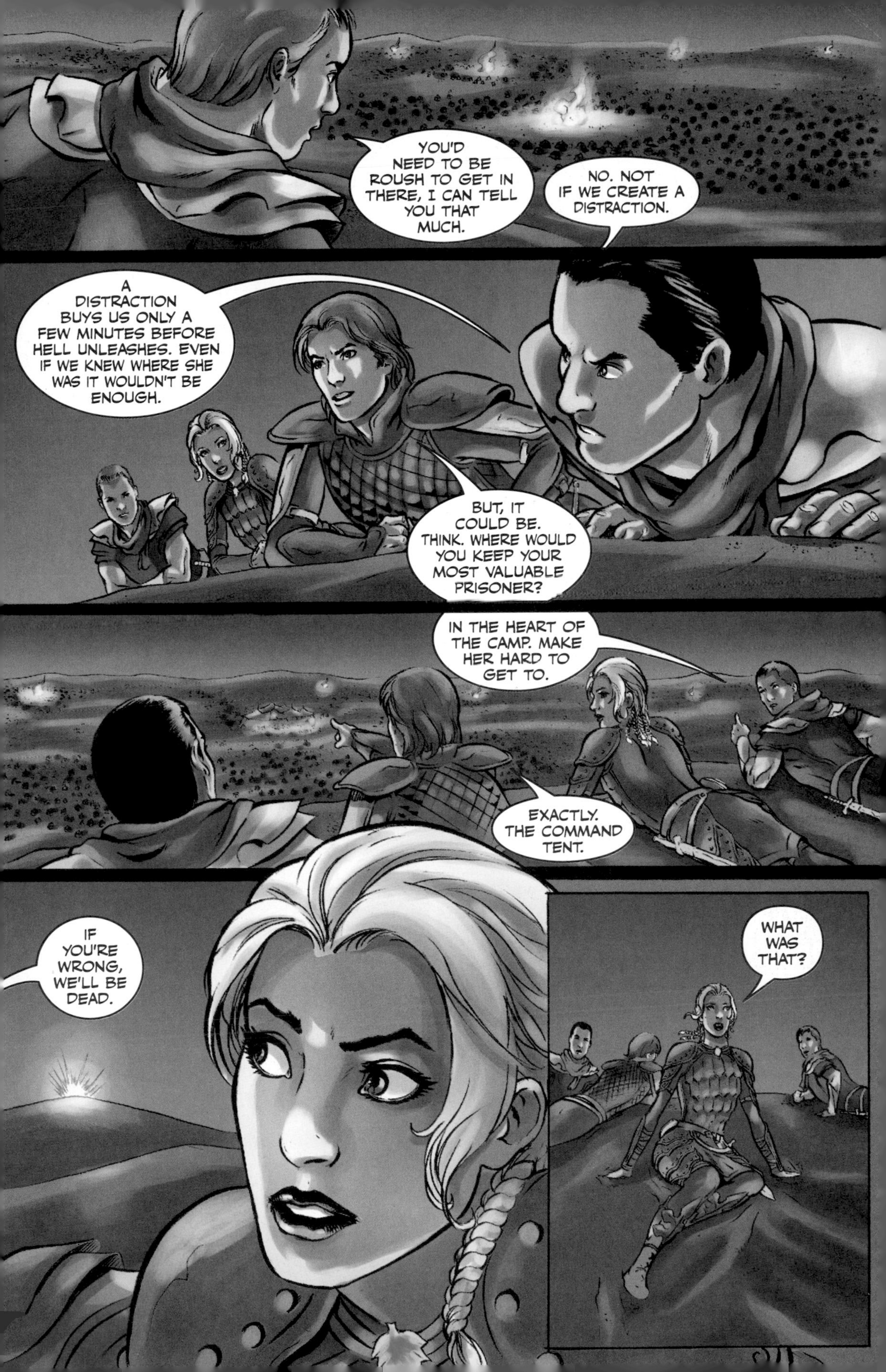
YOU'D NEED TO BE ROUSH TO GET IN THERE, I CAN TELL YOU THAT MUCH.
NO. NOT IF WE CREATE A DISTRACTION.
A DISTRACTION BUYS US ONLY A FEW MINUTES BEFORE HELL UNLEASHES. EVEN IF WE KNEW WHERE SHE WAS IT WOULDN'T BE ENOUGH.
BUT, IT COULD BE. THINK. WHERE WOULD YOU KEEP YOUR MOST VALUABLE PRISONER?
IN THE HEART OF THE CAMP. MAKE HER HARD TO GET TO.
EXACTLY. THE COMMAND TENT.
IF YOU'RE WRONG, WE'LL BE DEAD.
WHAT WAS THAT?

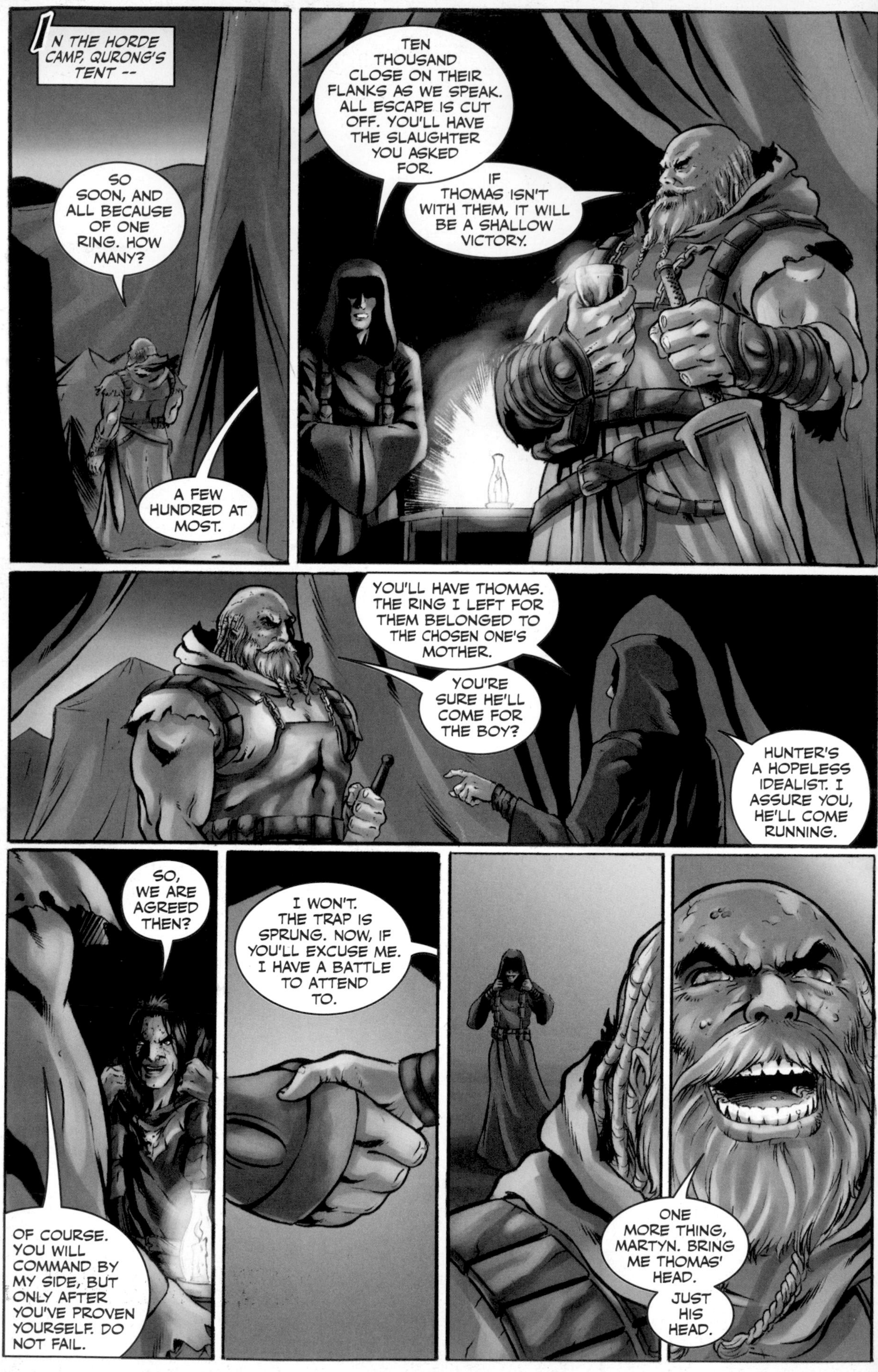
IN THE HORDE CAMP, QURONG'S TENT --
SO SOON, AND ALL BECAUSE OF ONE RING. HOW MANY?
A FEW HUNDRED AT MOST.
TEN THOUSAND CLOSE ON THEIR FLANKS AS WE SPEAK. ALL ESCAPE IS CUT OFF. YOU'LL HAVE THE SLAUGHTER YOU ASKED FOR.
IF THOMAS ISN'T WITH THEM, IT WILL BE A SHALLOW VICTORY.
YOU'LL HAVE THOMAS. THE RING I LEFT FOR THEM BELONGED TO THE CHOSEN ONE'S MOTHER.
YOU'RE SURE HE'LL COME FOR THE BOY?
HUNTER'S A HOPELESS IDEALIST. I ASSURE YOU, HE'LL COME RUNNING.
SO, WE ARE AGREED THEN?
OF COURSE. YOU WILL COMMAND BY MY SIDE, BUT ONLY AFTER YOU'VE PROVEN YOURSELF. DO NOT FAIL.
I WON'T. THE TRAP IS SPRUNG. NOW, IF YOU'LL EXCUSE ME. I HAVE A BATTLE TO ATTEND TO.
ONE MORE THING, MARTYN. BRING ME THOMAS' HEAD.
JUST HIS HEAD.

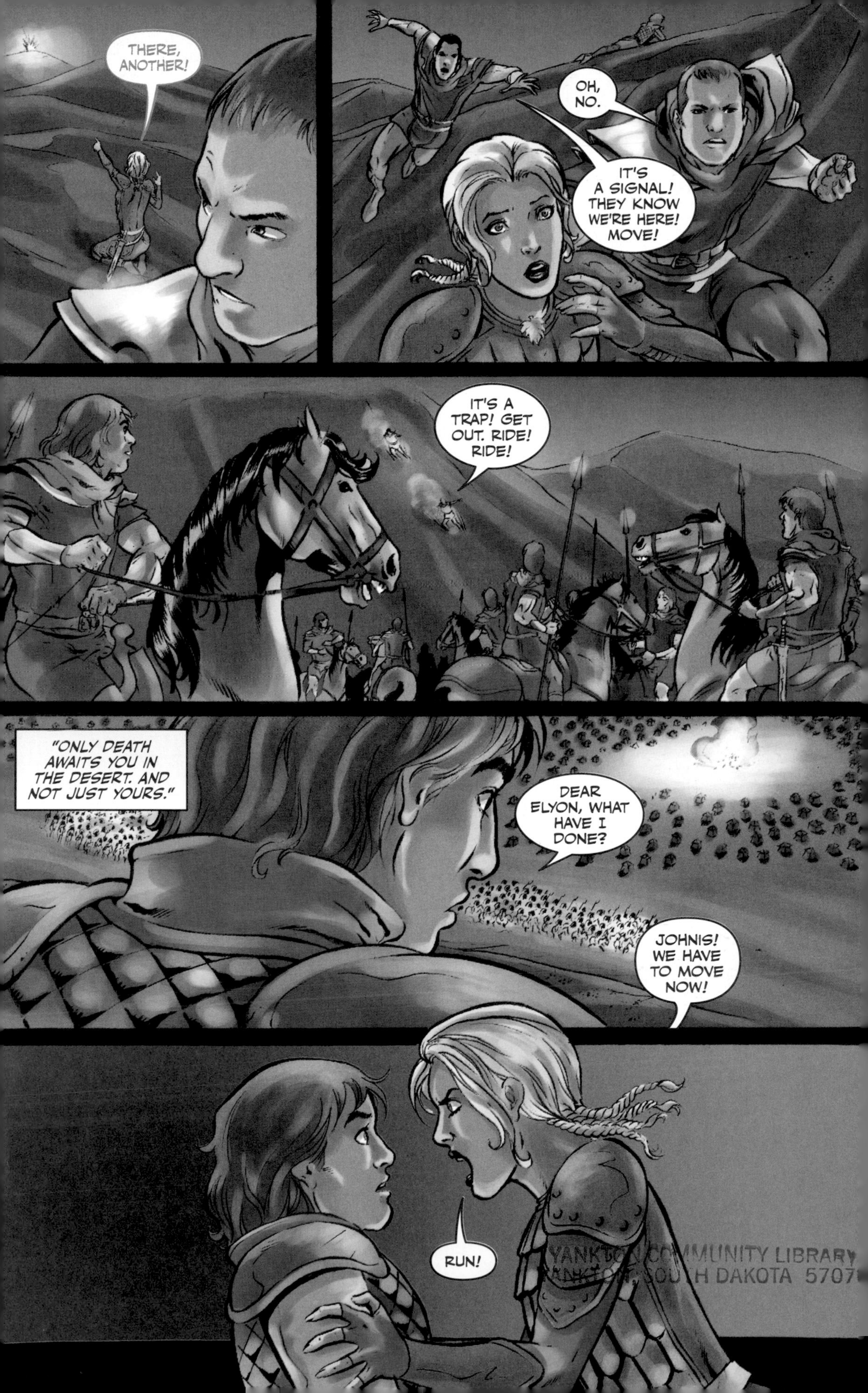
THERE, ANOTHER!
OH, NO.
IT'S A SIGNAL! THEY KNOW WE'RE HERE! MOVE!
IT'S A TRAP! GET OUT. RIDE! RIDE!
"ONLY DEATH AWAITS YOU IN THE DESERT. AND NOT JUST YOURS."
DEAR ELYON, WHAT HAVE I DONE?
JOHNIS! WE HAVE TO MOVE NOW!
RUN!

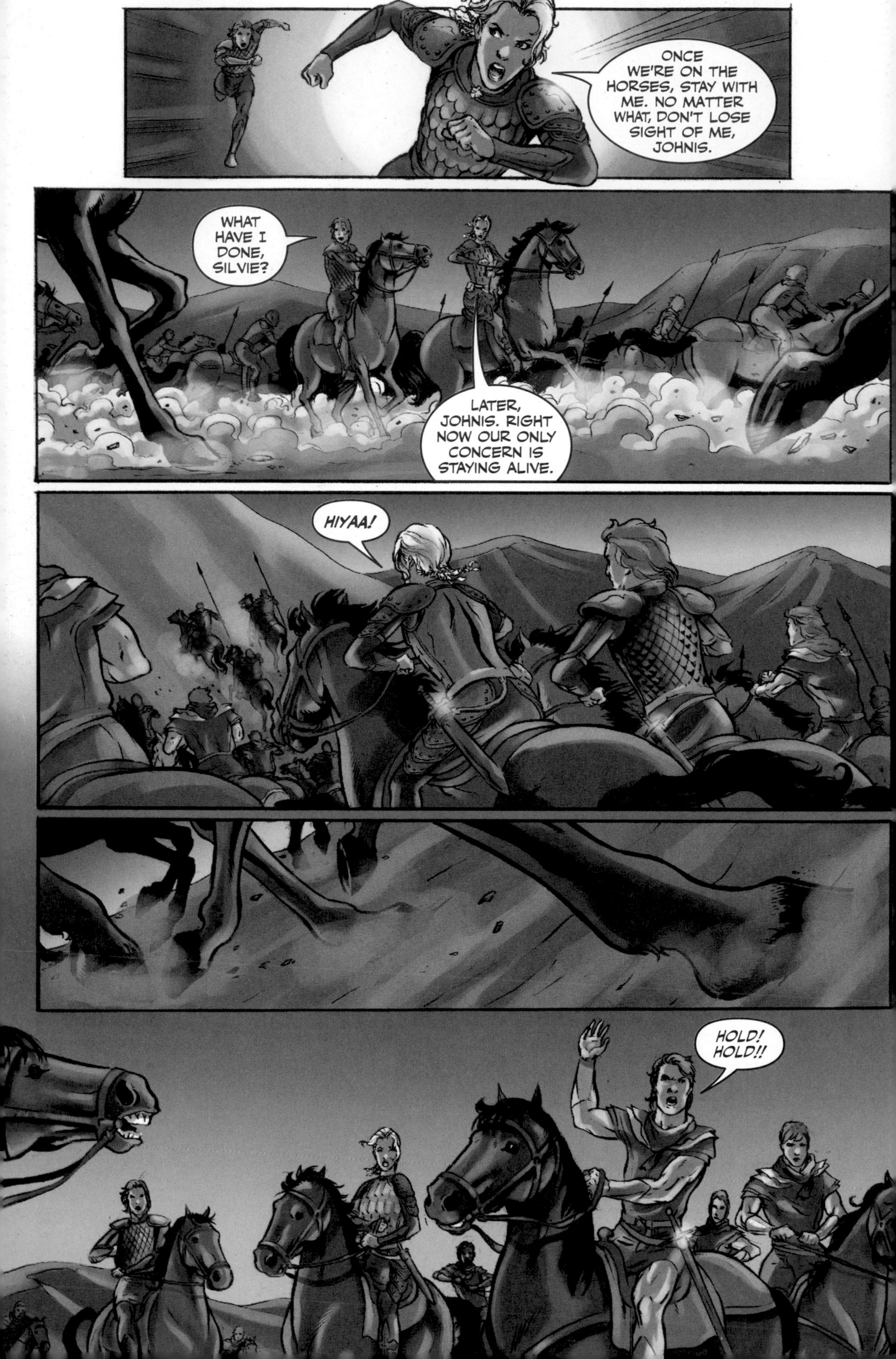
ONCE WE'RE ON THE HORSES, STAY WITH ME. NO MATTER WHAT, DON'T LOSE SIGHT OF ME, JOHNIS.
WHAT HAVE I DONE, SILVIE?
LATER, JOHNIS. RIGHT NOW OUR ONLY CONCERN IS STAYING ALIVE.
HIYAA!
HOLD! HOLD!!

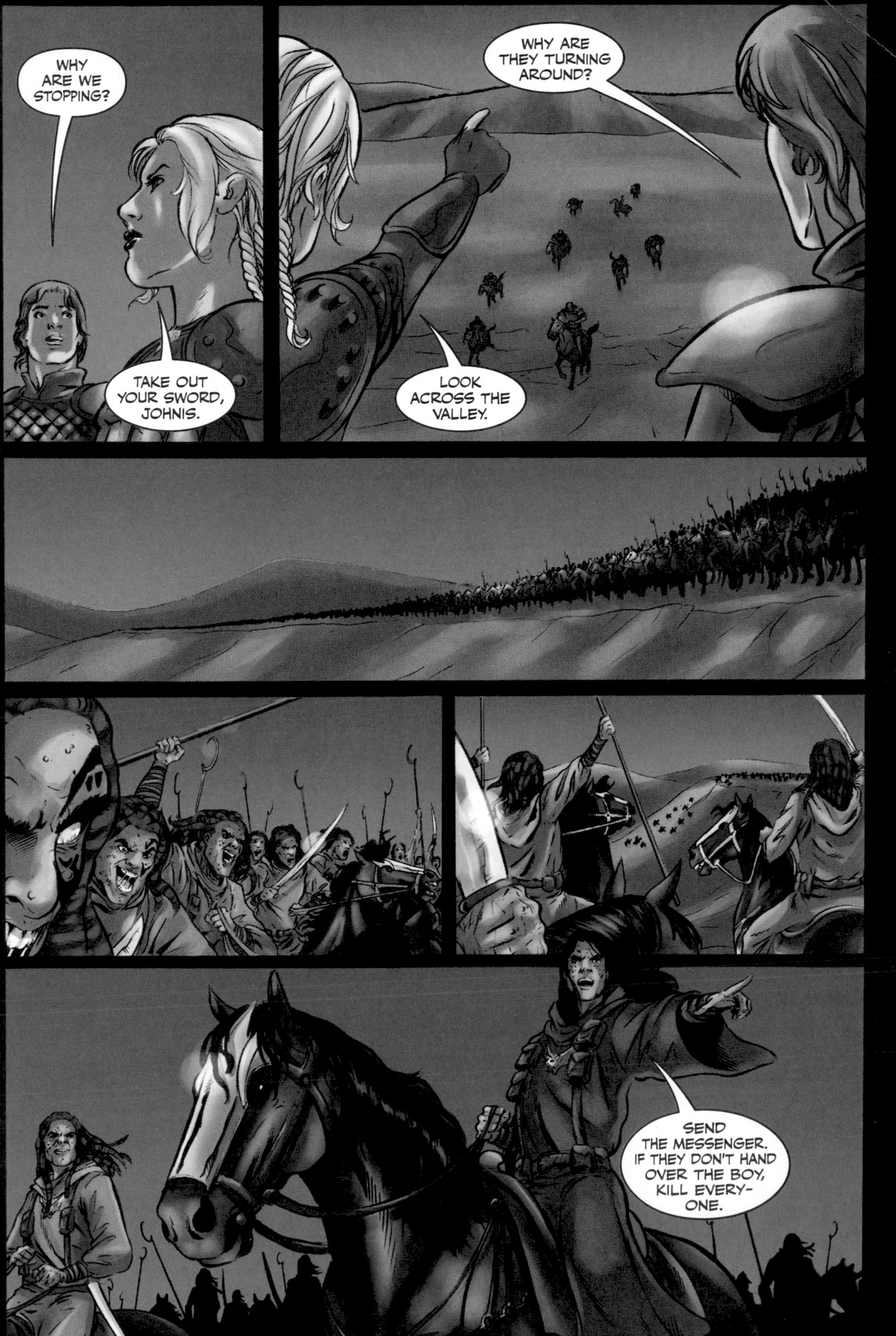
WHY ARE WE STOPPING?
TAKE OUT YOUR SWORD, JOHNIS.
WHY ARE THEY TURNING AROUND?
LOOK ACROSS THE VALLEY.
SEND THE MESSENGER. IF THEY DON'T HAND OVER THE BOY, KILL EVERY-ONE.

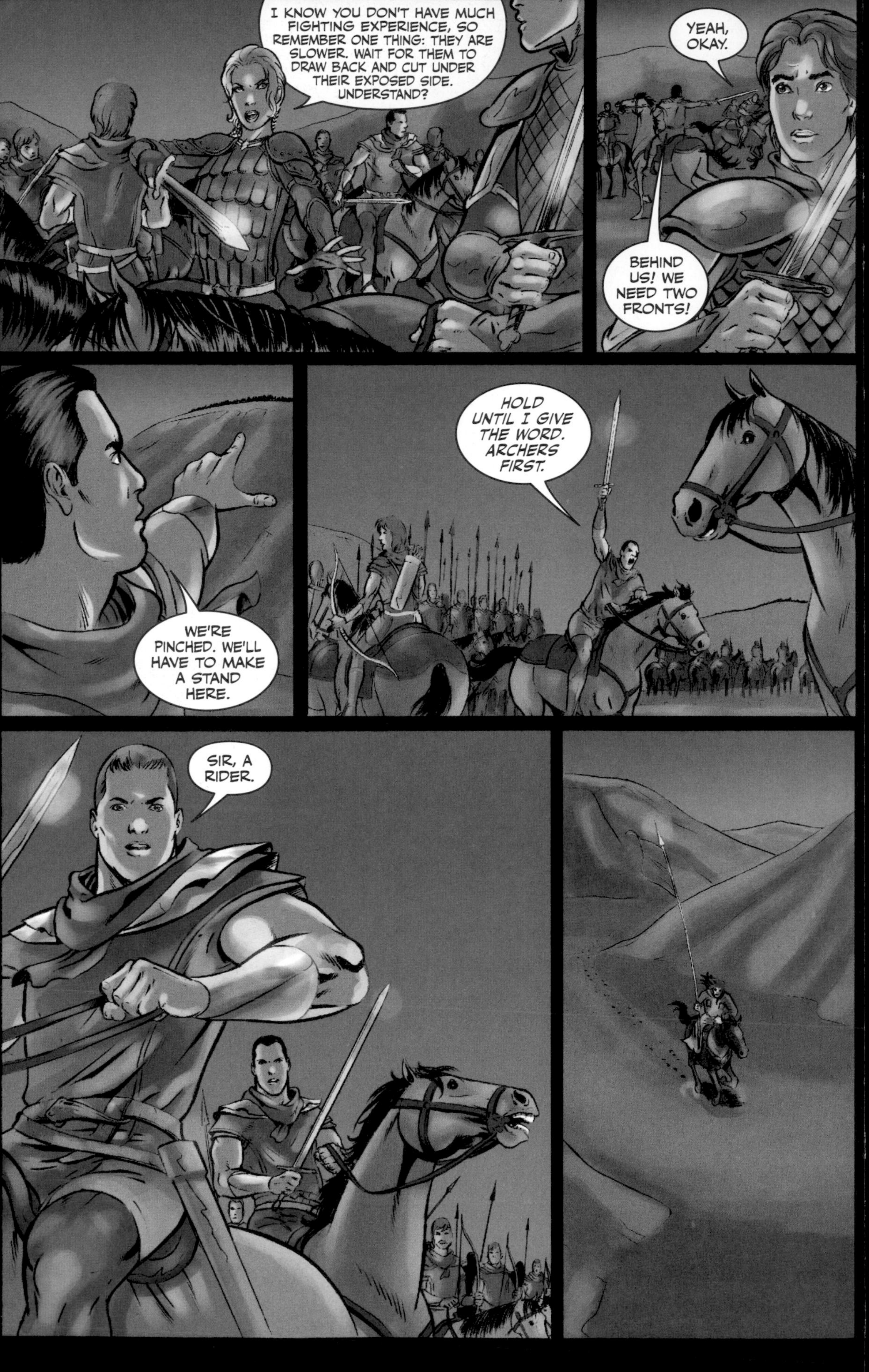
I KNOW YOU DON'T HAVE MUCH FIGHTING EXPERIENCE, SO REMEMBER ONE THING: THEY ARE SLOWER. WAIT FOR THEM TO DRAW BACK AND CUT UNDER THEIR EXPOSED SIDE. UNDERSTAND?
YEAH, OKAY.
BEHIND US! WE NEED TWO FRONTS!
WE'RE PINCHED. WE'LL HAVE TO MAKE A STAND HERE.
HOLD UNTIL I GIVE THE WORD. ARCHERS FIRST.
SIR, A RIDER.

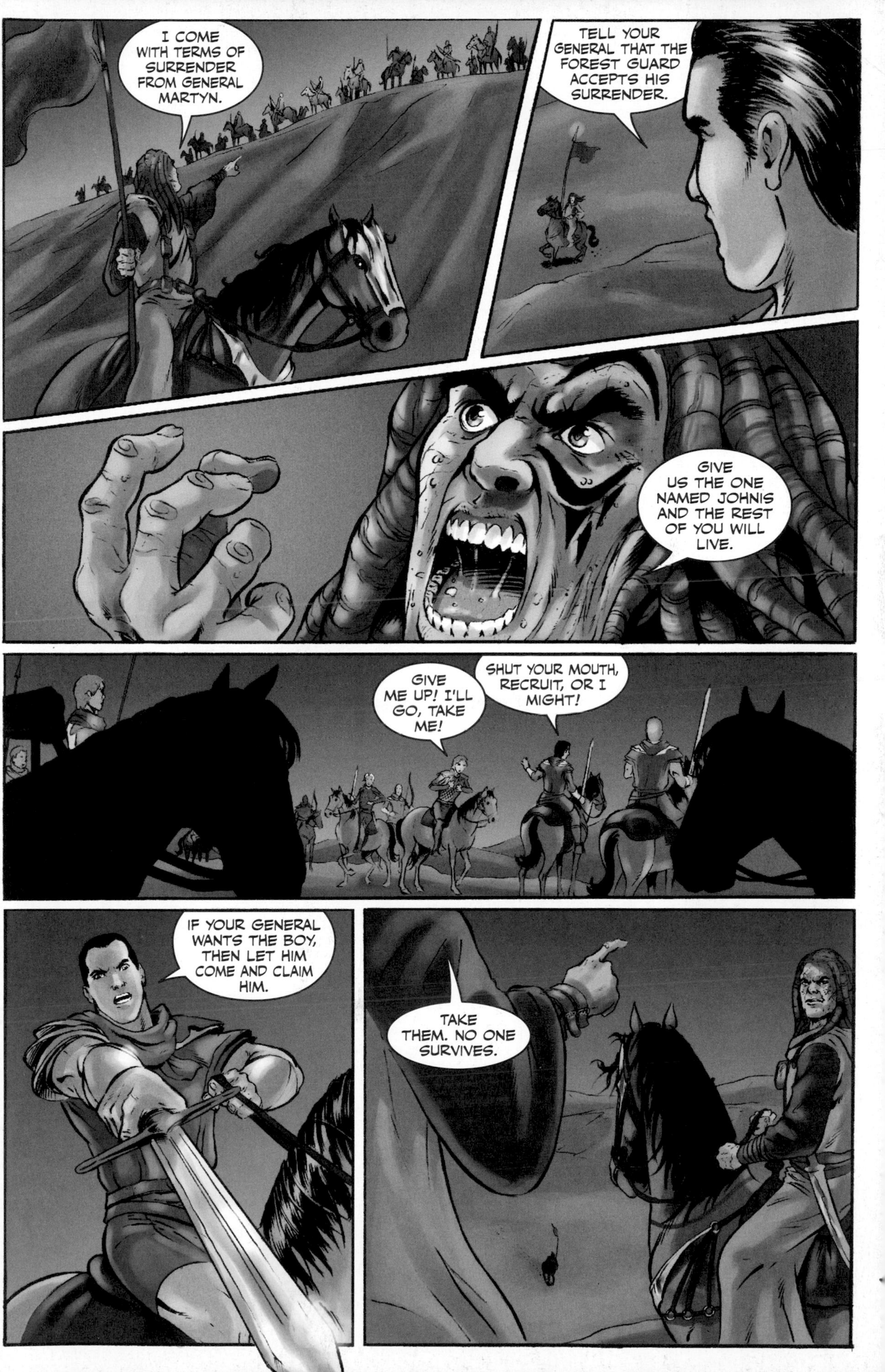
I COME WITH TERMS OF SURRENDER FROM GENERAL MARTYN.
TELL YOUR GENERAL THAT THE FOREST GUARD ACCEPTS HIS SURRENDER.
GIVE US THE ONE NAMED JOHNIS AND THE REST OF YOU WILL LIVE.
GIVE ME UP! I'LL GO, TAKE ME!
SHUT YOUR MOUTH, RECRUIT, OR I MIGHT!
IF YOUR GENERAL WANTS THE BOY, THEN LET HIM COME AND CLAIM HIM.
TAKE THEM. NO ONE SURVIVES.

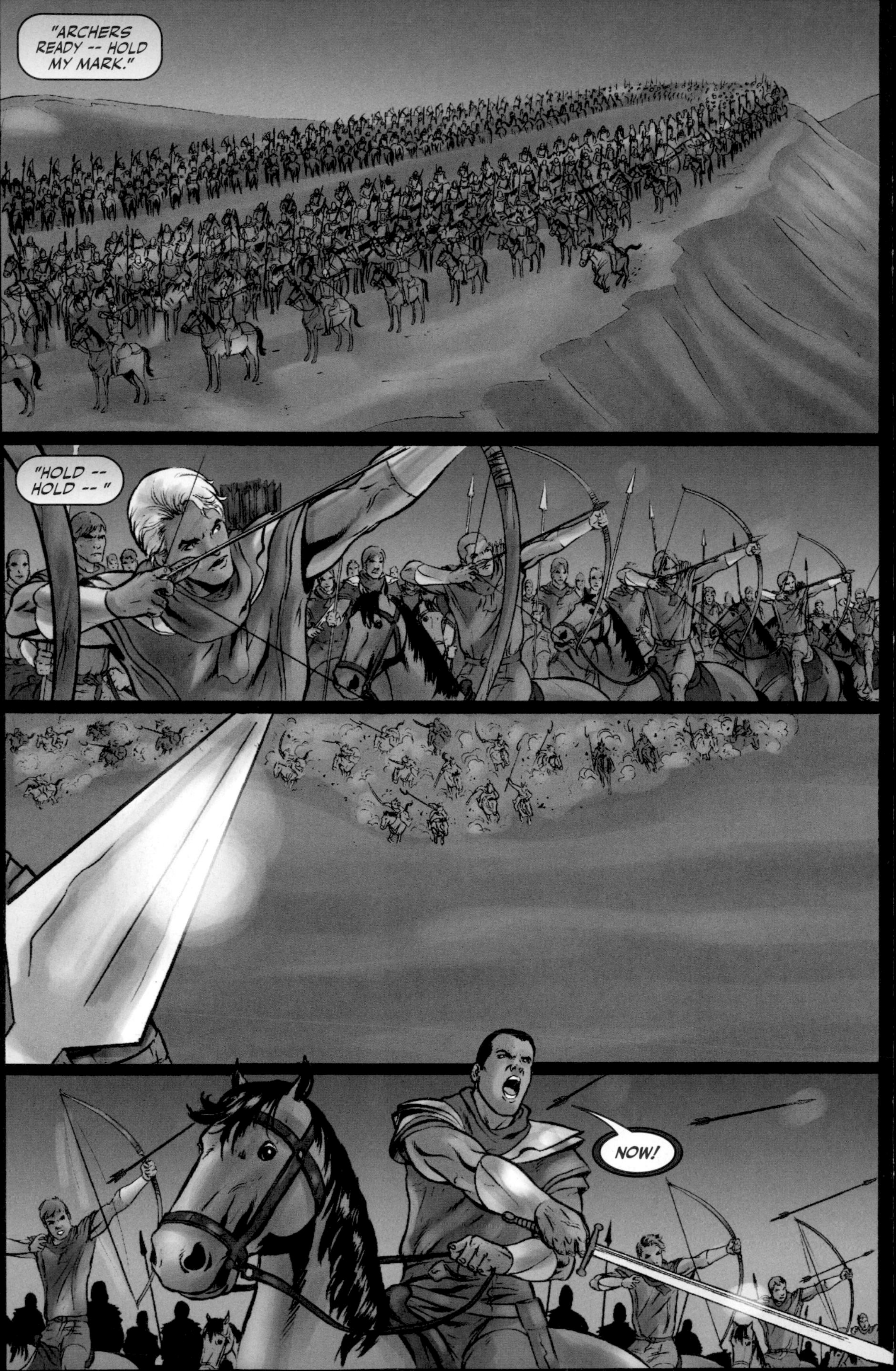
"ARCHERS READY -- HOLD MY MARK."
"HOLD -- HOLD -- "
NOW!

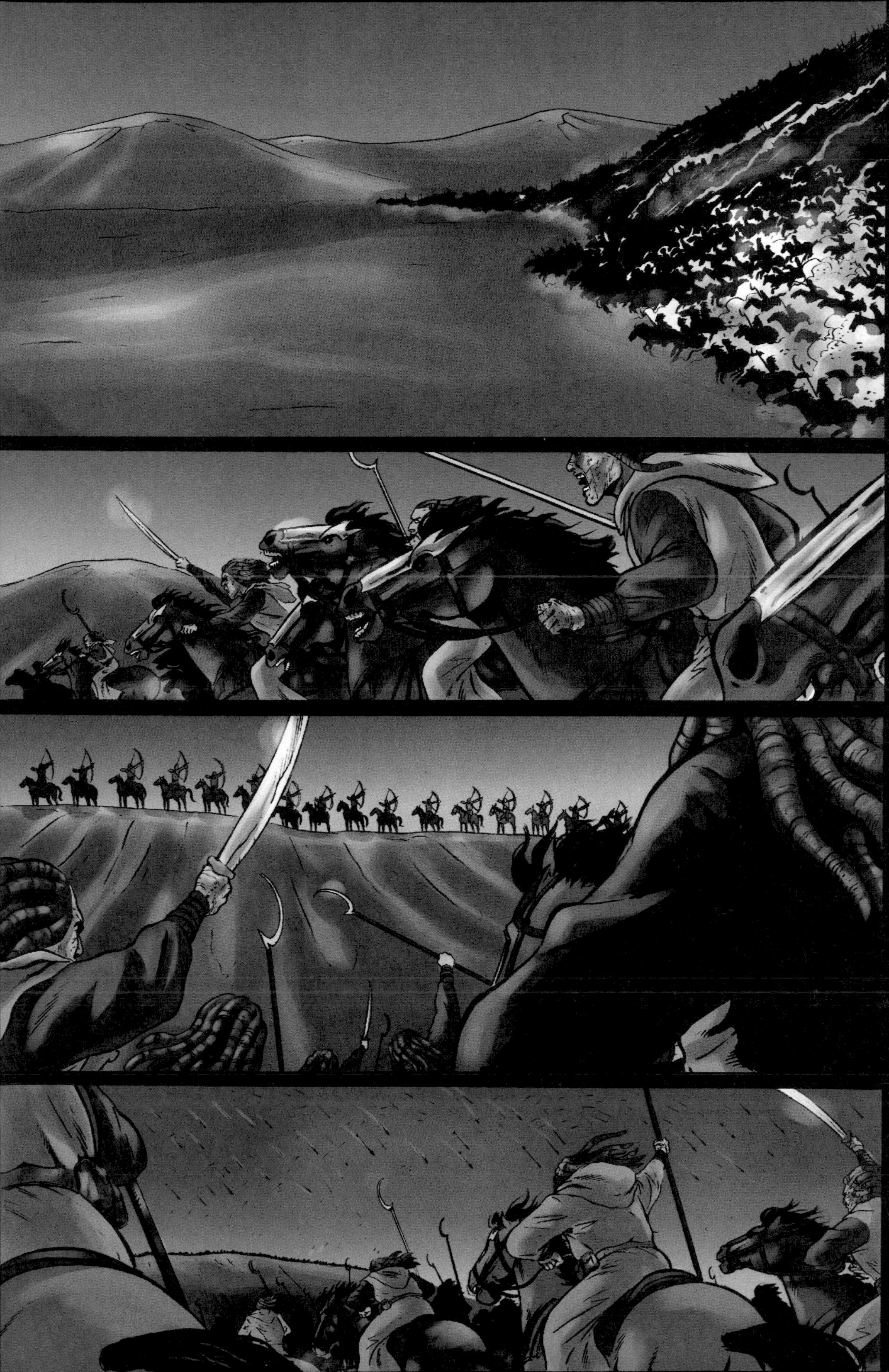

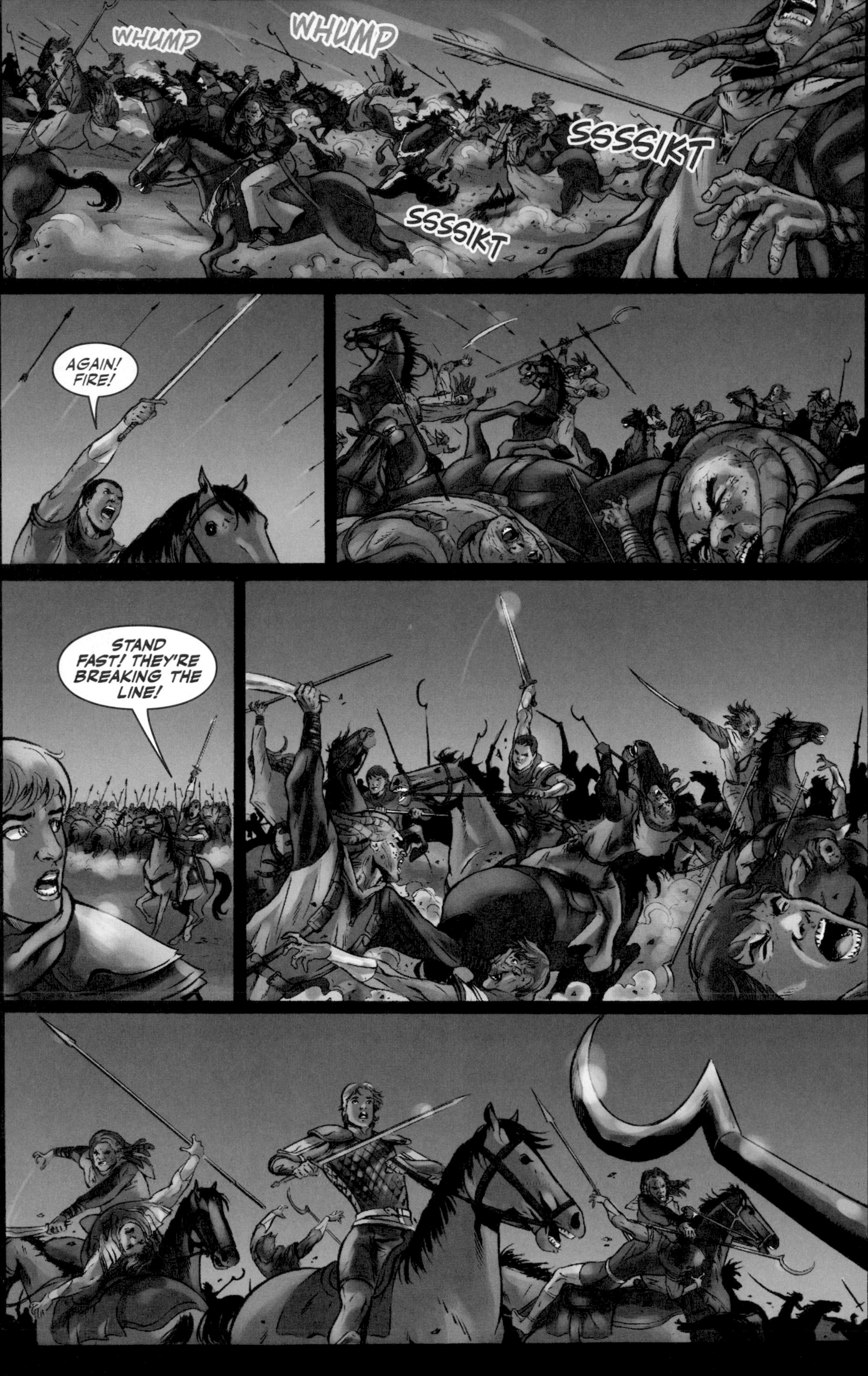
WHUMP
WHUMP
SSSSIKT
SSSSIKT
AGAIN! FIRE!
STAND FAST! THEY'RE BREAKING THE LINE!

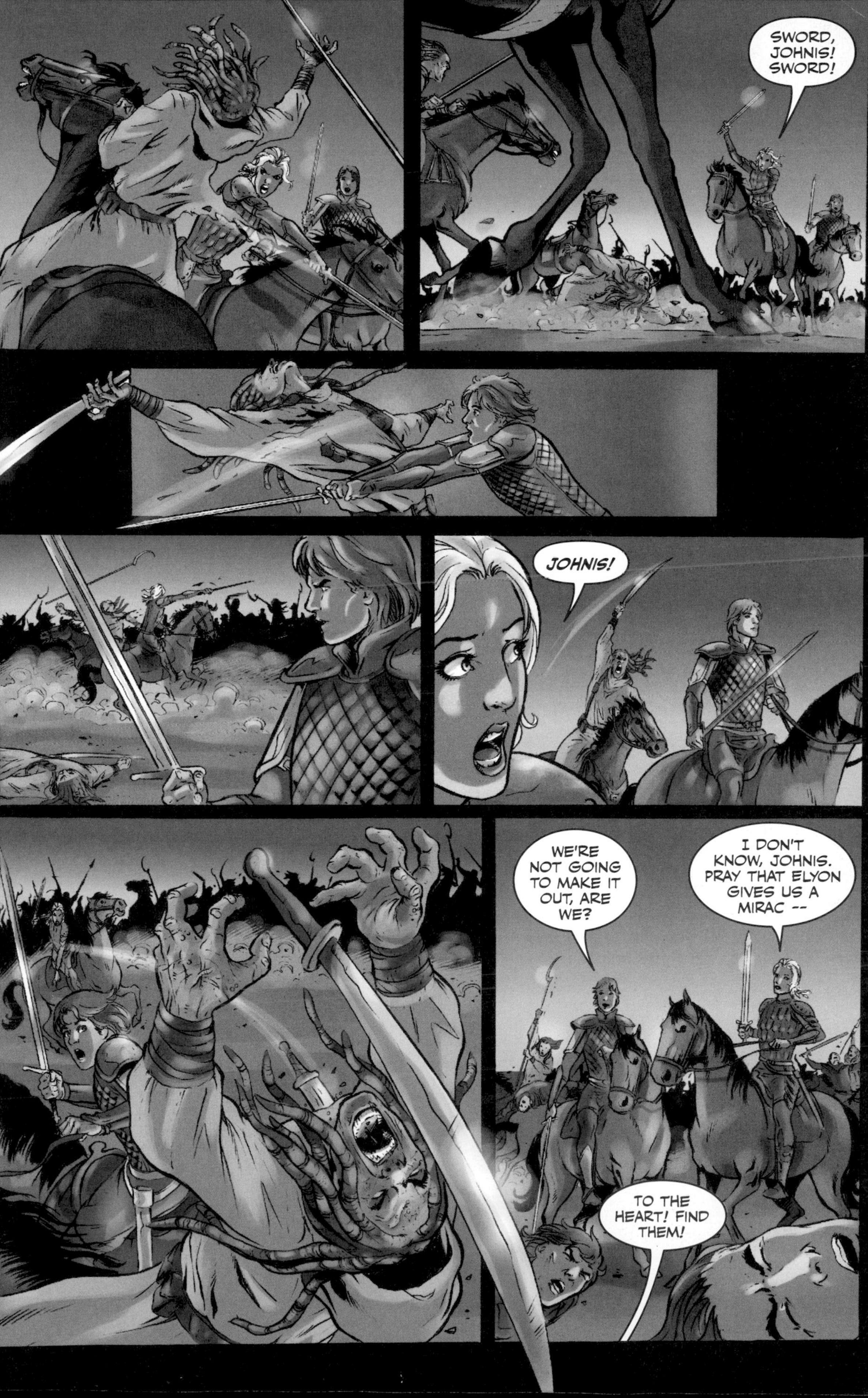
SWORD, JOHNIS! SWORD!
JOHNIS!
WE'RE NOT GOING TO MAKE IT OUT, ARE WE?
I DON'T KNOW, JOHNIS. PRAY THAT ELYON GIVES US A MIRAC --
TO THE HEART! FIND THEM!

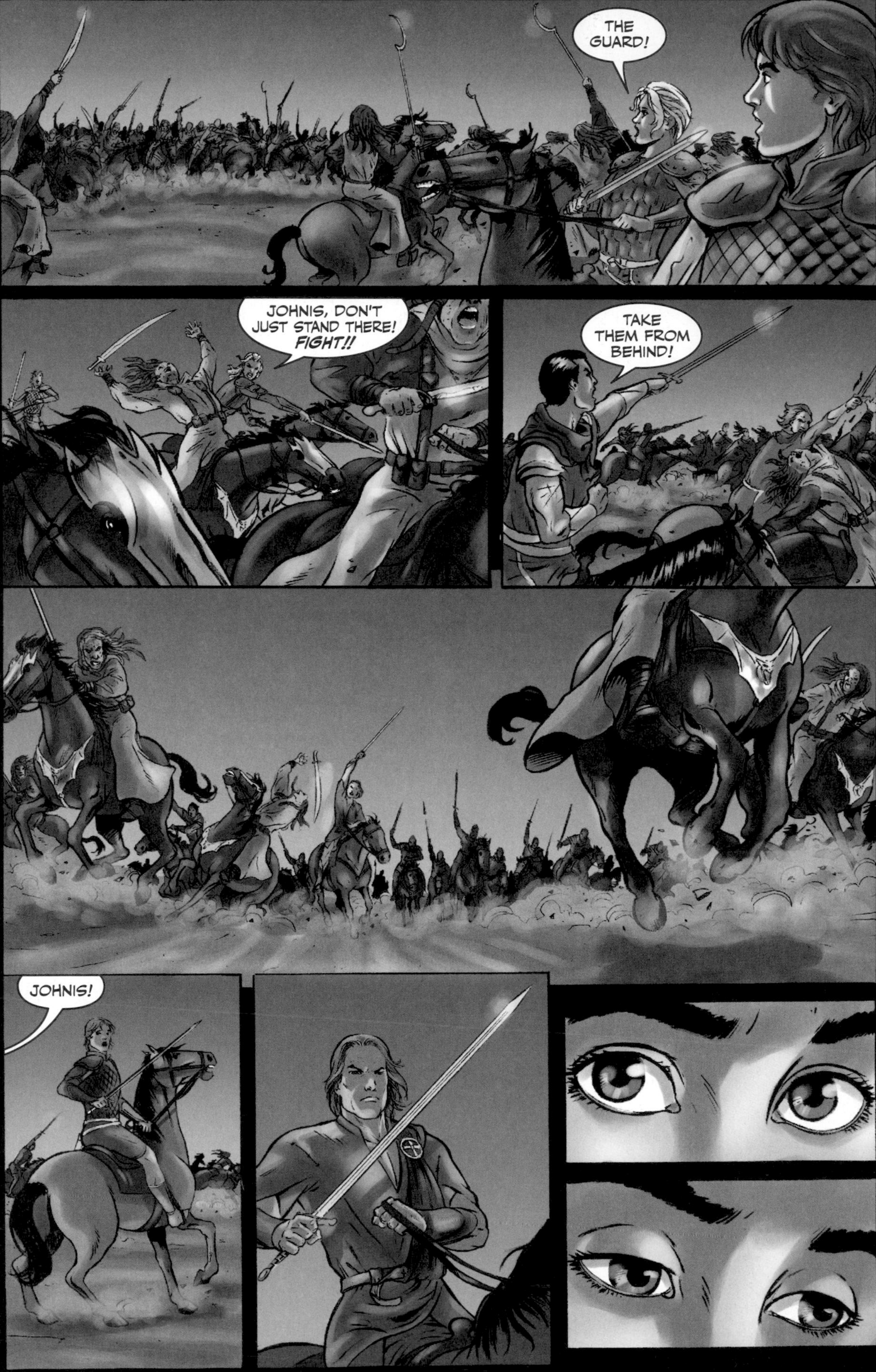
THE GUARD!
JOHNIS, DON'T JUST STAND THERE! *FIGHT!!*
TAKE THEM FROM BEHIND!
JOHNIS!

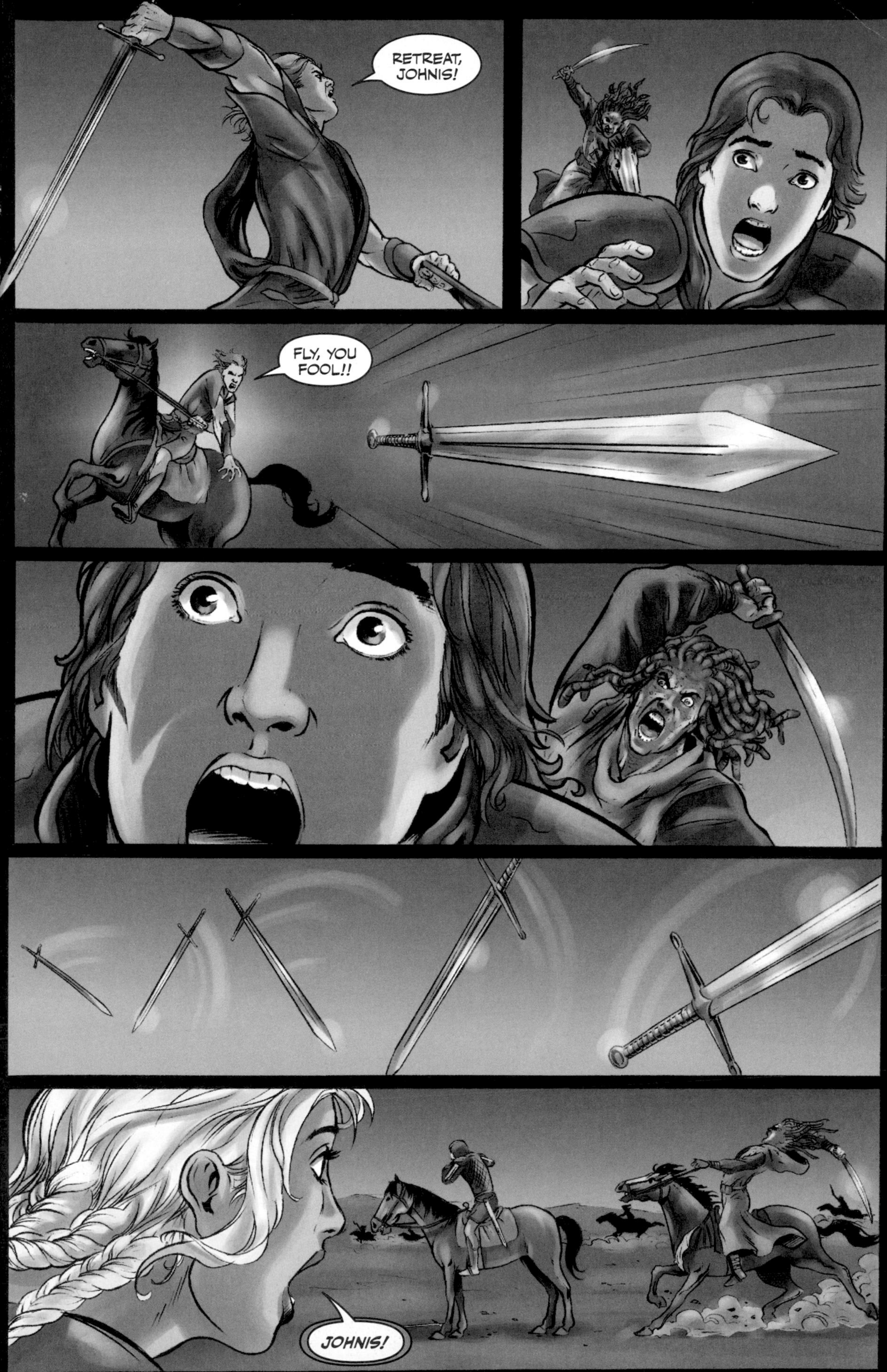
RETREAT, JOHNIS!
FLY, YOU FOOL!!
JOHNIS!

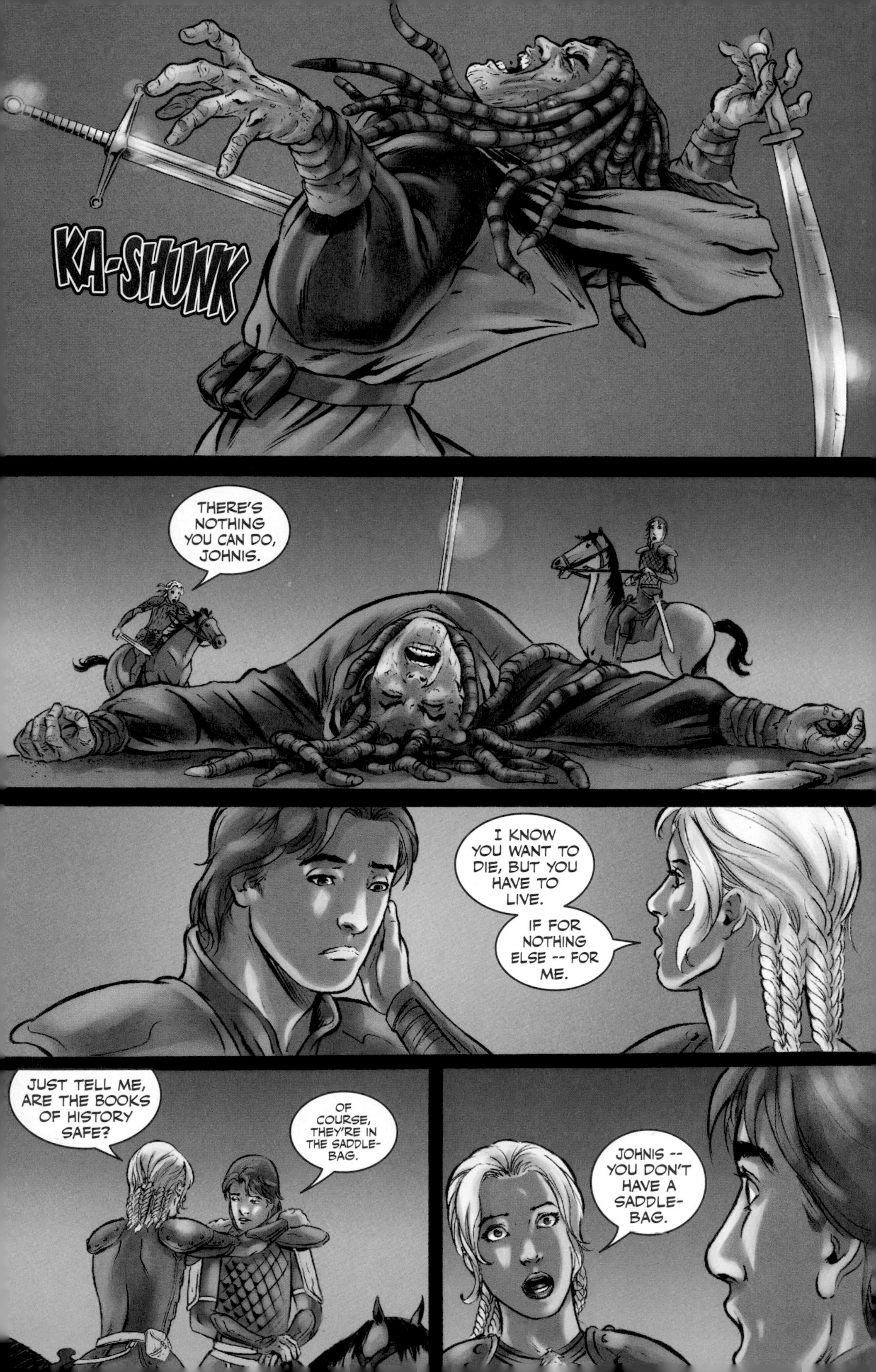
KA-SHUNK
THERE'S NOTHING YOU CAN DO, JOHNIS.
I KNOW YOU WANT TO DIE, BUT YOU HAVE TO LIVE.
IF FOR NOTHING ELSE -- FOR ME.
JUST TELL ME, ARE THE BOOKS OF HISTORY SAFE?
OF COURSE, THEY'RE IN THE SADDLE-BAG.
JOHNIS -- YOU DON'T HAVE A SADDLE-BAG.

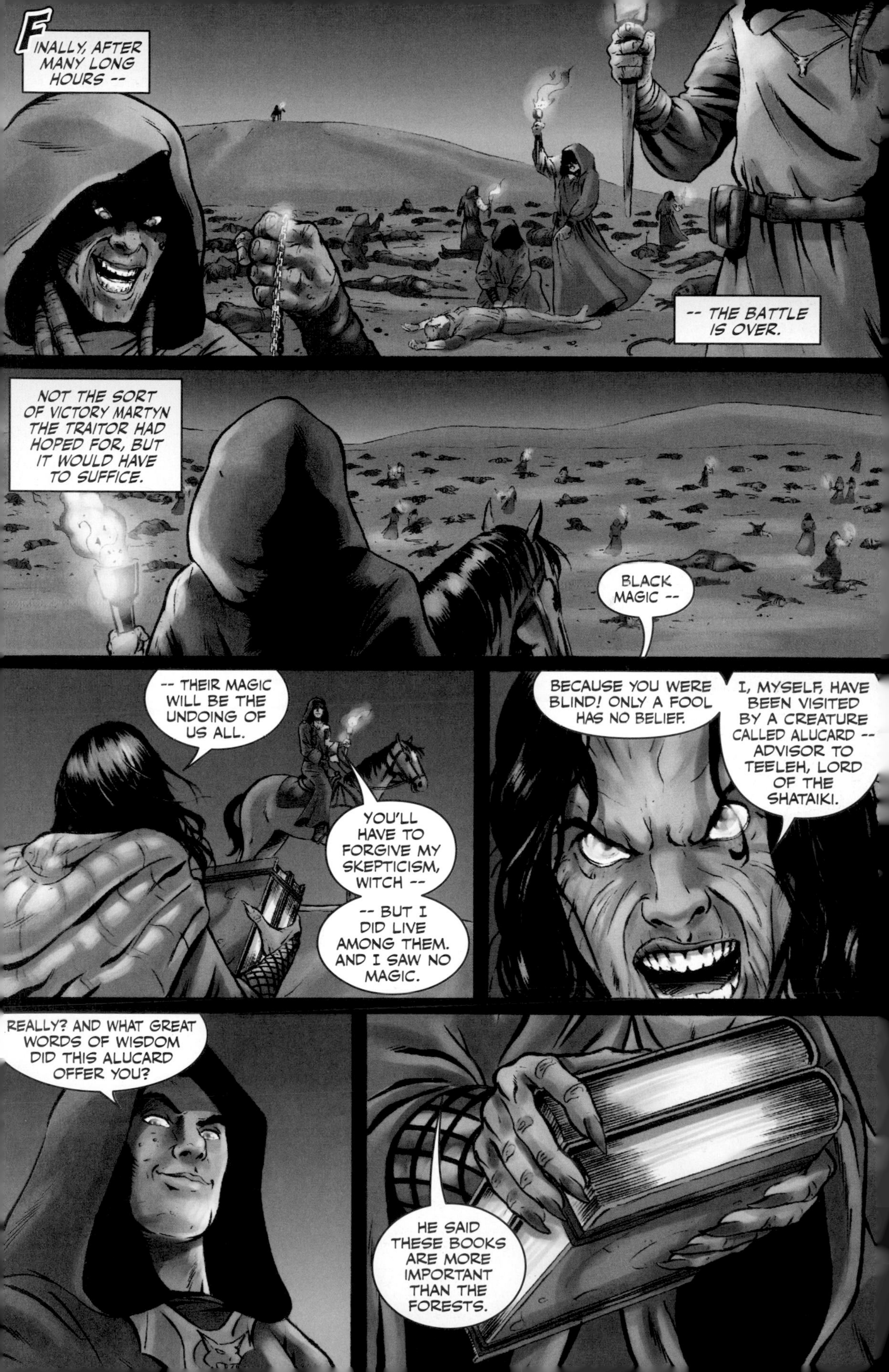
FINALLY, AFTER MANY LONG HOURS --
-- THE BATTLE IS OVER.
NOT THE SORT OF VICTORY MARTYN THE TRAITOR HAD HOPED FOR, BUT IT WOULD HAVE TO SUFFICE.
BLACK MAGIC --
-- THEIR MAGIC WILL BE THE UNDOING OF US ALL.
YOU'LL HAVE TO FORGIVE MY SKEPTICISM, WITCH --
-- BUT I DID LIVE AMONG THEM. AND I SAW NO MAGIC.
BECAUSE YOU WERE BLIND! ONLY A FOOL HAS NO BELIEF.
I, MYSELF, HAVE BEEN VISITED BY A CREATURE CALLED ALUCARD -- ADVISOR TO TEELEH, LORD OF THE SHATAIKI.
REALLY? AND WHAT GREAT WORDS OF WISDOM DID THIS ALUCARD OFFER YOU?
HE SAID THESE BOOKS ARE MORE IMPORTANT THAN THE FORESTS.

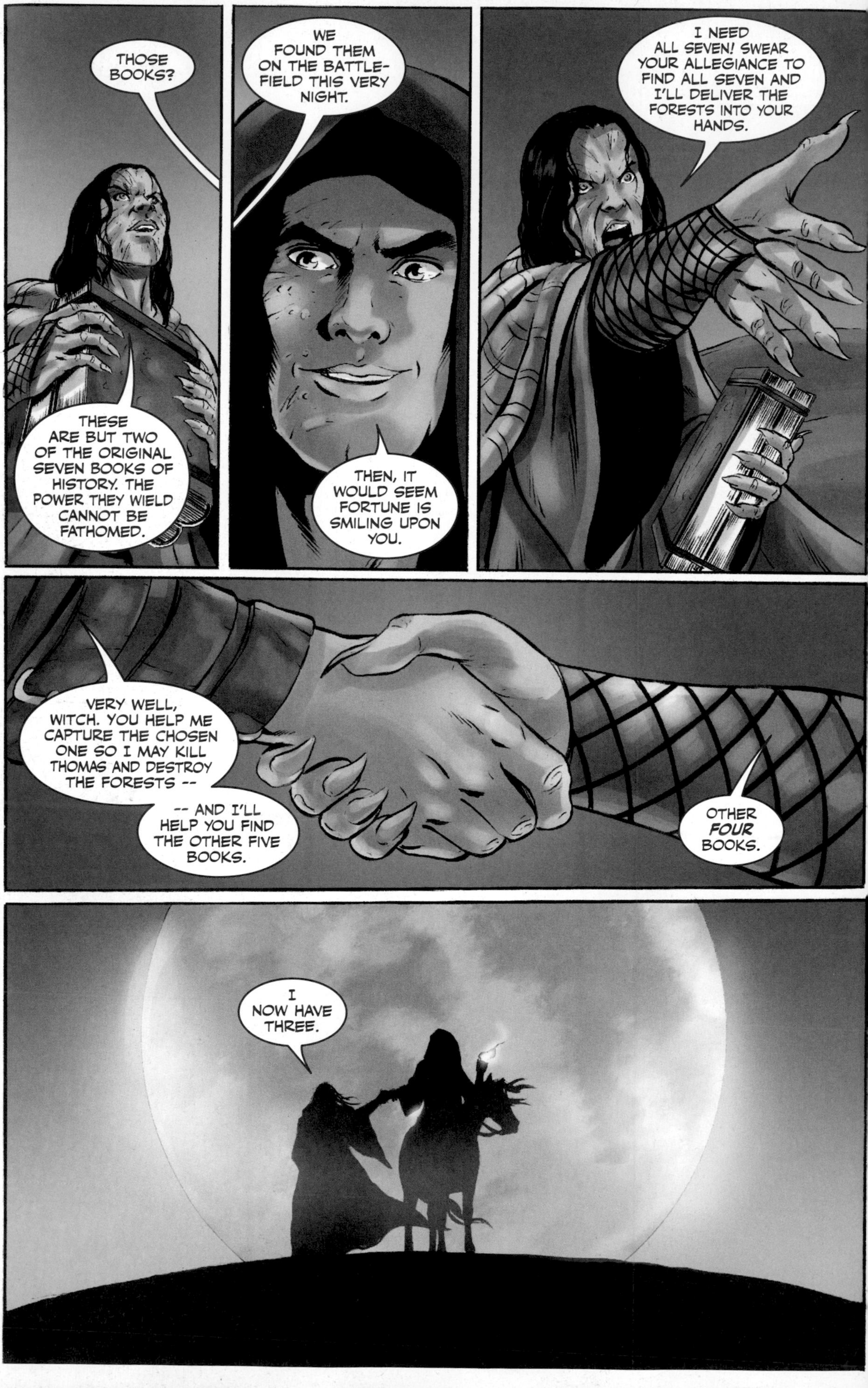
THOSE BOOKS?
WE FOUND THEM ON THE BATTLE-FIELD THIS VERY NIGHT.
I NEED ALL SEVEN! SWEAR YOUR ALLEGIANCE TO FIND ALL SEVEN AND I'LL DELIVER THE FORESTS INTO YOUR HANDS.
THESE ARE BUT TWO OF THE ORIGINAL SEVEN BOOKS OF HISTORY. THE POWER THEY WIELD CANNOT BE FATHOMED.
THEN, IT WOULD SEEM FORTUNE IS SMILING UPON YOU.
VERY WELL, WITCH. YOU HELP ME CAPTURE THE CHOSEN ONE SO I MAY KILL THOMAS AND DESTROY THE FORESTS --
-- AND I'LL HELP YOU FIND THE OTHER FIVE BOOKS.
OTHER *FOUR* BOOKS.
I NOW HAVE THREE.

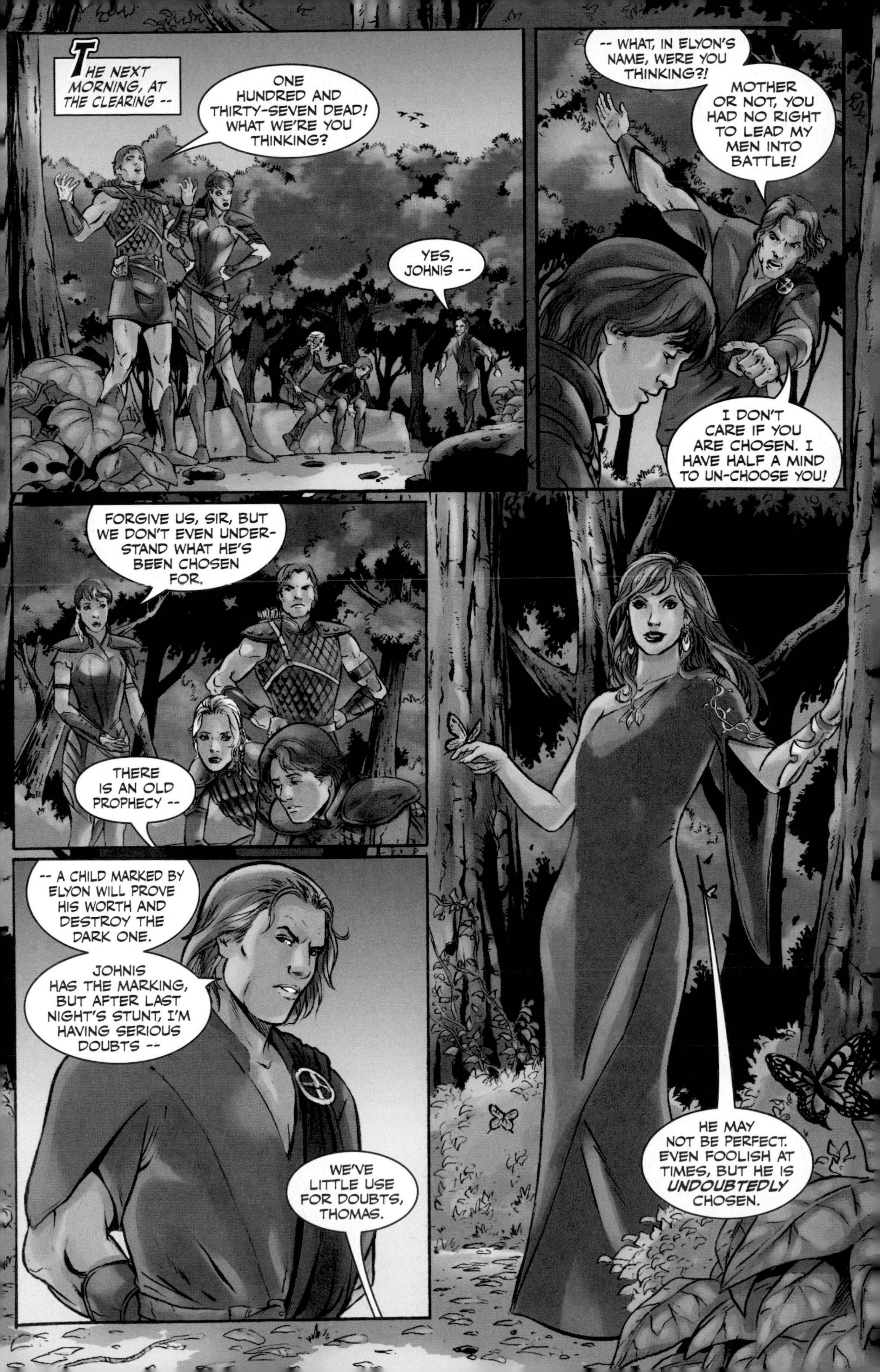
THE NEXT MORNING, AT THE CLEARING --
ONE HUNDRED AND THIRTY-SEVEN DEAD! WHAT WE'RE YOU THINKING?
YES, JOHNIS --
-- WHAT, IN ELYON'S NAME, WERE YOU THINKING?!
MOTHER OR NOT, YOU HAD NO RIGHT TO LEAD MY MEN INTO BATTLE!
I DON'T CARE IF YOU ARE CHOSEN. I HAVE HALF A MIND TO UN-CHOOSE YOU!
FORGIVE US, SIR, BUT WE DON'T EVEN UNDER-STAND WHAT HE'S BEEN CHOSEN FOR.
THERE IS AN OLD PROPHECY --
-- A CHILD MARKED BY ELYON WILL PROVE HIS WORTH AND DESTROY THE DARK ONE.
JOHNIS HAS THE MARKING, BUT AFTER LAST NIGHT'S STUNT, I'M HAVING SERIOUS DOUBTS --
WE'VE LITTLE USE FOR DOUBTS, THOMAS.
HE MAY NOT BE PERFECT. EVEN FOOLISH AT TIMES, BUT HE IS *UNDOUBTEDLY* CHOSEN.

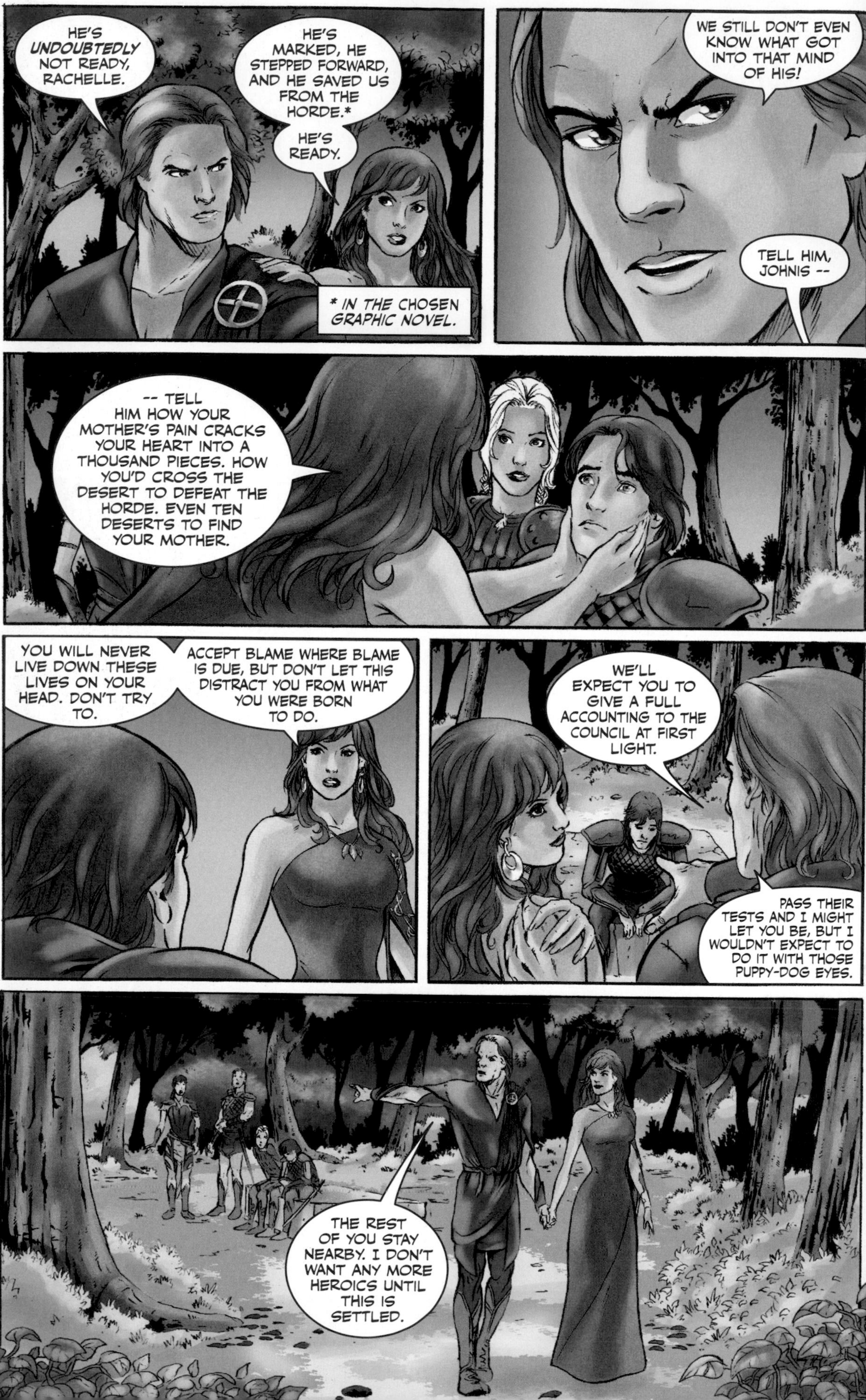
HE'S *UNDOUBTEDLY* NOT READY, RACHELLE.
HE'S MARKED, HE STEPPED FORWARD, AND HE SAVED US FROM THE HORDE.*
HE'S READY.
* IN THE CHOSEN GRAPHIC NOVEL.
WE STILL DON'T EVEN KNOW WHAT GOT INTO THAT MIND OF HIS!
TELL HIM, JOHNIS --
-- TELL HIM HOW YOUR MOTHER'S PAIN CRACKS YOUR HEART INTO A THOUSAND PIECES. HOW YOU'D CROSS THE DESERT TO DEFEAT THE HORDE. EVEN TEN DESERTS TO FIND YOUR MOTHER.
YOU WILL NEVER LIVE DOWN THESE LIVES ON YOUR HEAD. DON'T TRY TO.
ACCEPT BLAME WHERE BLAME IS DUE, BUT DON'T LET THIS DISTRACT YOU FROM WHAT YOU WERE BORN TO DO.
WE'LL EXPECT YOU TO GIVE A FULL ACCOUNTING TO THE COUNCIL AT FIRST LIGHT.
PASS THEIR TESTS AND I MIGHT LET YOU BE, BUT I WOULDN'T EXPECT TO DO IT WITH THOSE PUPPY-DOG EYES.
THE REST OF YOU STAY NEARBY. I DON'T WANT ANY MORE HEROICS UNTIL THIS IS SETTLED.

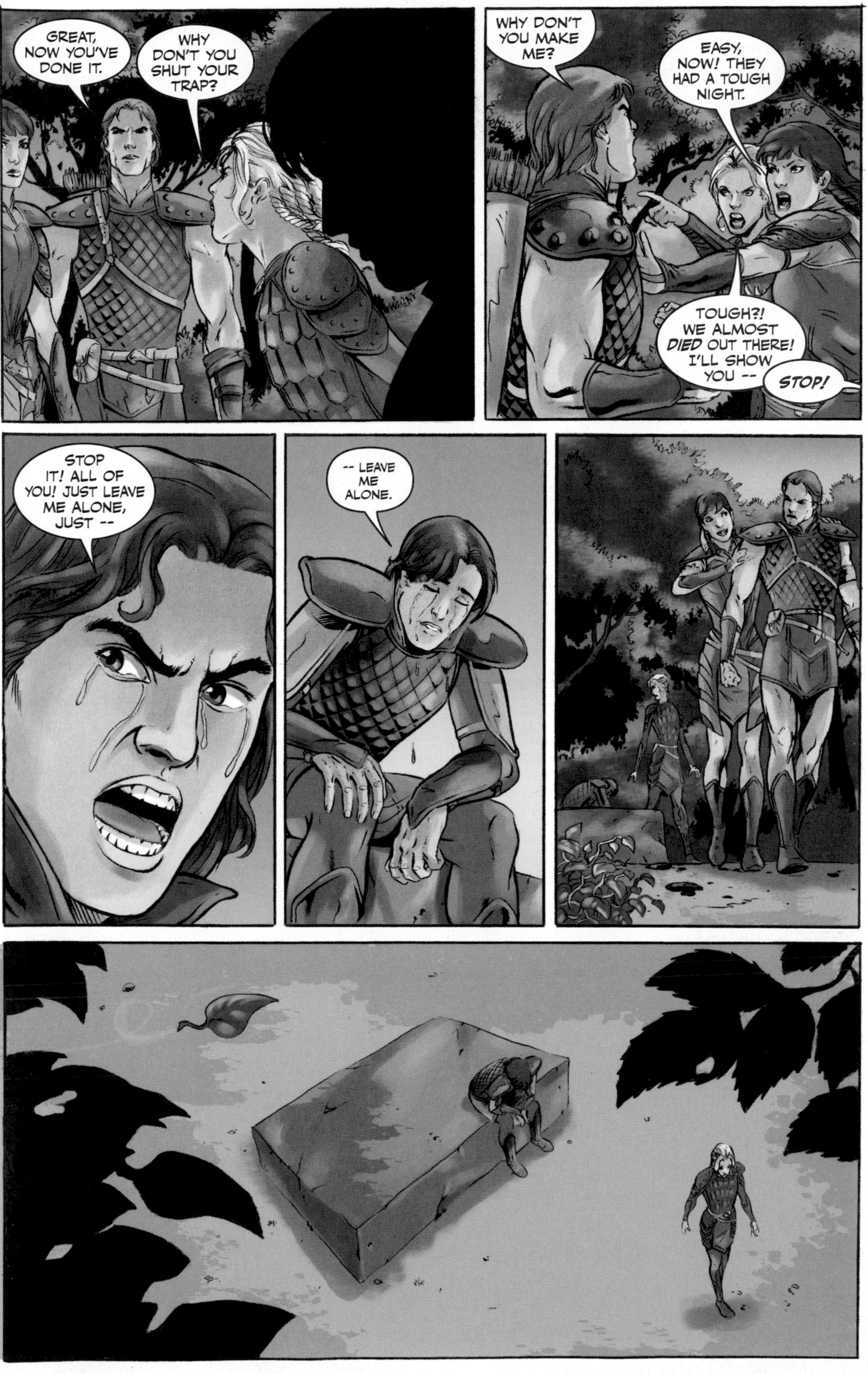
GREAT, NOW YOU'VE DONE IT.
WHY DON'T YOU SHUT YOUR TRAP?
WHY DON'T YOU MAKE ME?
EASY, NOW! THEY HAD A TOUGH NIGHT.
TOUGH?! WE ALMOST DIED OUT THERE! I'LL SHOW YOU --
STOP!
STOP IT! ALL OF YOU! JUST LEAVE ME ALONE, JUST --
-- LEAVE ME ALONE.

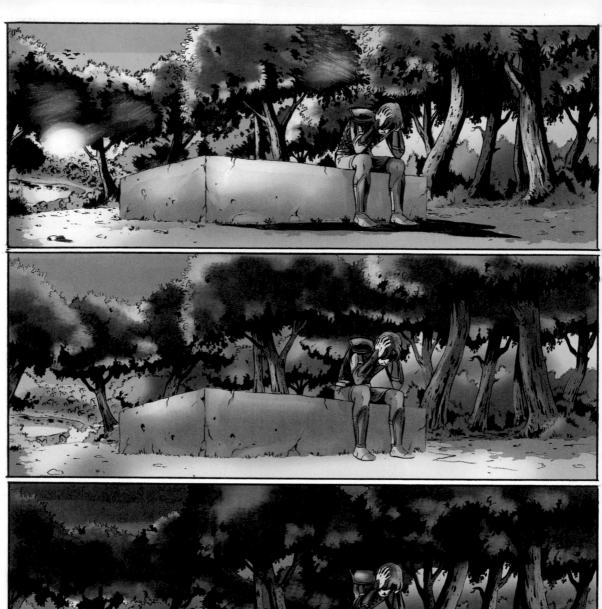

YOU GONNA SIT THERE ALL NIGHT?

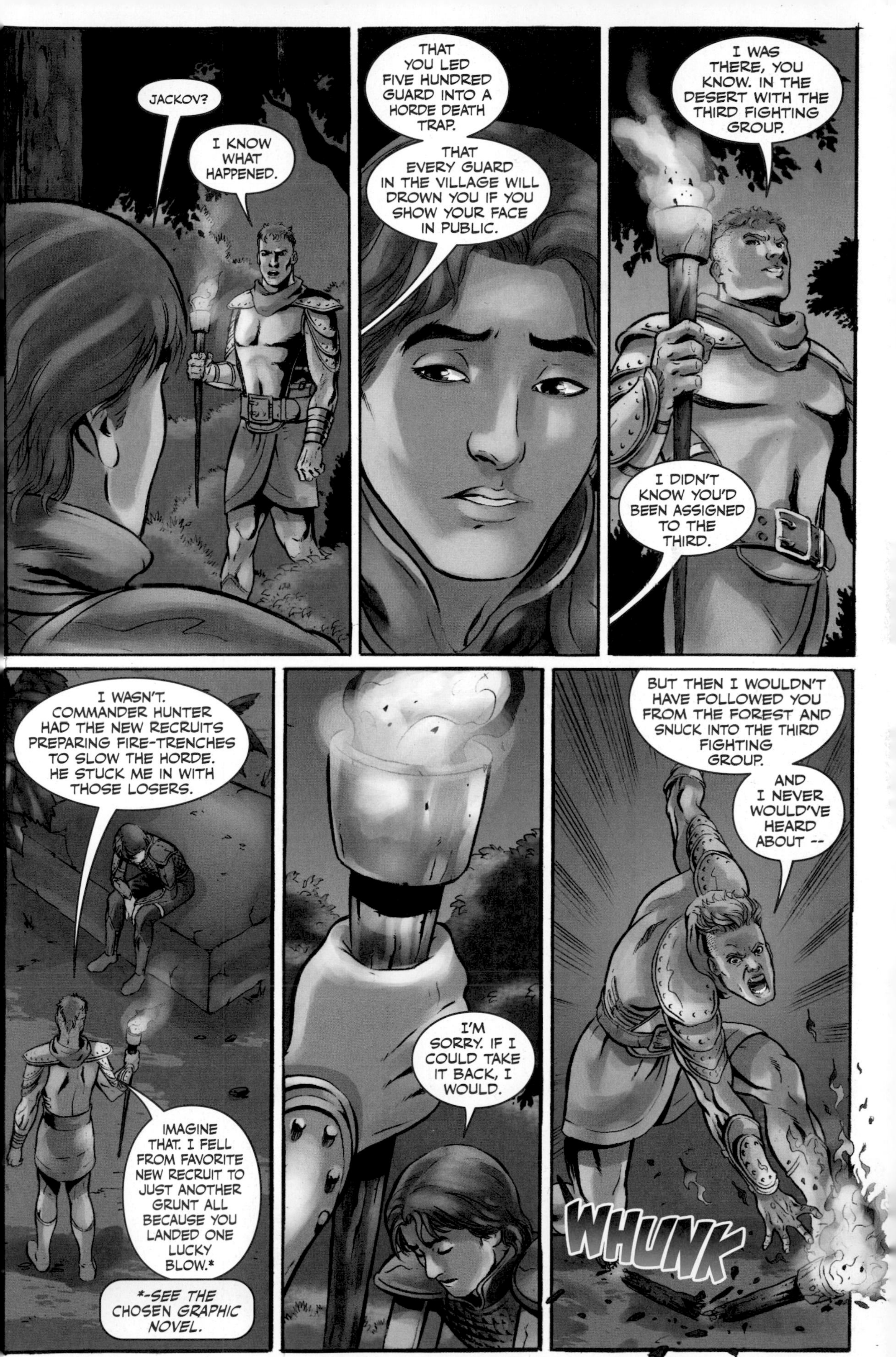
JACKOV?
I KNOW WHAT HAPPENED.
THAT YOU LED FIVE HUNDRED GUARD INTO A HORDE DEATH TRAP.
THAT EVERY GUARD IN THE VILLAGE WILL DROWN YOU IF YOU SHOW YOUR FACE IN PUBLIC.
I WAS THERE, YOU KNOW. IN THE DESERT WITH THE THIRD FIGHTING GROUP.
I DIDN'T KNOW YOU'D BEEN ASSIGNED TO THE THIRD.
I WASN'T. COMMANDER HUNTER HAD THE NEW RECRUITS PREPARING FIRE-TRENCHES TO SLOW THE HORDE. HE STUCK ME IN WITH THOSE LOSERS.
IMAGINE THAT. I FELL FROM FAVORITE NEW RECRUIT TO JUST ANOTHER GRUNT ALL BECAUSE YOU LANDED ONE LUCKY BLOW.*
*-SEE THE CHOSEN GRAPHIC NOVEL.
I'M SORRY. IF I COULD TAKE IT BACK, I WOULD.
BUT THEN I WOULDN'T HAVE FOLLOWED YOU FROM THE FOREST AND SNUCK INTO THE THIRD FIGHTING GROUP.
AND I NEVER WOULD'VE HEARD ABOUT --
WHUNK

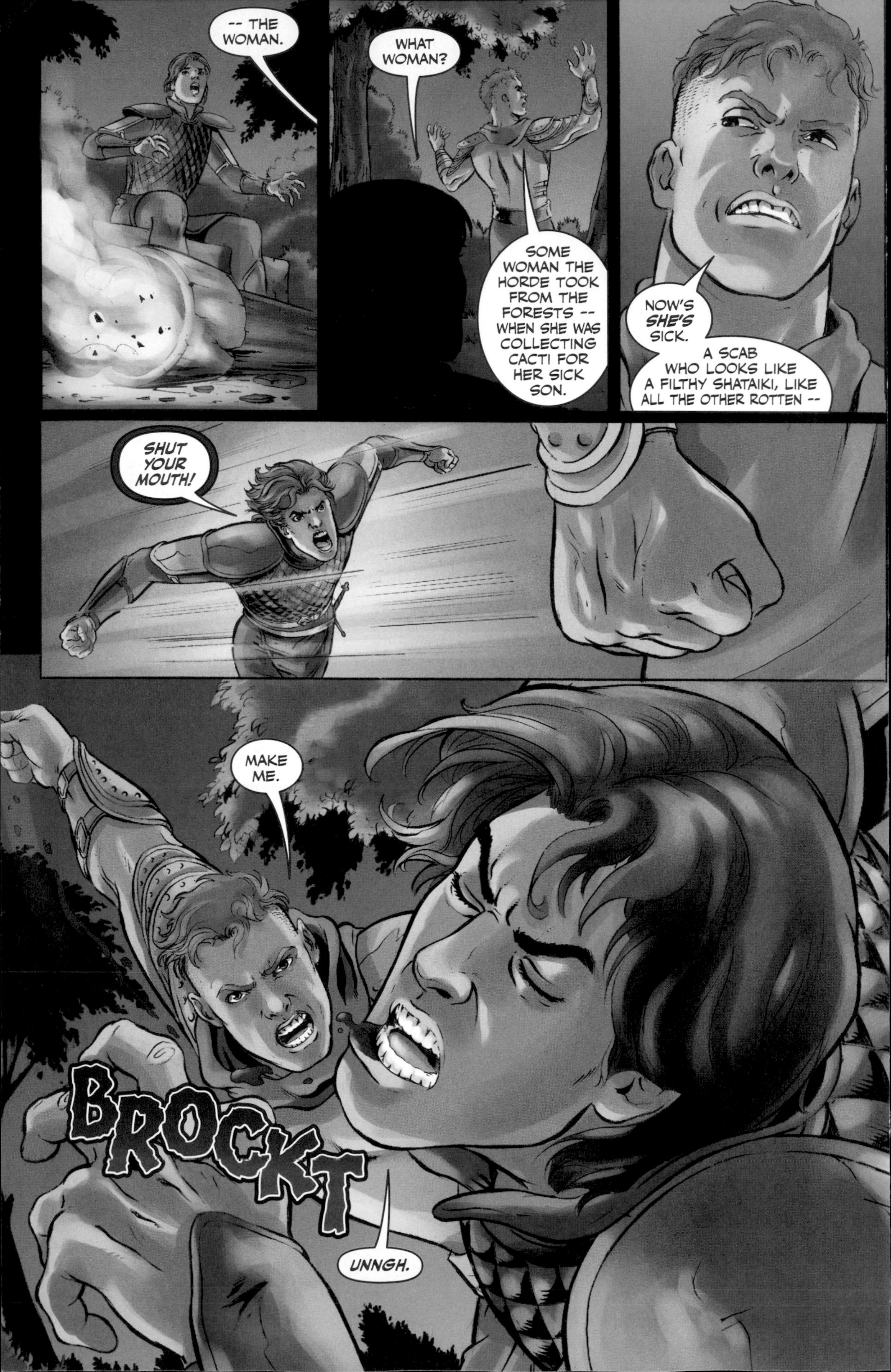
-- THE WOMAN.
WHAT WOMAN?
SOME WOMAN THE HORDE TOOK FROM THE FORESTS -- WHEN SHE WAS COLLECTING CACTI FOR HER SICK SON.
NOW'S *SHE'S* SICK.
A SCAB WHO LOOKS LIKE A FILTHY SHATAIKI, LIKE ALL THE OTHER ROTTEN --
SHUT YOUR MOUTH!
MAKE ME.
BROCKT
UNNGH.

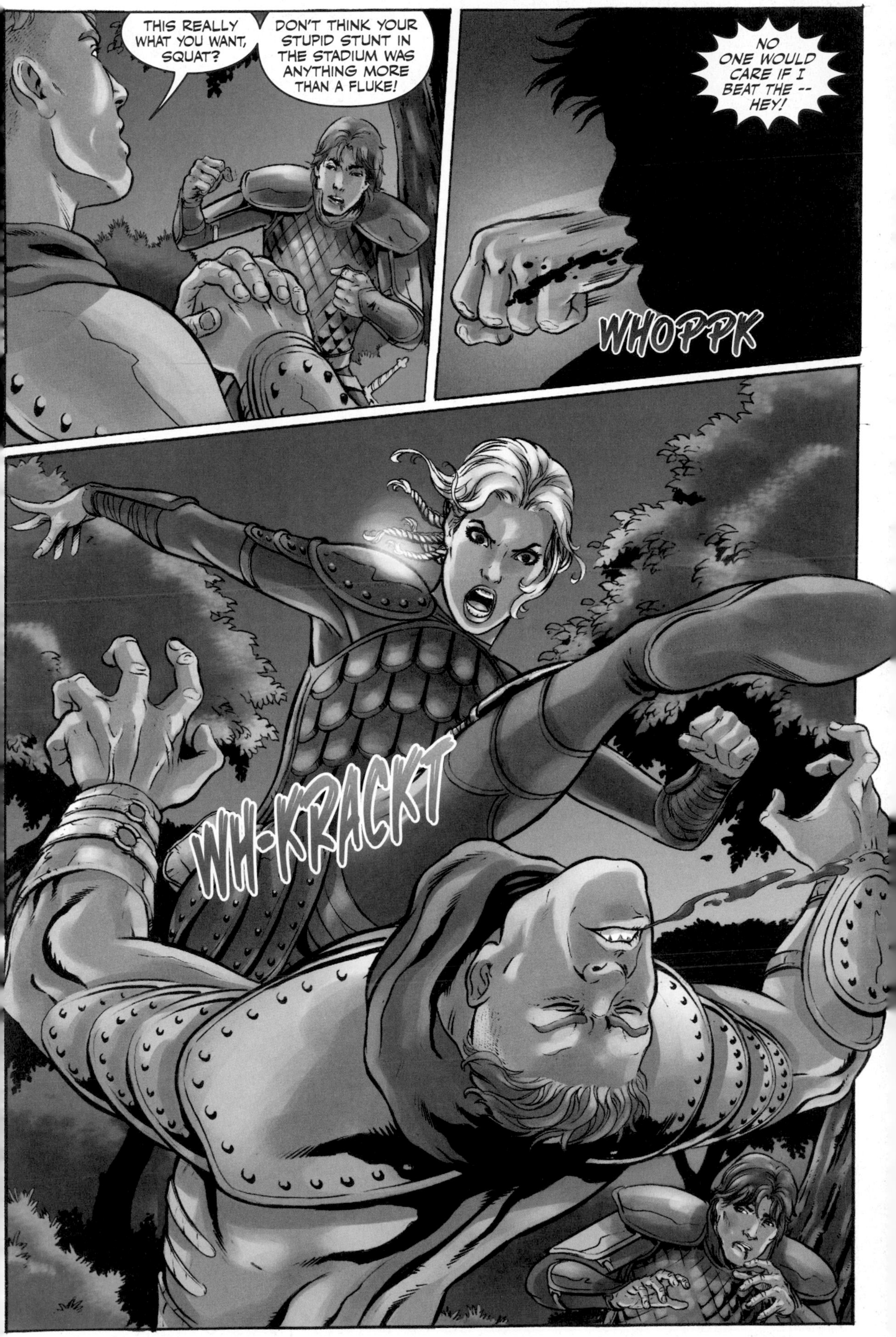
THIS REALLY WHAT YOU WANT, SQUAT?
DON'T THINK YOUR STUPID STUNT IN THE STADIUM WAS ANYTHING MORE THAN A FLUKE!
NO ONE WOULD CARE IF I BEAT THE -- HEY!
WHOPPK
WH-KRACKT

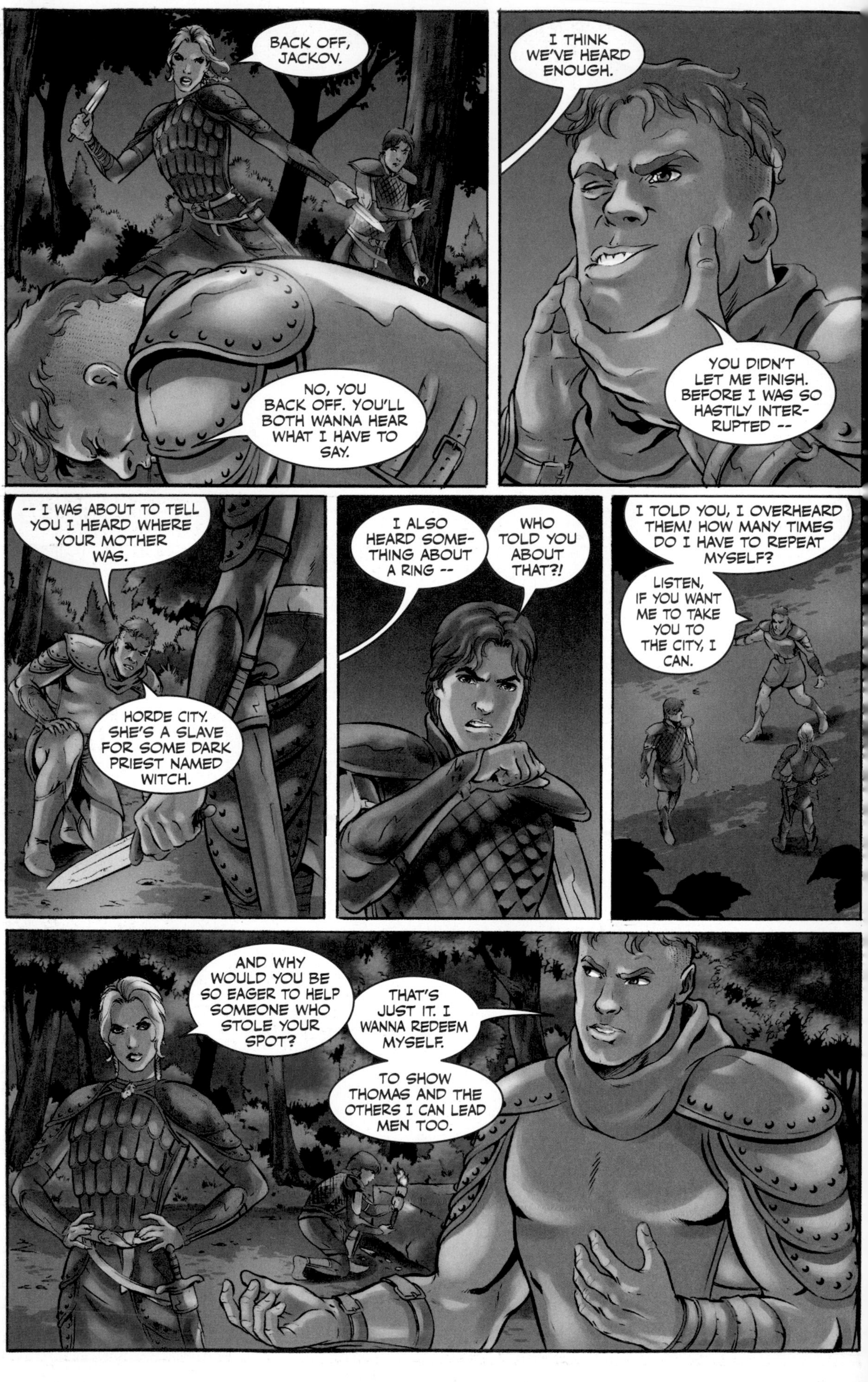
BACK OFF, JACKOV.
NO, YOU BACK OFF. YOU'LL BOTH WANNA HEAR WHAT I HAVE TO SAY.
I THINK WE'VE HEARD ENOUGH.
YOU DIDN'T LET ME FINISH. BEFORE I WAS SO HASTILY INTER-RUPTED --
-- I WAS ABOUT TO TELL YOU I HEARD WHERE YOUR MOTHER WAS.
HORDE CITY. SHE'S A SLAVE FOR SOME DARK PRIEST NAMED WITCH.
I ALSO HEARD SOME-THING ABOUT A RING --
WHO TOLD YOU ABOUT THAT?!
I TOLD YOU, I OVERHEARD THEM! HOW MANY TIMES DO I HAVE TO REPEAT MYSELF?
LISTEN, IF YOU WANT ME TO TAKE YOU TO THE CITY, I CAN.
AND WHY WOULD YOU BE SO EAGER TO HELP SOMEONE WHO STOLE YOUR SPOT?
THAT'S JUST IT. I WANNA REDEEM MYSELF.
TO SHOW THOMAS AND THE OTHERS I CAN LEAD MEN TOO.

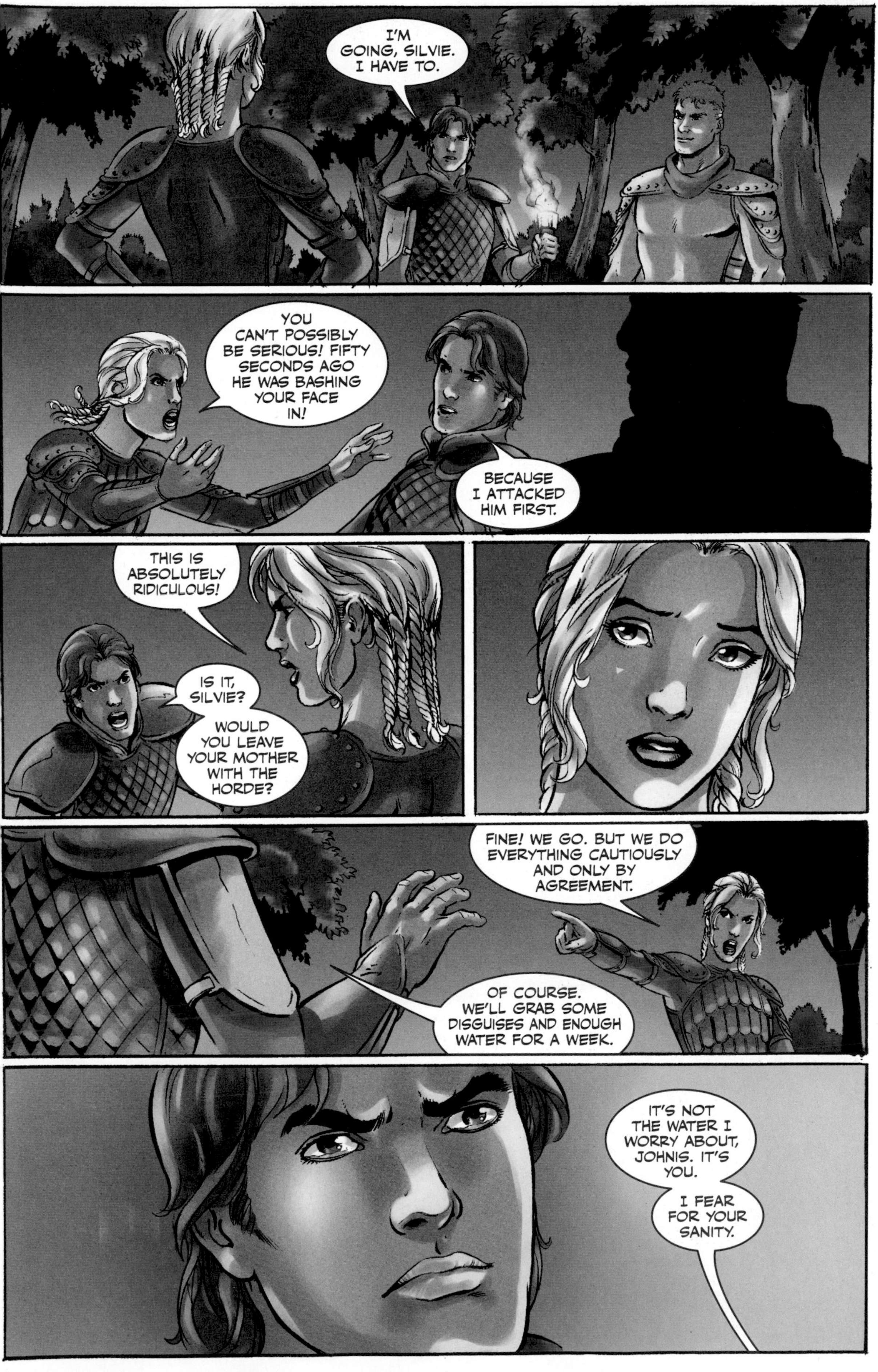
I'M GOING, SILVIE. I HAVE TO.
YOU CAN'T POSSIBLY BE SERIOUS! FIFTY SECONDS AGO HE WAS BASHING YOUR FACE IN!
BECAUSE I ATTACKED HIM FIRST.
THIS IS ABSOLUTELY RIDICULOUS!
IS IT, SILVIE?
WOULD YOU LEAVE YOUR MOTHER WITH THE HORDE?
FINE! WE GO. BUT WE DO EVERYTHING CAUTIOUSLY AND ONLY BY AGREEMENT.
OF COURSE. WE'LL GRAB SOME DISGUISES AND ENOUGH WATER FOR A WEEK.
IT'S NOT THE WATER I WORRY ABOUT, JOHNIS. IT'S YOU.
I FEAR FOR YOUR SANITY.

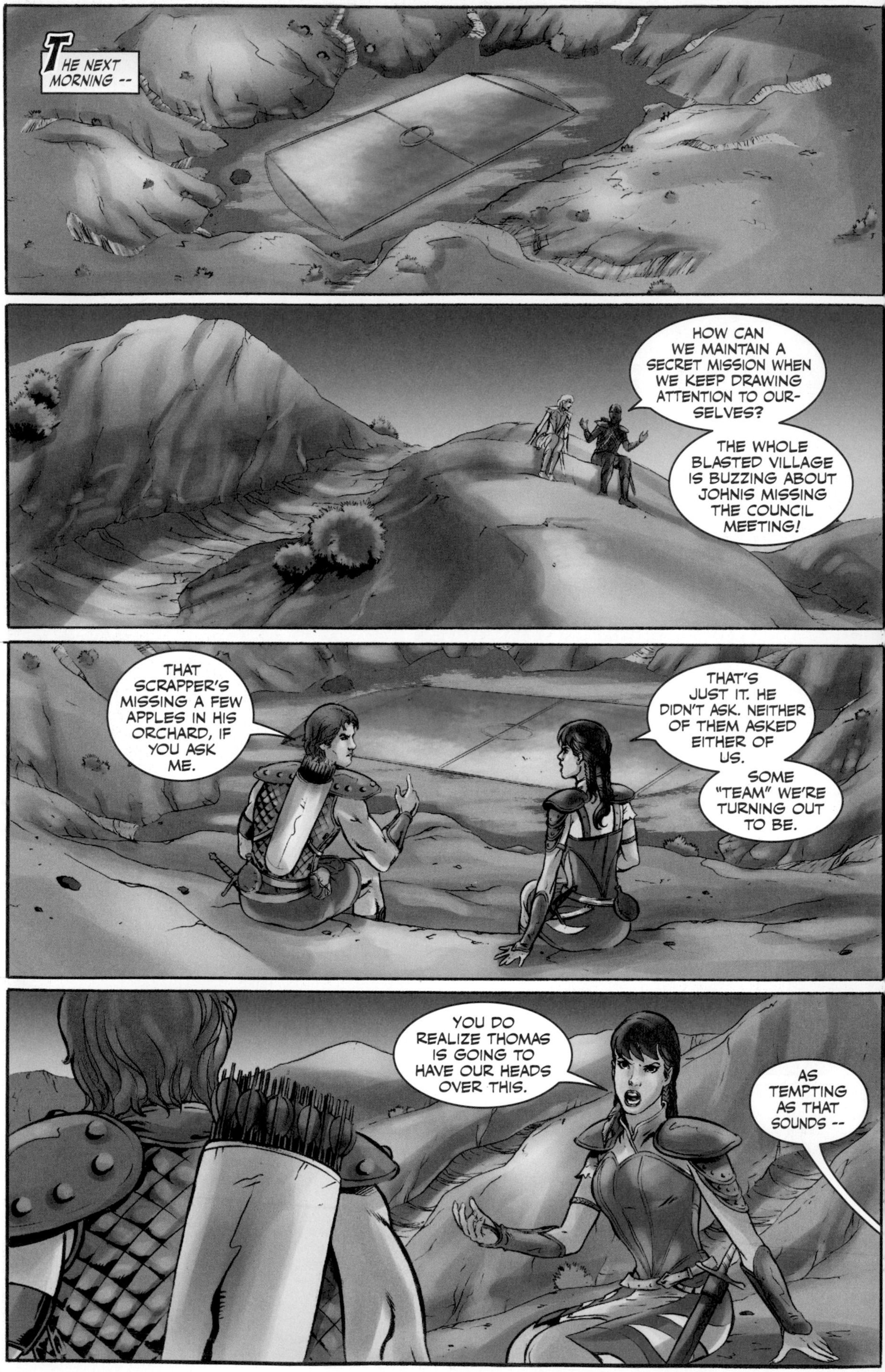
THE NEXT MORNING --
HOW CAN WE MAINTAIN A SECRET MISSION WHEN WE KEEP DRAWING ATTENTION TO OURSELVES?
THE WHOLE BLASTED VILLAGE IS BUZZING ABOUT JOHNIS MISSING THE COUNCIL MEETING!
THAT SCRAPPER'S MISSING A FEW APPLES IN HIS ORCHARD, IF YOU ASK ME.
THAT'S JUST IT. HE DIDN'T ASK. NEITHER OF THEM ASKED EITHER OF US.
SOME "TEAM" WE'RE TURNING OUT TO BE.
YOU DO REALIZE THOMAS IS GOING TO HAVE OUR HEADS OVER THIS.
AS TEMPTING AS THAT SOUNDS --

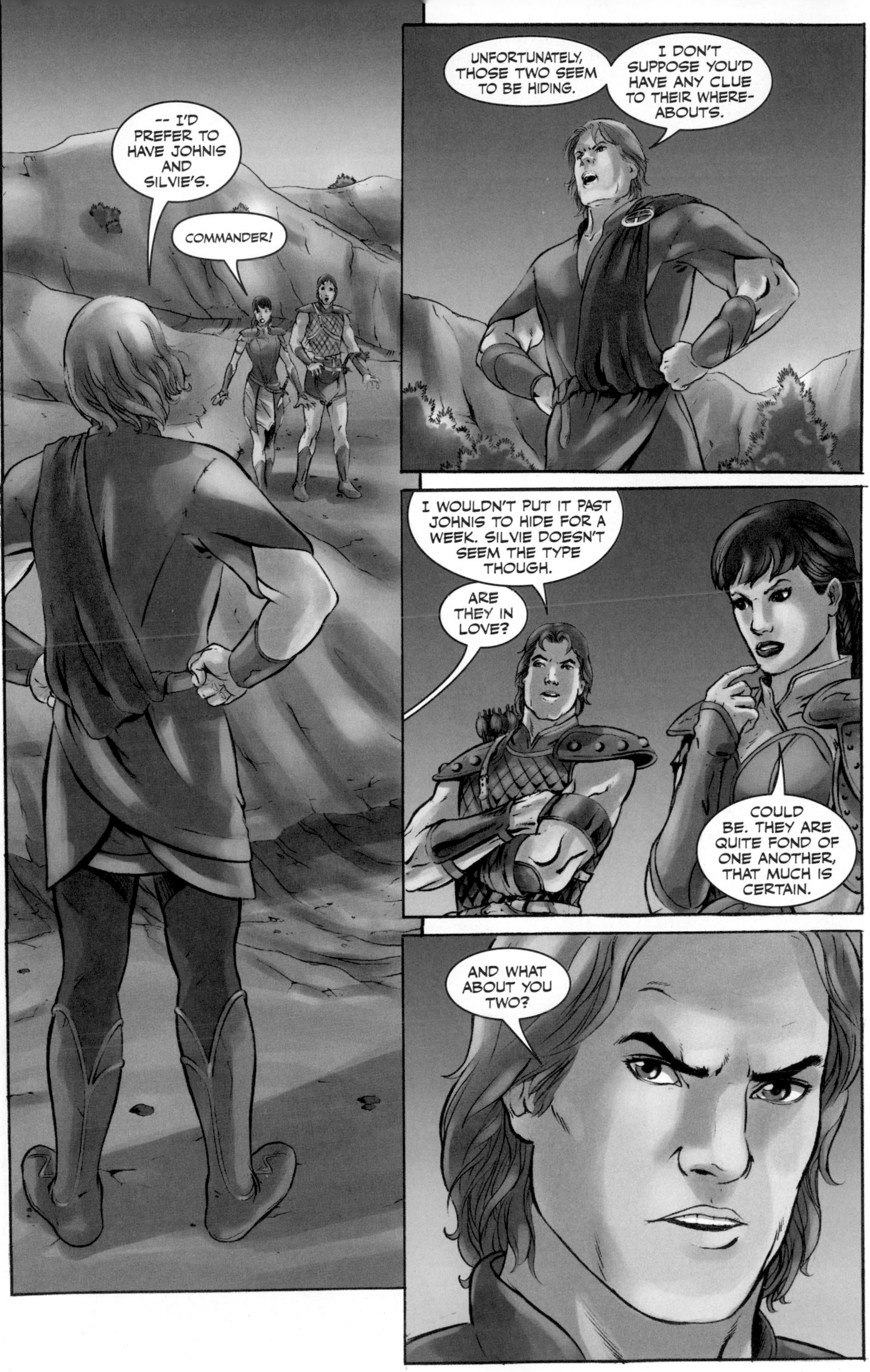
-- I'D PREFER TO HAVE JOHNIS AND SILVIE'S.
COMMANDER!
UNFORTUNATELY, THOSE TWO SEEM TO BE HIDING.
I DON'T SUPPOSE YOU'D HAVE ANY CLUE TO THEIR WHERE-ABOUTS.
I WOULDN'T PUT IT PAST JOHNIS TO HIDE FOR A WEEK. SILVIE DOESN'T SEEM THE TYPE THOUGH.
ARE THEY IN LOVE?
COULD BE. THEY ARE QUITE FOND OF ONE ANOTHER, THAT MUCH IS CERTAIN.
AND WHAT ABOUT YOU TWO?

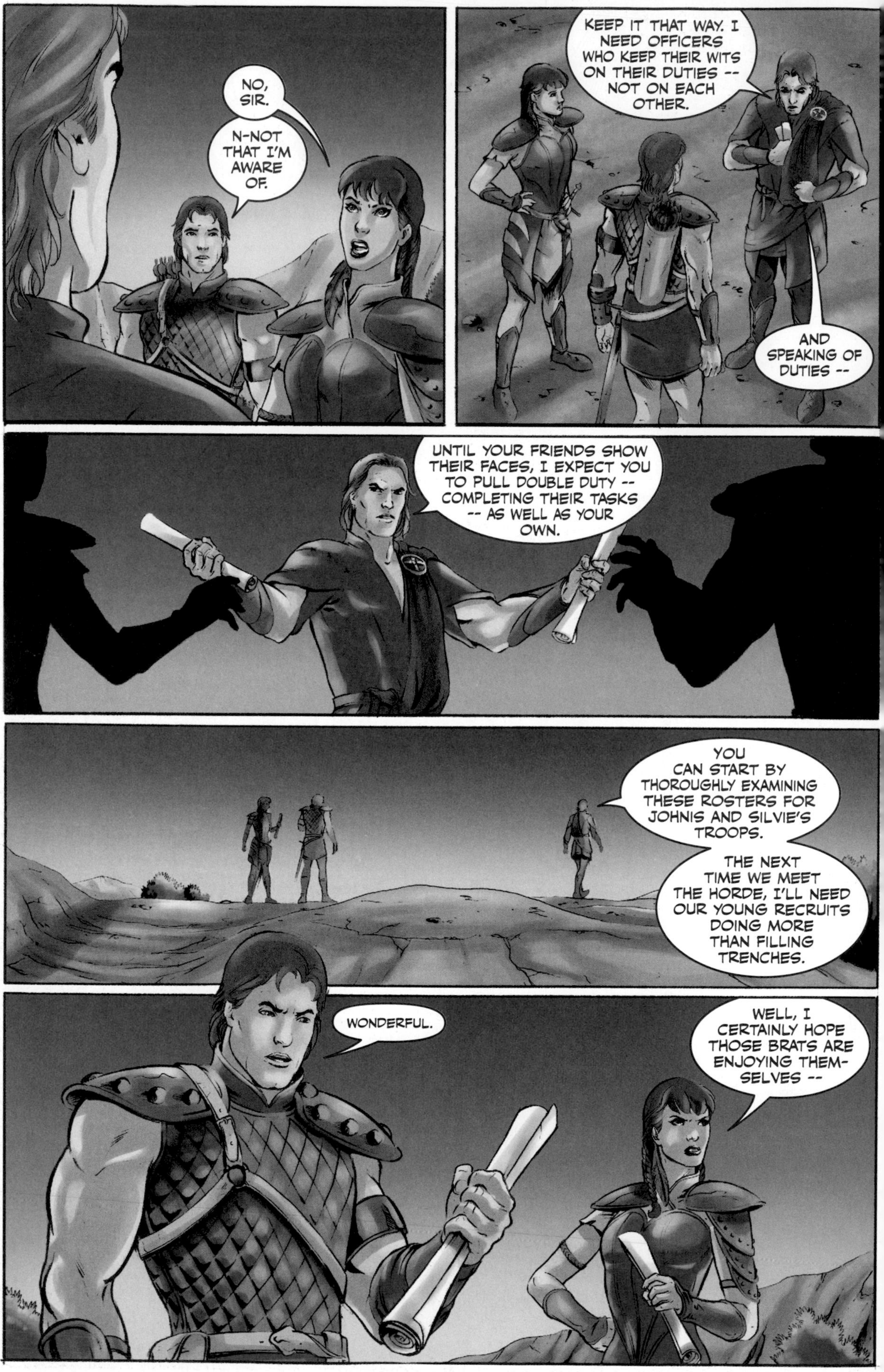
NO, SIR.
N-NOT THAT I'M AWARE OF.
KEEP IT THAT WAY. I NEED OFFICERS WHO KEEP THEIR WITS ON THEIR DUTIES -- NOT ON EACH OTHER.
AND SPEAKING OF DUTIES --
UNTIL YOUR FRIENDS SHOW THEIR FACES, I EXPECT YOU TO PULL DOUBLE DUTY -- COMPLETING THEIR TASKS -- AS WELL AS YOUR OWN.
YOU CAN START BY THOROUGHLY EXAMINING THESE ROSTERS FOR JOHNIS AND SILVIE'S TROOPS.
THE NEXT TIME WE MEET THE HORDE, I'LL NEED OUR YOUNG RECRUITS DOING MORE THAN FILLING TRENCHES.
WONDERFUL.
WELL, I CERTAINLY HOPE THOSE BRATS ARE ENJOYING THEM-SELVES --

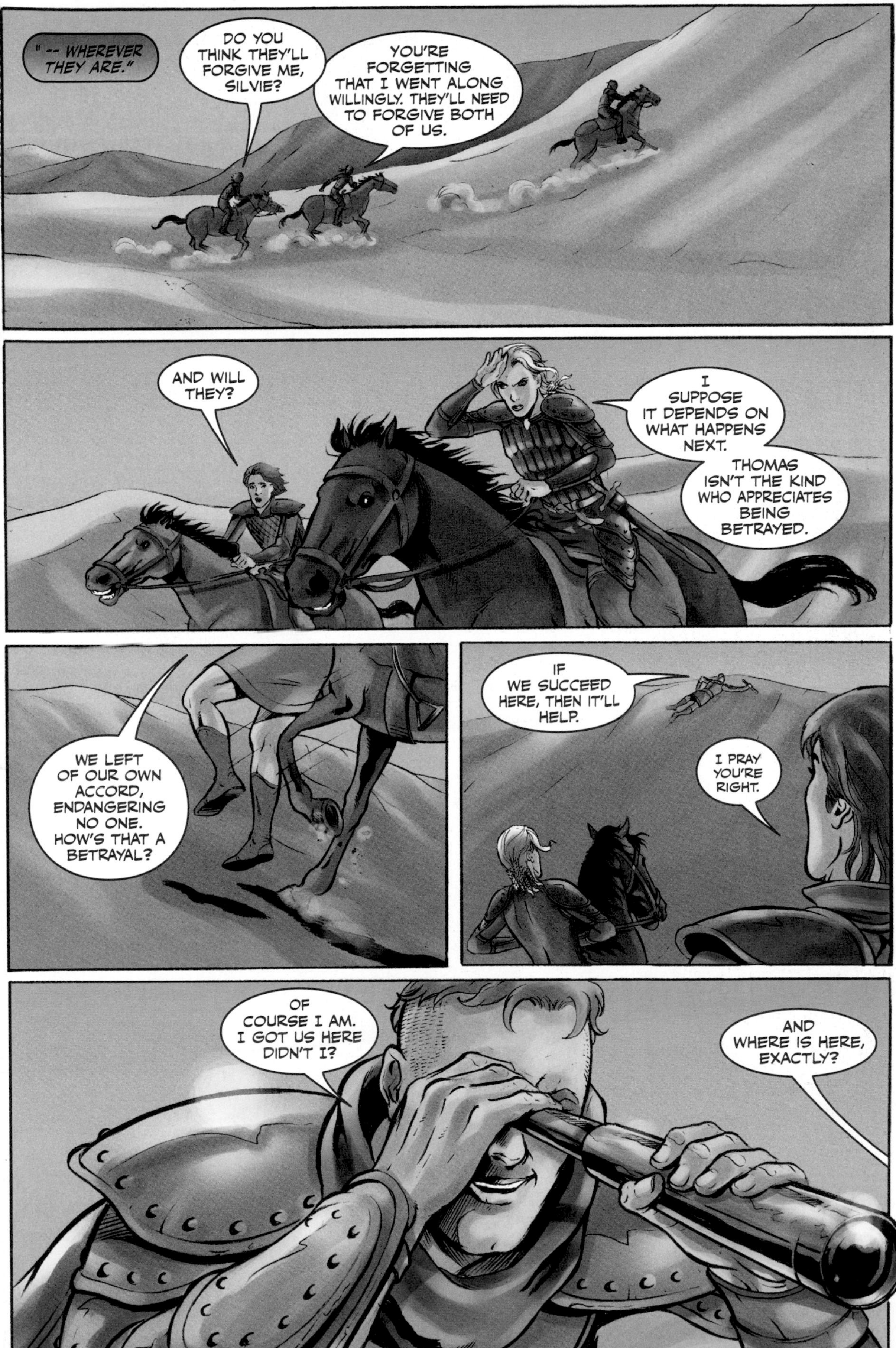
" -- WHEREVER THEY ARE."
DO YOU THINK THEY'LL FORGIVE ME, SILVIE?
YOU'RE FORGETTING THAT I WENT ALONG WILLINGLY. THEY'LL NEED TO FORGIVE BOTH OF US.
AND WILL THEY?
I SUPPOSE IT DEPENDS ON WHAT HAPPENS NEXT.
THOMAS ISN'T THE KIND WHO APPRECIATES BEING BETRAYED.
WE LEFT OF OUR OWN ACCORD, ENDANGERING NO ONE. HOW'S THAT A BETRAYAL?
IF WE SUCCEED HERE, THEN IT'LL HELP.
I PRAY YOU'RE RIGHT.
OF COURSE I AM. I GOT US HERE DIDN'T I?
AND WHERE IS HERE, EXACTLY?

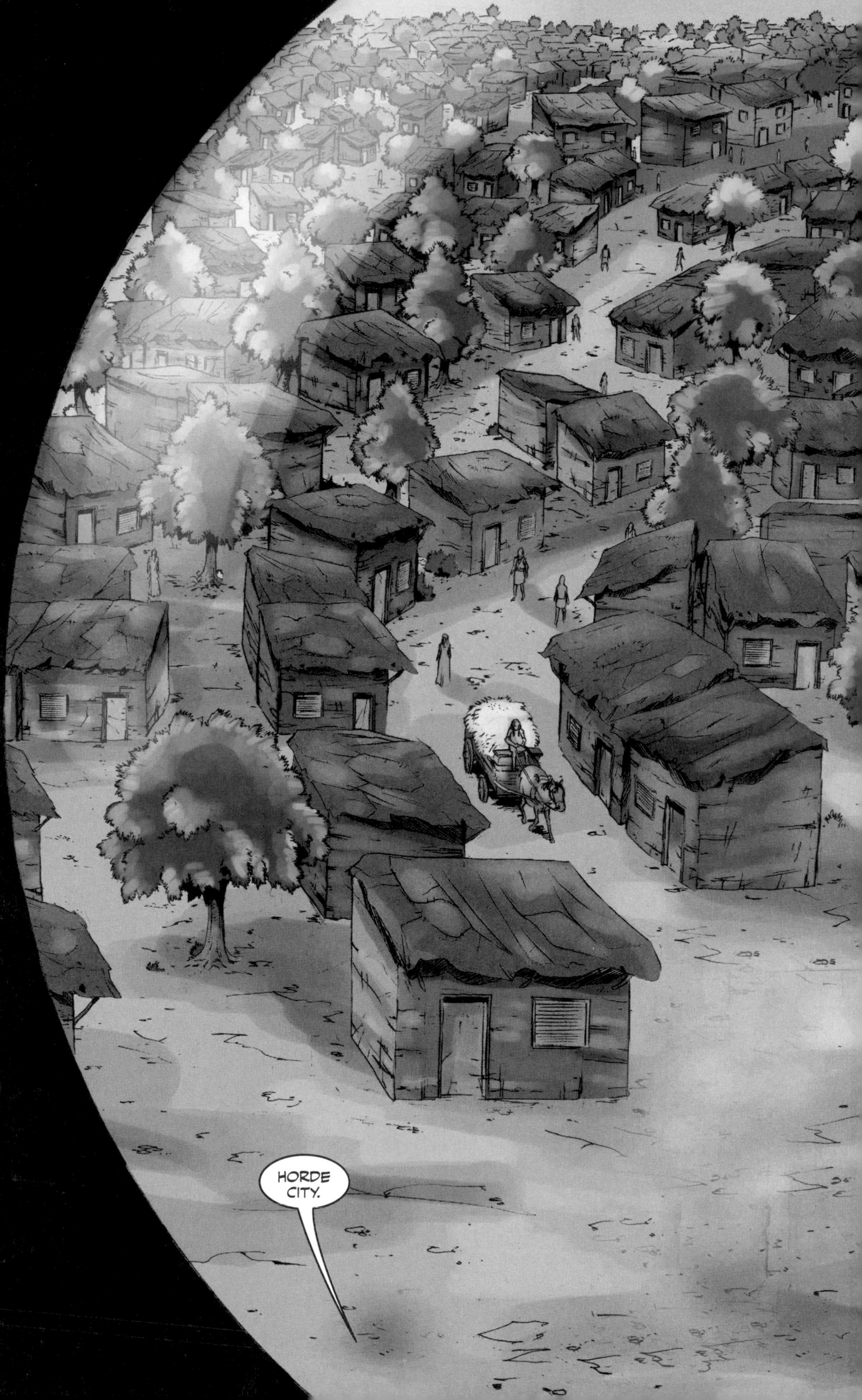
HORDE CITY.

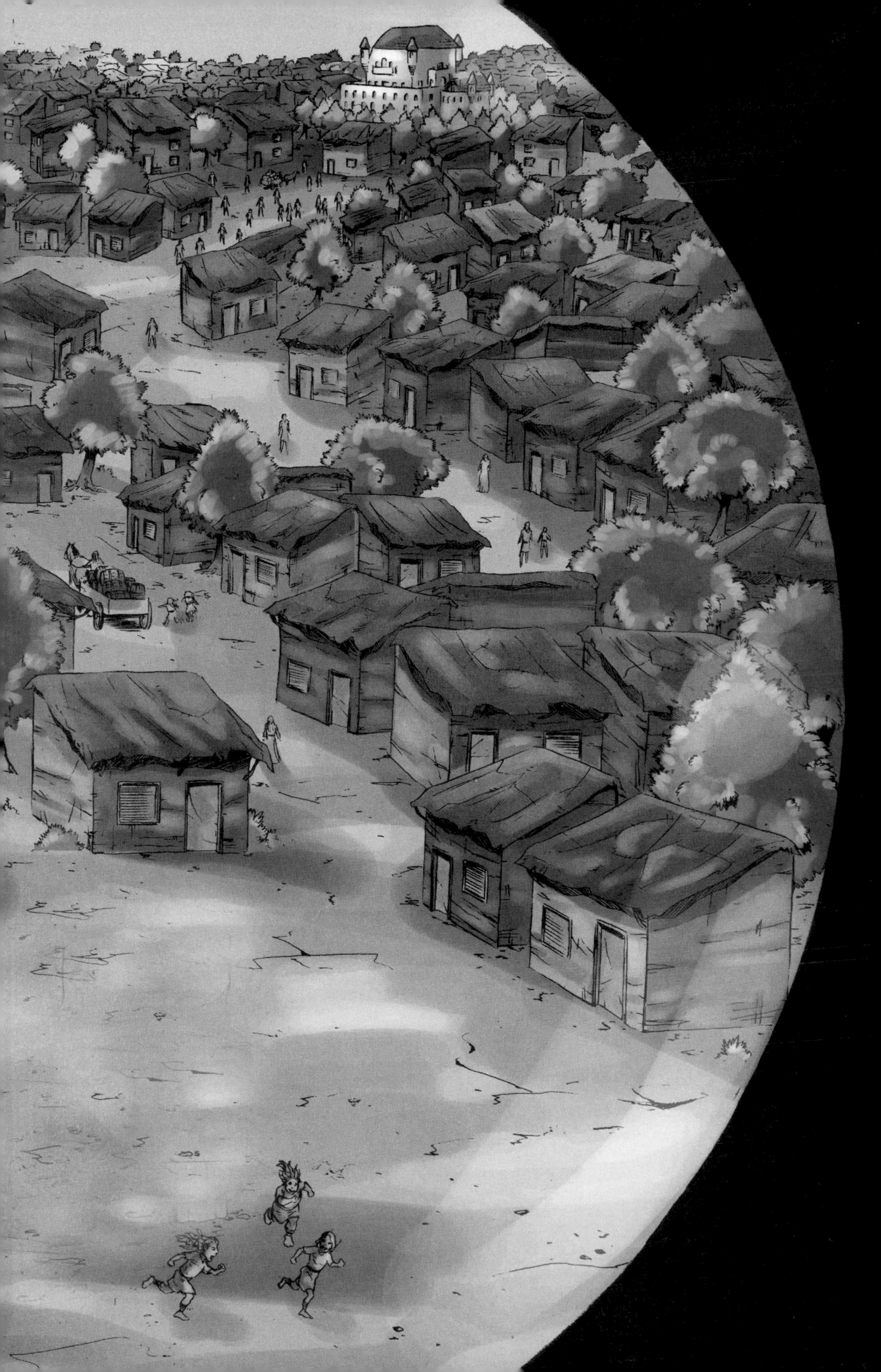

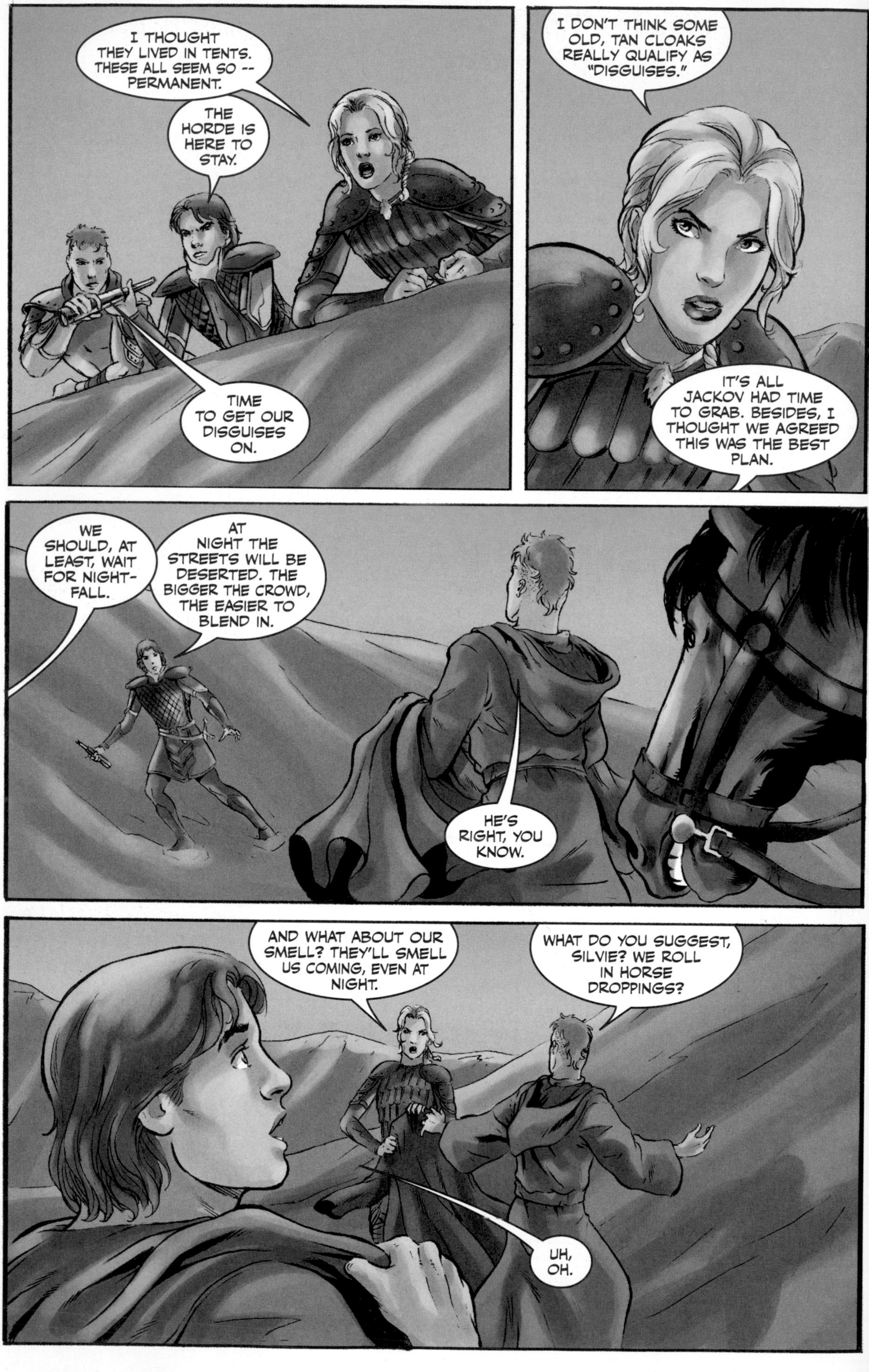
I THOUGHT THEY LIVED IN TENTS. THESE ALL SEEM SO -- PERMANENT.
THE HORDE IS HERE TO STAY.
TIME TO GET OUR DISGUISES ON.
I DON'T THINK SOME OLD, TAN CLOAKS REALLY QUALIFY AS "DISGUISES."
IT'S ALL JACKOV HAD TIME TO GRAB. BESIDES, I THOUGHT WE AGREED THIS WAS THE BEST PLAN.
WE SHOULD, AT LEAST, WAIT FOR NIGHT-FALL.
AT NIGHT THE STREETS WILL BE DESERTED. THE BIGGER THE CROWD, THE EASIER TO BLEND IN.
HE'S RIGHT, YOU KNOW.
AND WHAT ABOUT OUR SMELL? THEY'LL SMELL US COMING, EVEN AT NIGHT.
WHAT DO YOU SUGGEST, SILVIE? WE ROLL IN HORSE DROPPINGS?
UH, OH.

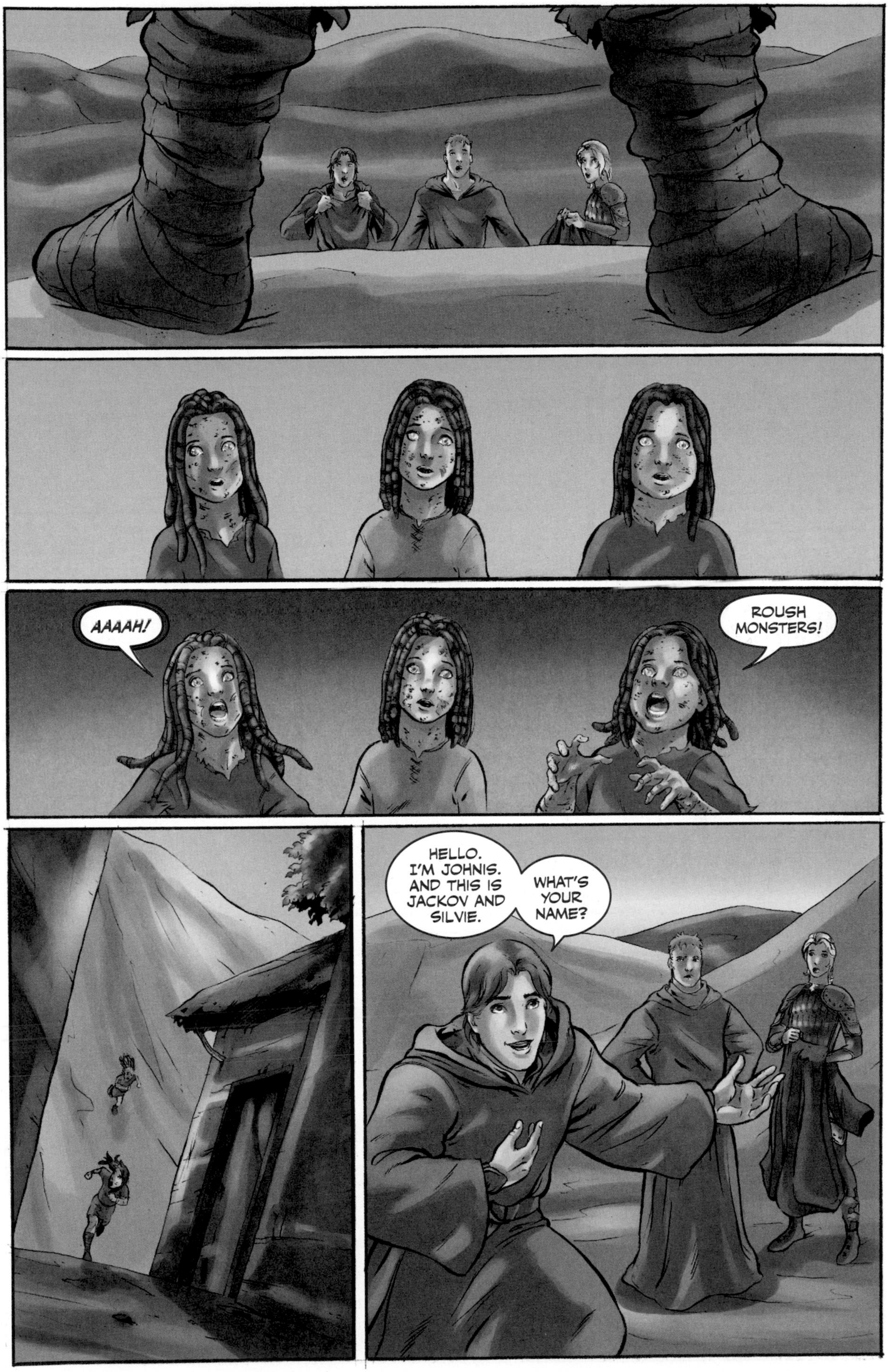
AAAAH!
ROUSH MONSTERS!
HELLO. I'M JOHNIS. AND THIS IS JACKOV AND SILVIE.
WHAT'S YOUR NAME?

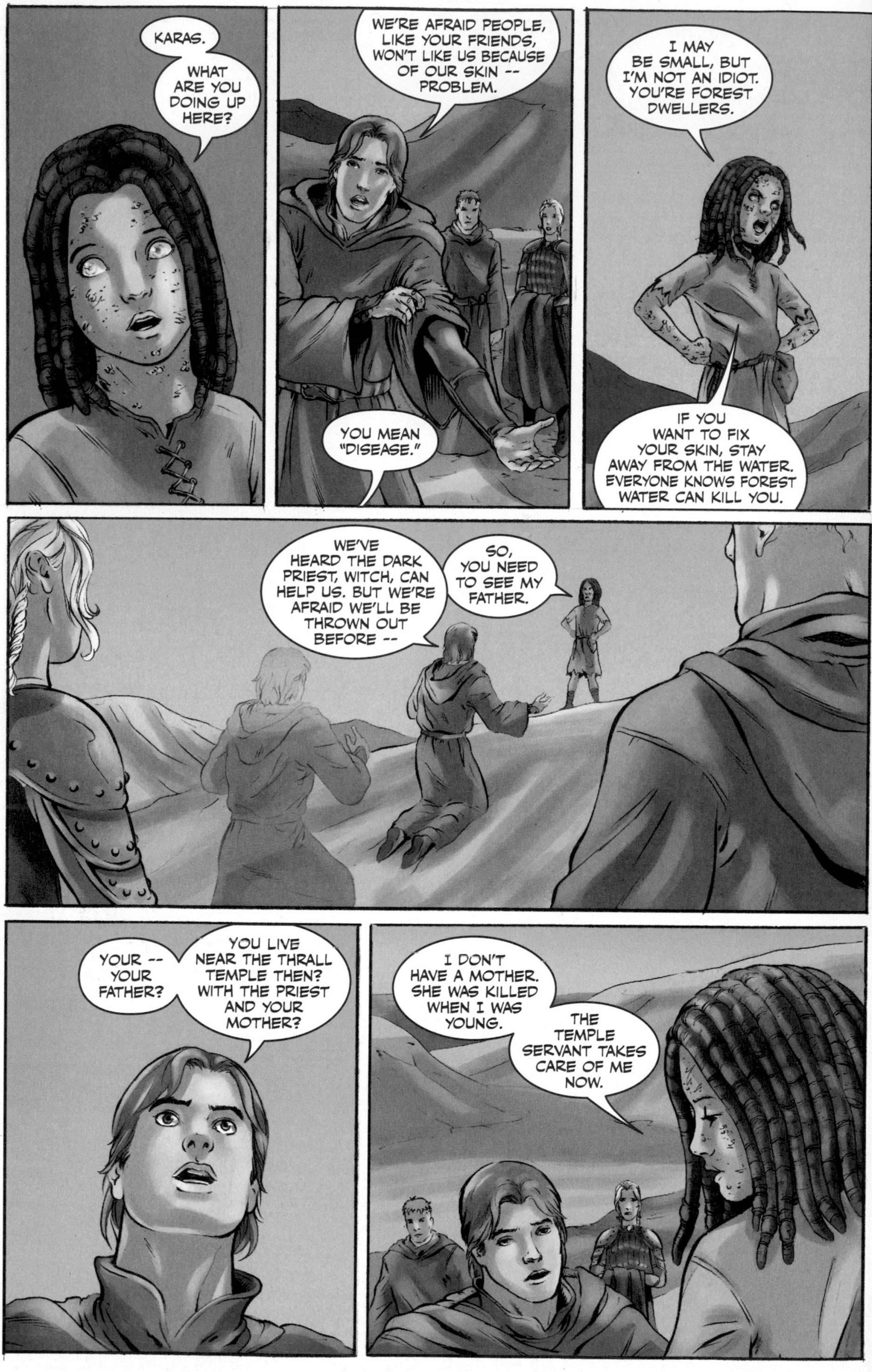

KARAS.
WHAT ARE YOU DOING UP HERE?
WE'RE AFRAID PEOPLE, LIKE YOUR FRIENDS, WON'T LIKE US BECAUSE OF OUR SKIN -- PROBLEM.
YOU MEAN "DISEASE."
I MAY BE SMALL, BUT I'M NOT AN IDIOT. YOU'RE FOREST DWELLERS.
IF YOU WANT TO FIX YOUR SKIN, STAY AWAY FROM THE WATER. EVERYONE KNOWS FOREST WATER CAN KILL YOU.
WE'VE HEARD THE DARK PRIEST, WITCH, CAN HELP US. BUT WE'RE AFRAID WE'LL BE THROWN OUT BEFORE --
SO, YOU NEED TO SEE MY FATHER.
YOUR -- YOUR FATHER?
YOU LIVE NEAR THE THRALL TEMPLE THEN? WITH THE PRIEST AND YOUR MOTHER?
I DON'T HAVE A MOTHER. SHE WAS KILLED WHEN I WAS YOUNG.
THE TEMPLE SERVANT TAKES CARE OF ME NOW.

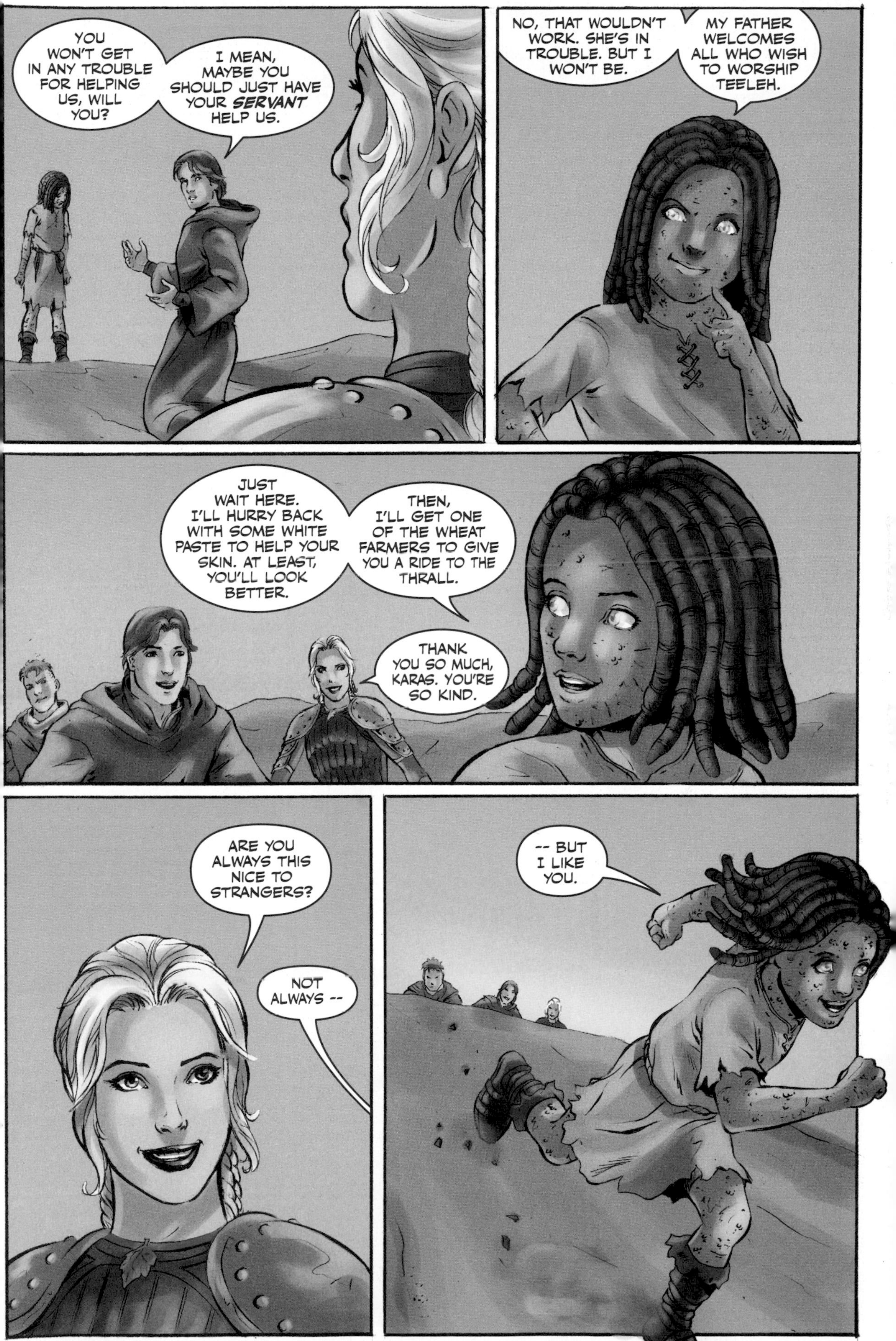
YOU WON'T GET IN ANY TROUBLE FOR HELPING US, WILL YOU?
I MEAN, MAYBE YOU SHOULD JUST HAVE YOUR SERVANT HELP US.
NO, THAT WOULDN'T WORK. SHE'S IN TROUBLE. BUT I WON'T BE.
MY FATHER WELCOMES ALL WHO WISH TO WORSHIP TEELEH.
JUST WAIT HERE. I'LL HURRY BACK WITH SOME WHITE PASTE TO HELP YOUR SKIN. AT LEAST, YOU'LL LOOK BETTER.
THEN, I'LL GET ONE OF THE WHEAT FARMERS TO GIVE YOU A RIDE TO THE THRALL.
THANK YOU SO MUCH, KARAS. YOU'RE SO KIND.
ARE YOU ALWAYS THIS NICE TO STRANGERS?
NOT ALWAYS --
-- BUT I LIKE YOU.

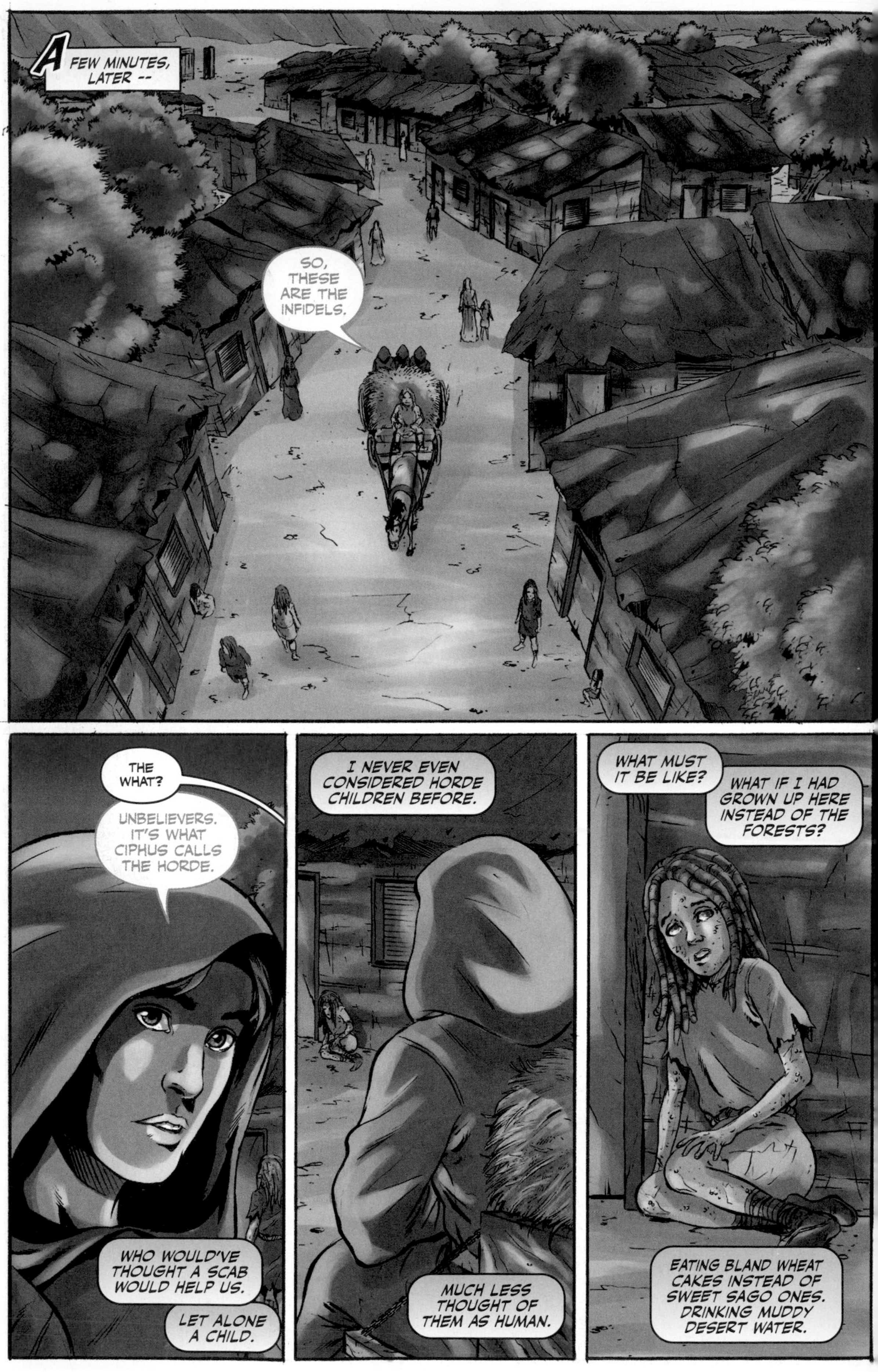
A FEW MINUTES, LATER --
SO, THESE ARE THE INFIDELS.
THE WHAT?
UNBELIEVERS. IT'S WHAT CIPHUS CALLS THE HORDE.
WHO WOULD'VE THOUGHT A SCAB WOULD HELP US.
LET ALONE A CHILD.
I NEVER EVEN CONSIDERED HORDE CHILDREN BEFORE.
MUCH LESS THOUGHT OF THEM AS HUMAN.
WHAT MUST IT BE LIKE?
WHAT IF I HAD GROWN UP HERE INSTEAD OF THE FORESTS?
EATING BLAND WHEAT CAKES INSTEAD OF SWEET SAGO ONES. DRINKING MUDDY DESERT WATER.

HOW BLESSED WE ARE.

HOW FORTUNATE.

THANK ELYON FOR HIS GRACE.

PERHAPS -- WE WOULD DO WELL TO SHARE THAT GRACE.

INSTEAD OF SLAUGHTERING THE HORDE, PERHAPS WE SHOULD FLOOD THE DESERTS WITH ELYON'S WATER --

-- THAT THEY MIGHT WASH AWAY THIS DISEASE OF THE FLESH AND MIND.

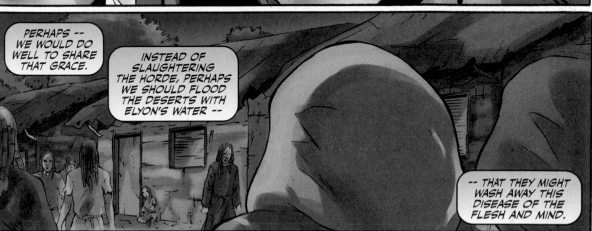

IF WE WERE TO EMPTY EACH LAKE, I HAVE A FEELING THERE'D BE ENOUGH FOR EVERY ONE OF THESE.

OFF!

AND ELYON ONLY KNOWS WHAT HIDDEN WATERS WE MIGHT FIND. MAYBE, ONE DAY --

WE'RE HERE.

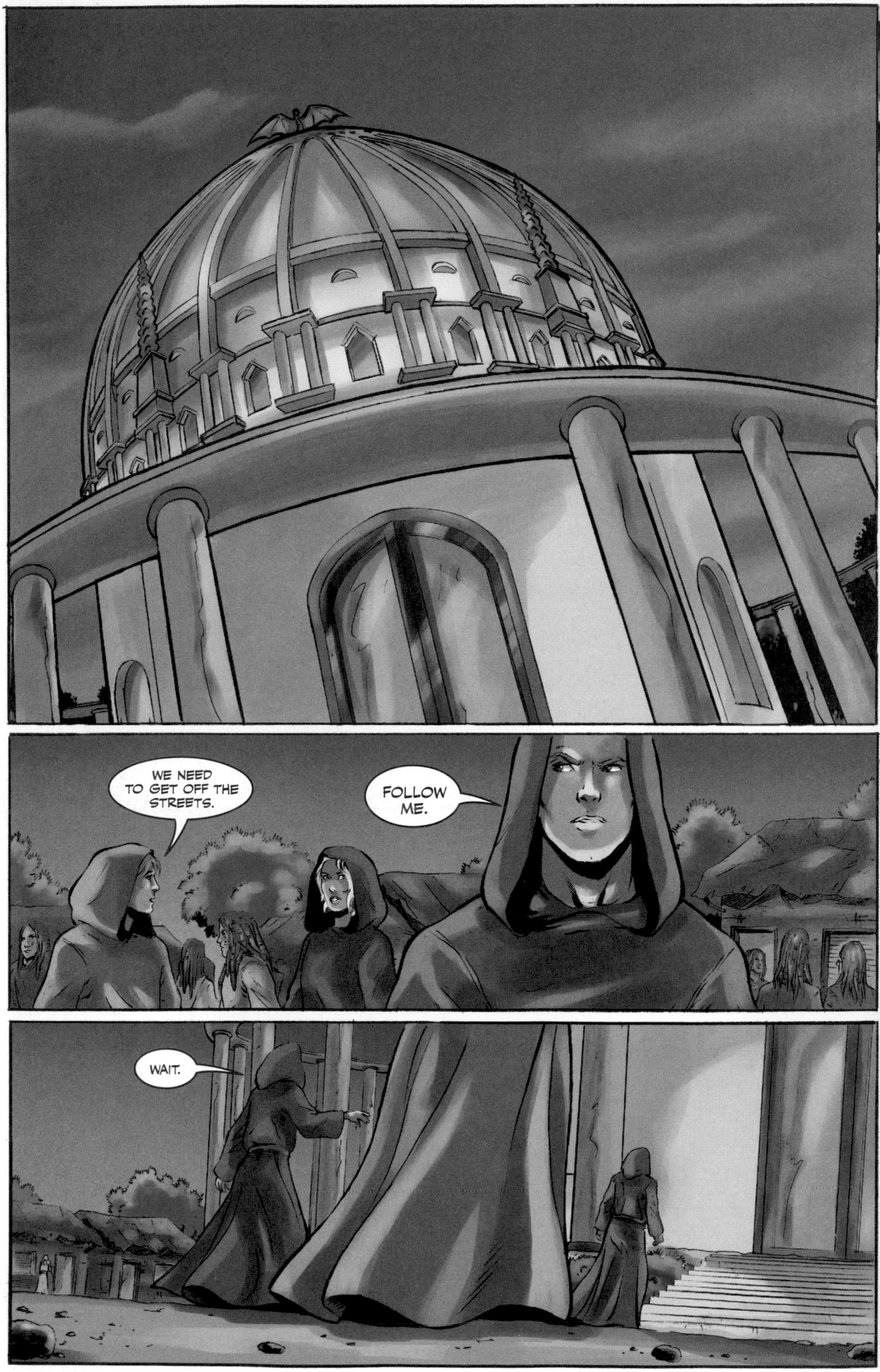
WE NEED TO GET OFF THE STREETS.
FOLLOW ME.
WAIT.

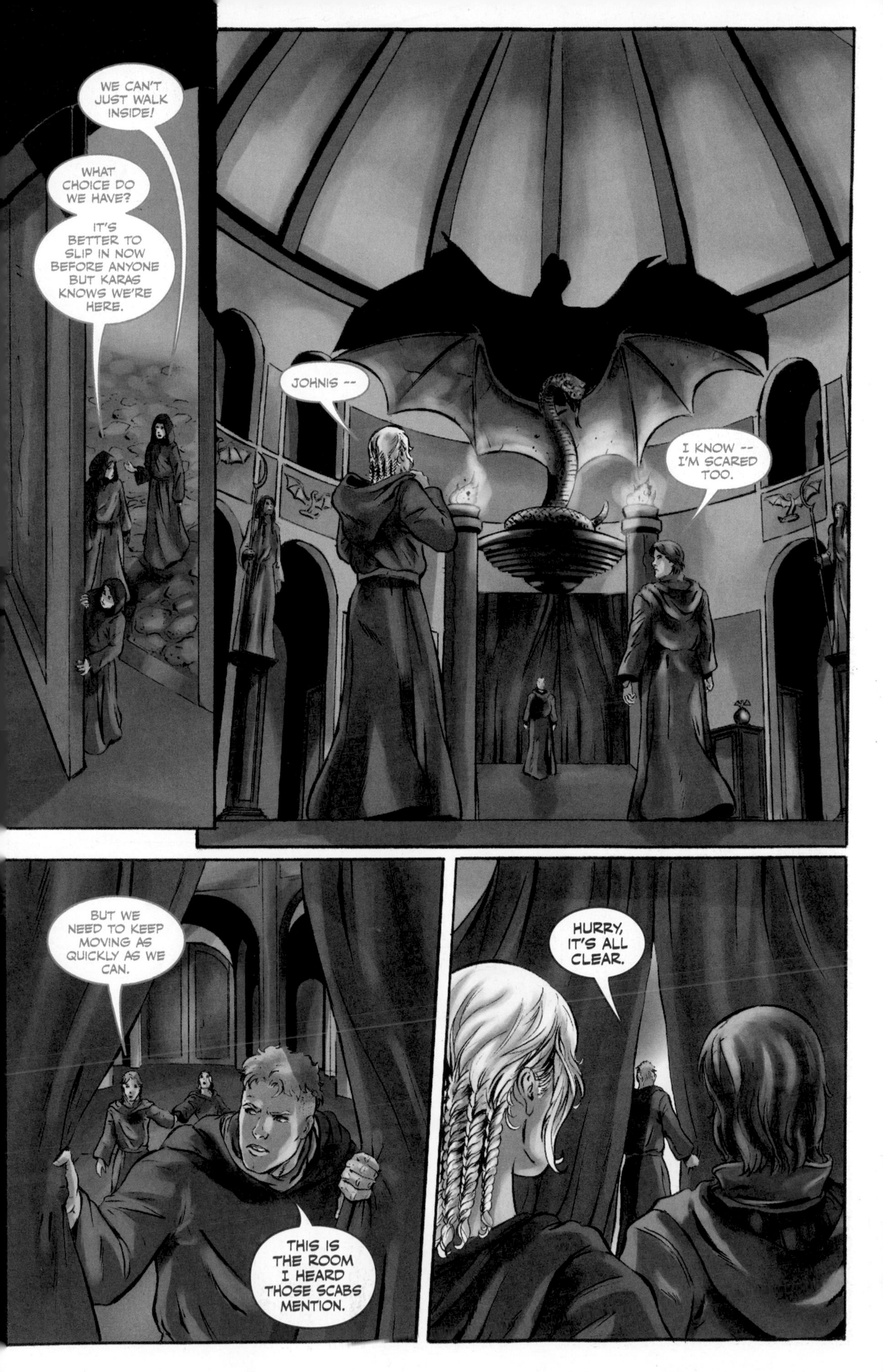
WE CAN'T JUST WALK INSIDE!
WHAT CHOICE DO WE HAVE?
IT'S BETTER TO SLIP IN NOW BEFORE ANYONE BUT KARAS KNOWS WE'RE HERE.
JOHNIS --
I KNOW -- I'M SCARED TOO.
BUT WE NEED TO KEEP MOVING AS QUICKLY AS WE CAN.
THIS IS THE ROOM I HEARD THOSE SCABS MENTION.
HURRY, IT'S ALL CLEAR.

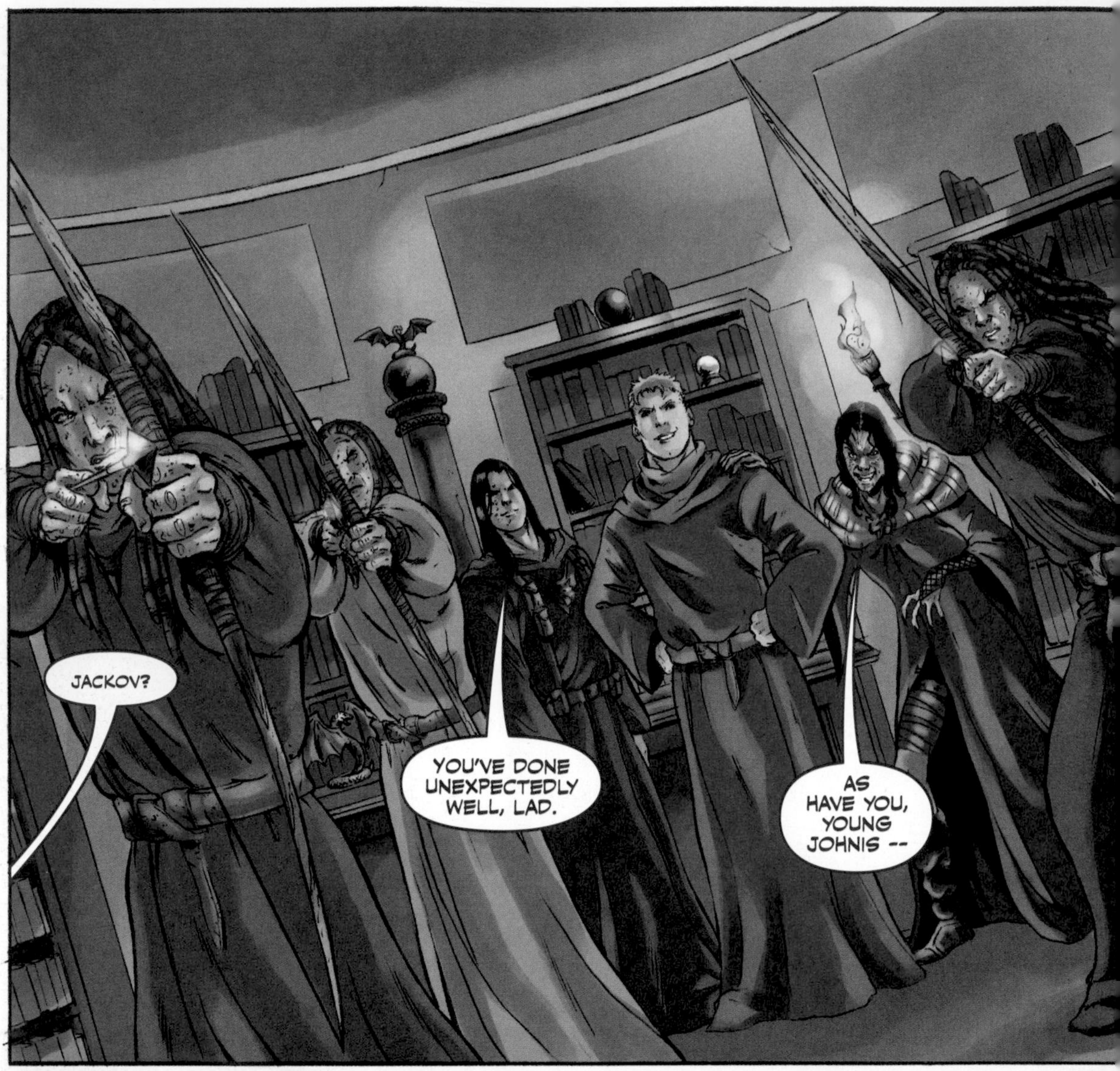
JACKOV?
YOU'VE DONE UNEXPECTEDLY WELL, LAD.
AS HAVE YOU, YOUNG JOHNIS --

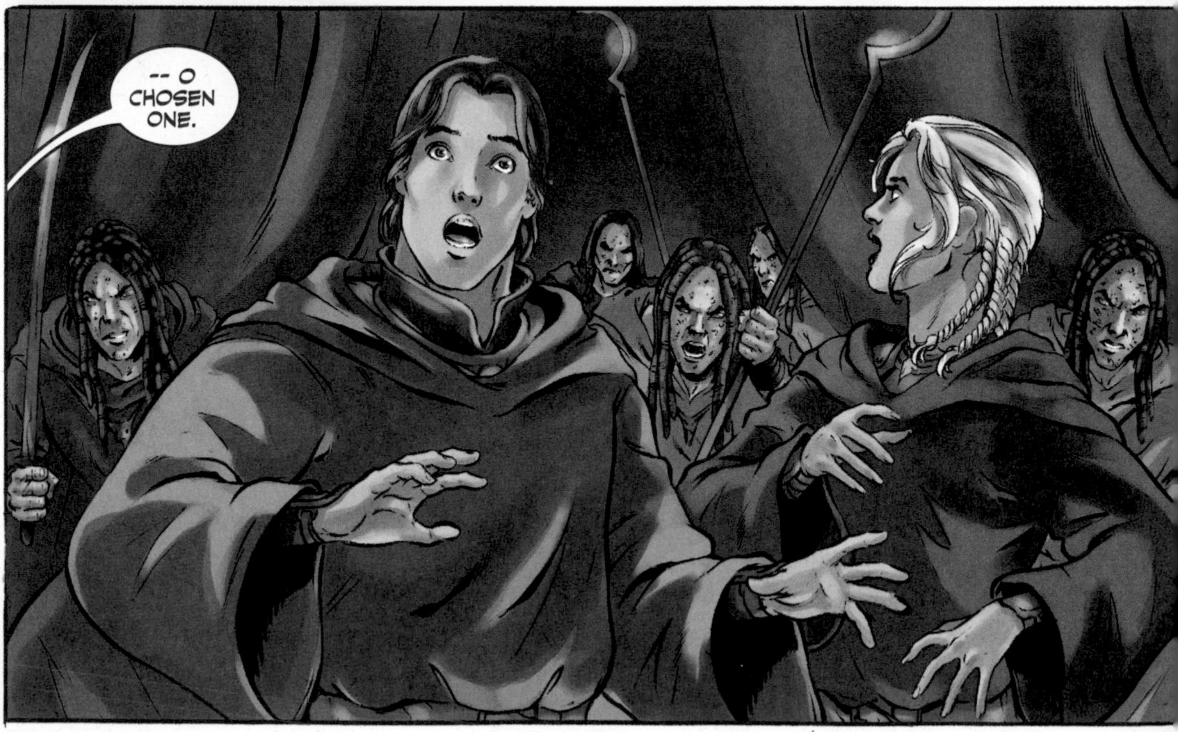
-- O CHOSEN ONE.

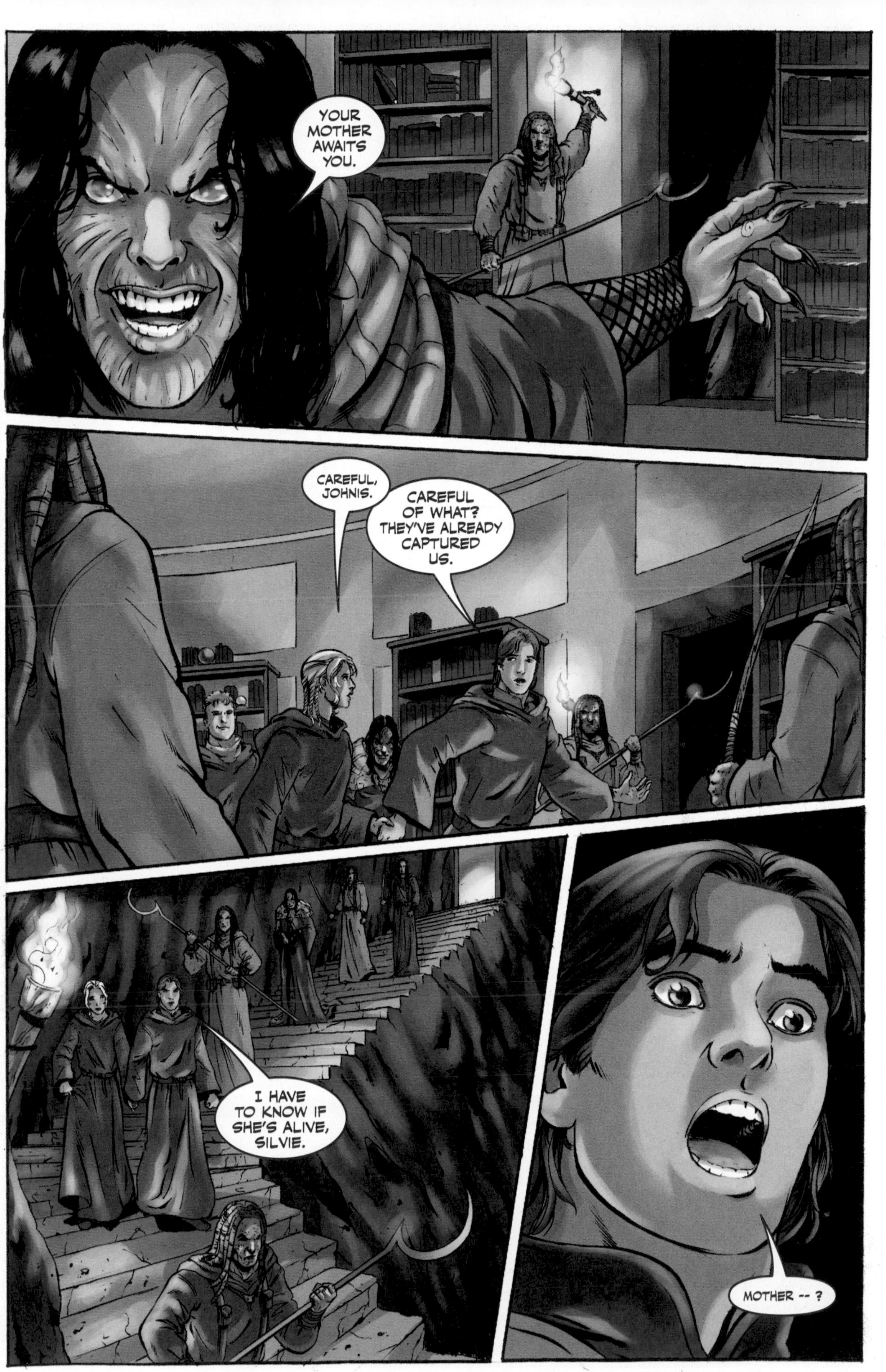
YOUR MOTHER AWAITS YOU.
CAREFUL, JOHNIS.
CAREFUL OF WHAT? THEY'VE ALREADY CAPTURED US.
I HAVE TO KNOW IF SHE'S ALIVE, SILVIE.
MOTHER -- ?

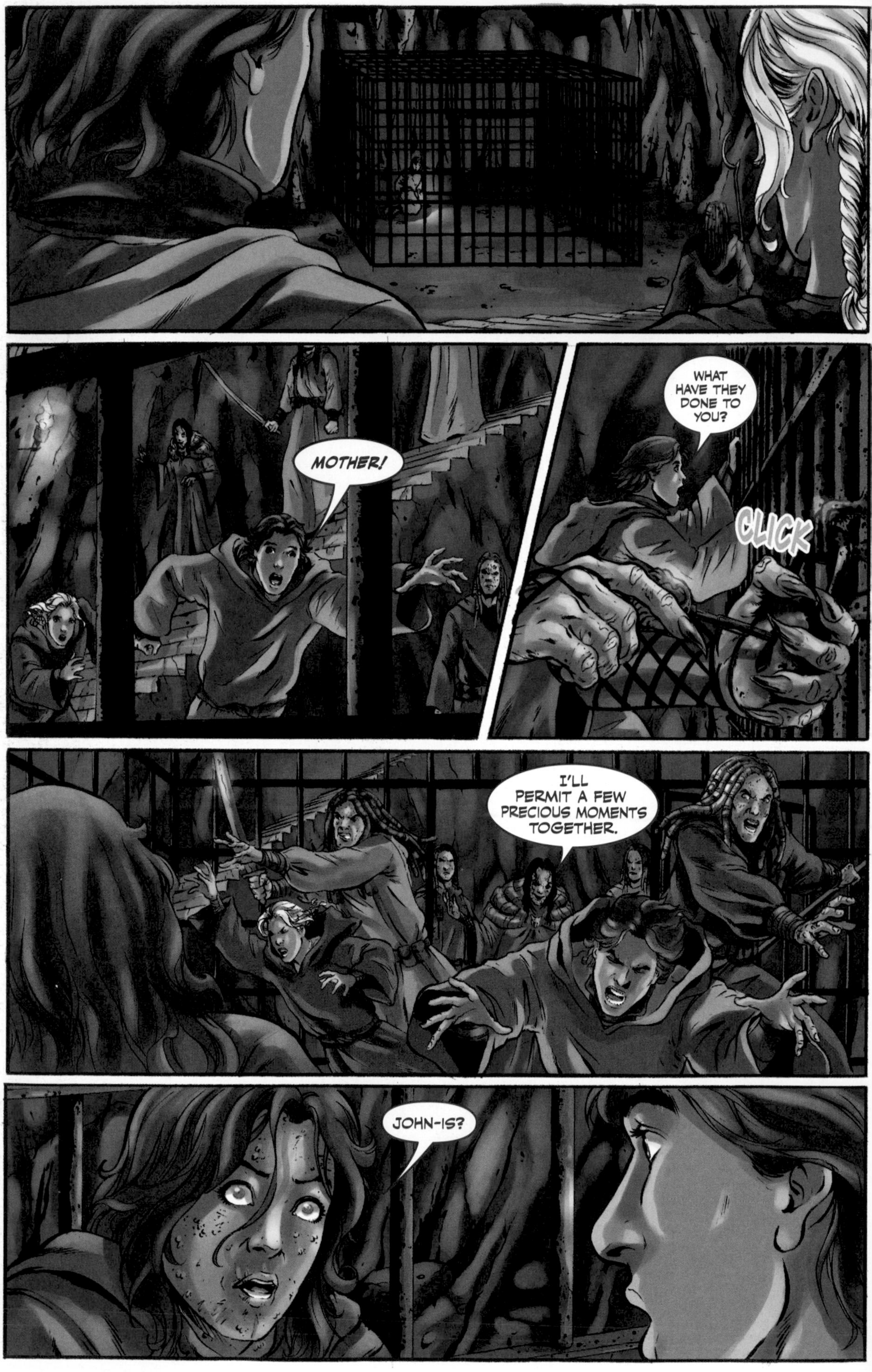
MOTHER!
WHAT HAVE THEY DONE TO YOU?
CLICK
I'LL PERMIT A FEW PRECIOUS MOMENTS TOGETHER.
JOHN-IS?

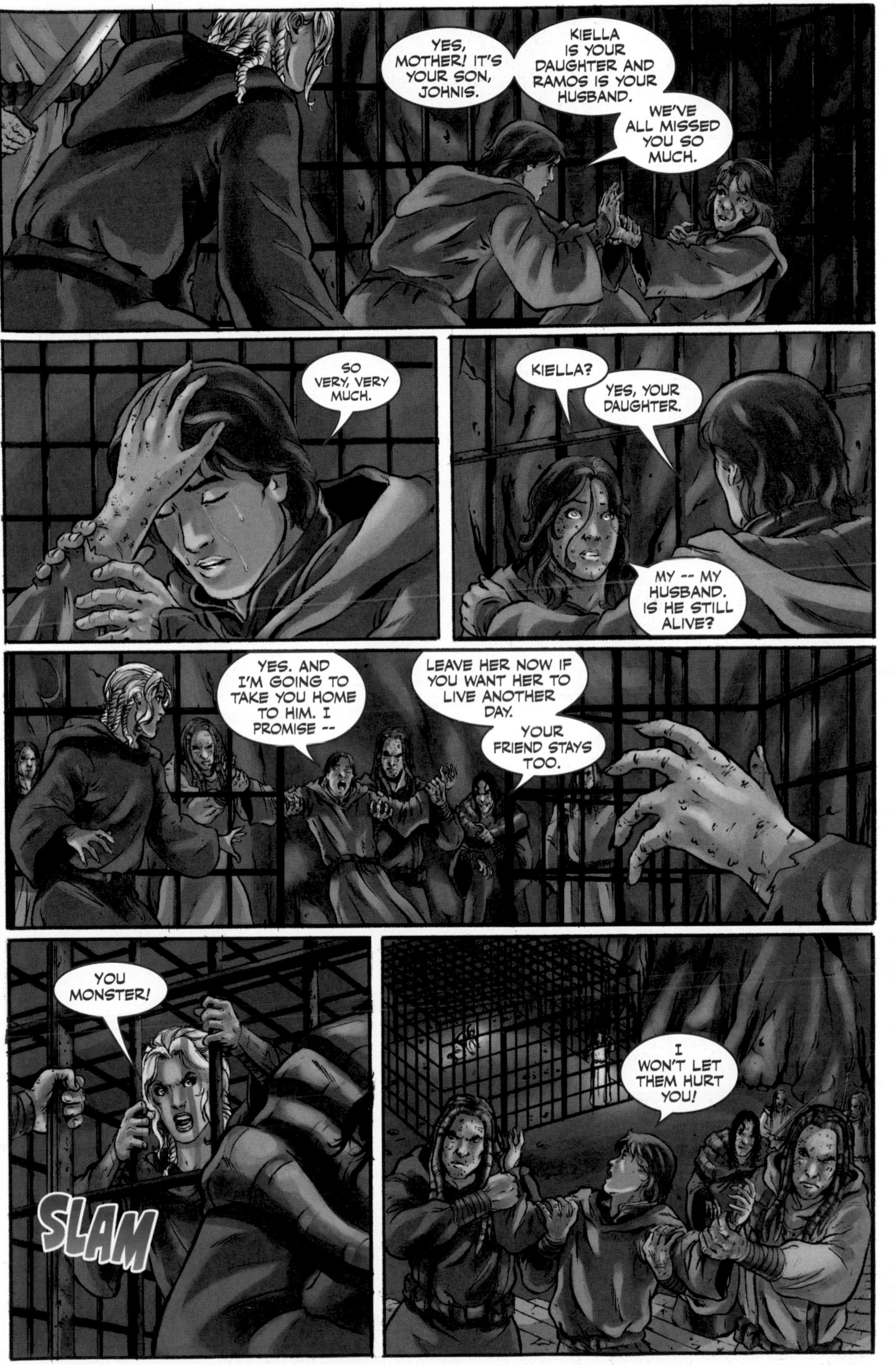
YES, MOTHER! IT'S YOUR SON, JOHNIS.
KIELLA IS YOUR DAUGHTER AND RAMOS IS YOUR HUSBAND.
WE'VE ALL MISSED YOU SO MUCH.
SO VERY, VERY MUCH.
KIELLA?
YES, YOUR DAUGHTER.
MY -- MY HUSBAND. IS HE STILL ALIVE?
YES. AND I'M GOING TO TAKE YOU HOME TO HIM. I PROMISE --
LEAVE HER NOW IF YOU WANT HER TO LIVE ANOTHER DAY.
YOUR FRIEND STAYS TOO.
YOU MONSTER!
SLAM
I WON'T LET THEM HURT YOU!

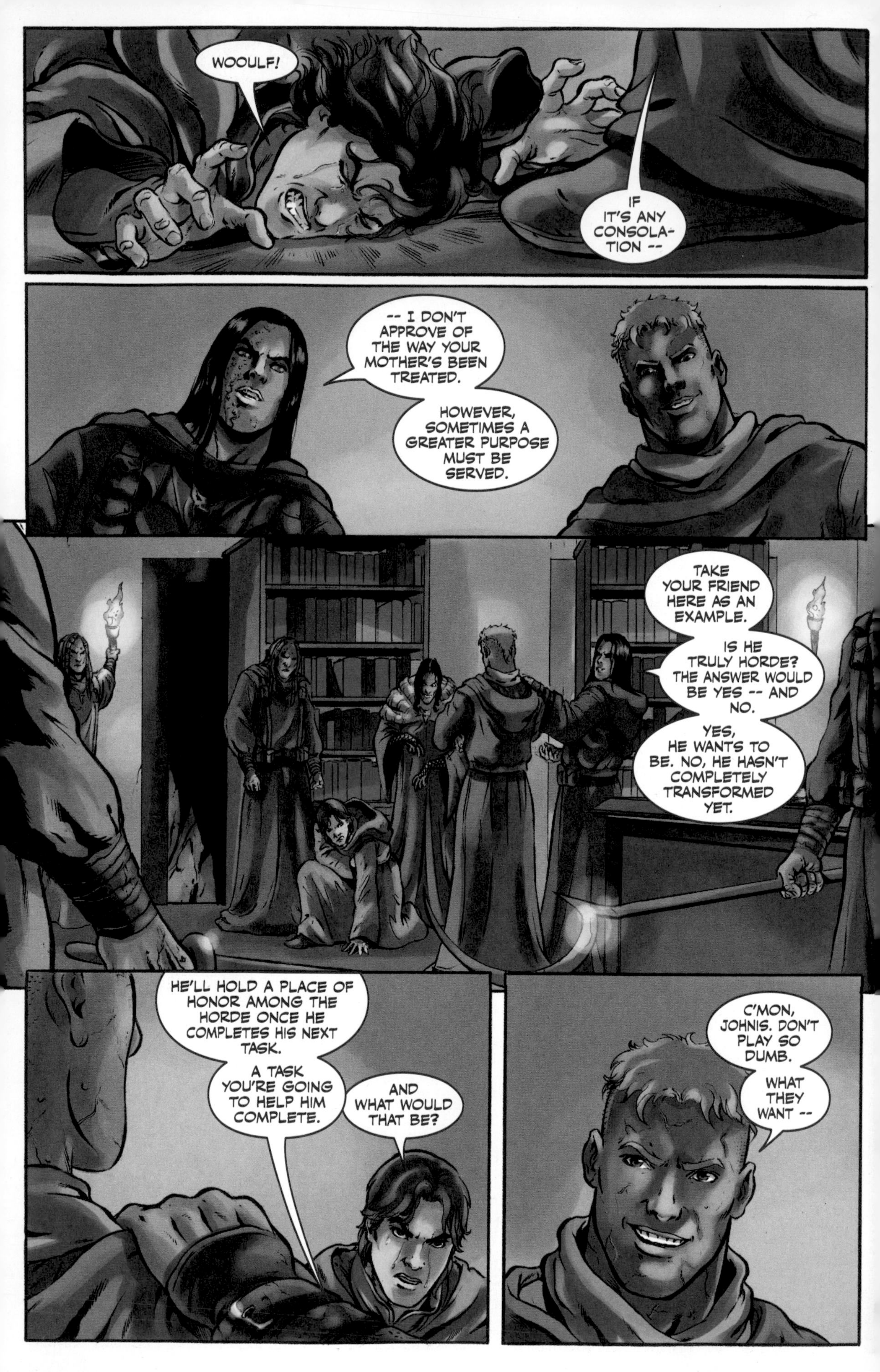
WOOULF!
IF IT'S ANY CONSOLATION --
-- I DON'T APPROVE OF THE WAY YOUR MOTHER'S BEEN TREATED.
HOWEVER, SOMETIMES A GREATER PURPOSE MUST BE SERVED.
TAKE YOUR FRIEND HERE AS AN EXAMPLE.
IS HE TRULY HORDE? THE ANSWER WOULD BE YES -- AND NO.
YES, HE WANTS TO BE. NO, HE HASN'T COMPLETELY TRANSFORMED YET.
HE'LL HOLD A PLACE OF HONOR AMONG THE HORDE ONCE HE COMPLETES HIS NEXT TASK.
A TASK YOU'RE GOING TO HELP HIM COMPLETE.
AND WHAT WOULD THAT BE?
C'MON, JOHNIS. DON'T PLAY SO DUMB.
WHAT THEY WANT --

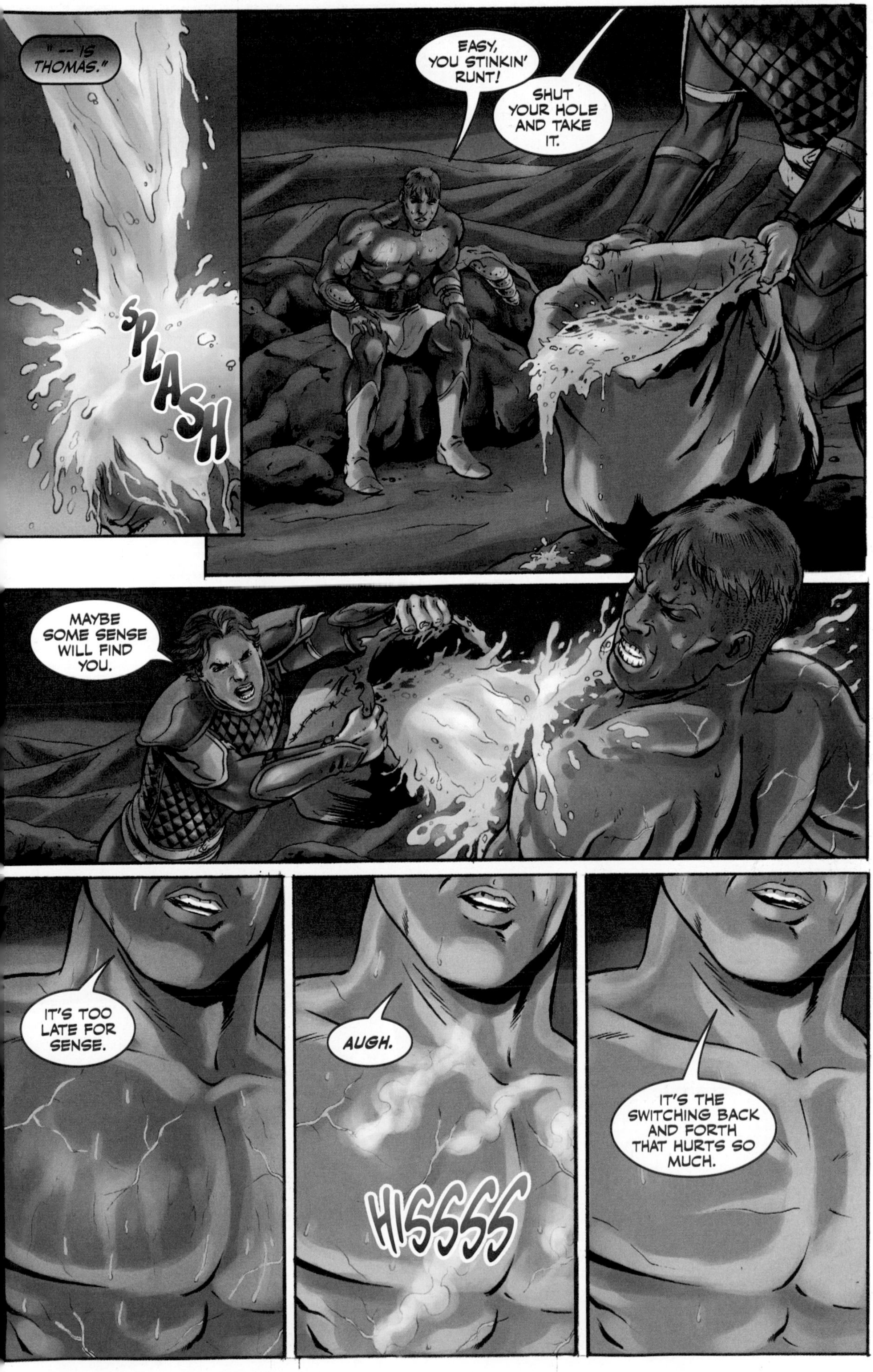
" -- IS THOMAS."
SPLASH
EASY, YOU STINKIN' RUNT!
SHUT YOUR HOLE AND TAKE IT.
MAYBE SOME SENSE WILL FIND YOU.
IT'S TOO LATE FOR SENSE.
AUGH.
HISSSS
IT'S THE SWITCHING BACK AND FORTH THAT HURTS SO MUCH.

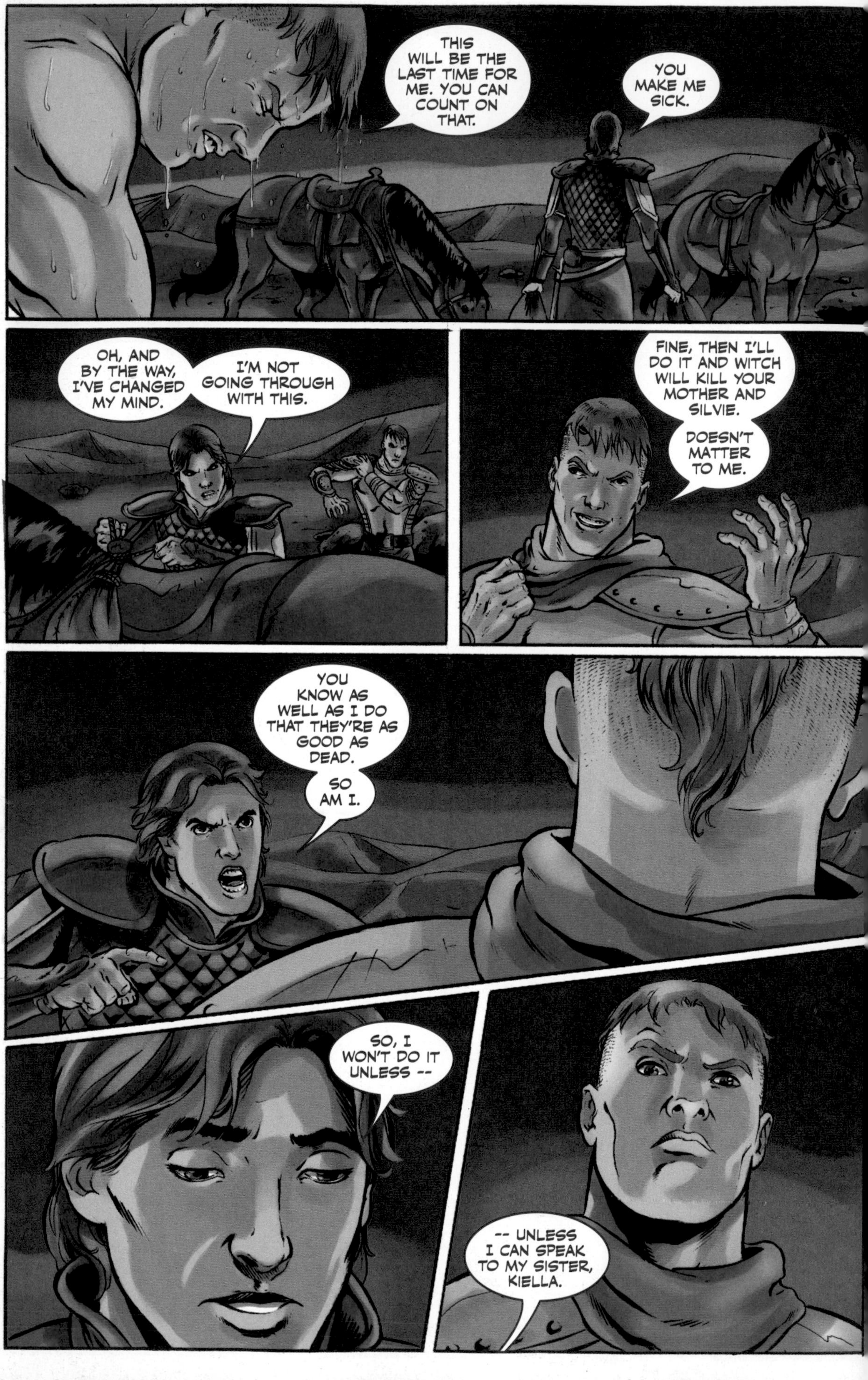
THIS WILL BE THE LAST TIME FOR ME. YOU CAN COUNT ON THAT.
YOU MAKE ME SICK.
OH, AND BY THE WAY, I'VE CHANGED MY MIND.
I'M NOT GOING THROUGH WITH THIS.
FINE, THEN I'LL DO IT AND WITCH WILL KILL YOUR MOTHER AND SILVIE.
DOESN'T MATTER TO ME.
YOU KNOW AS WELL AS I DO THAT THEY'RE AS GOOD AS DEAD.
SO AM I.
SO, I WON'T DO IT UNLESS --
-- UNLESS I CAN SPEAK TO MY SISTER, KIELLA.

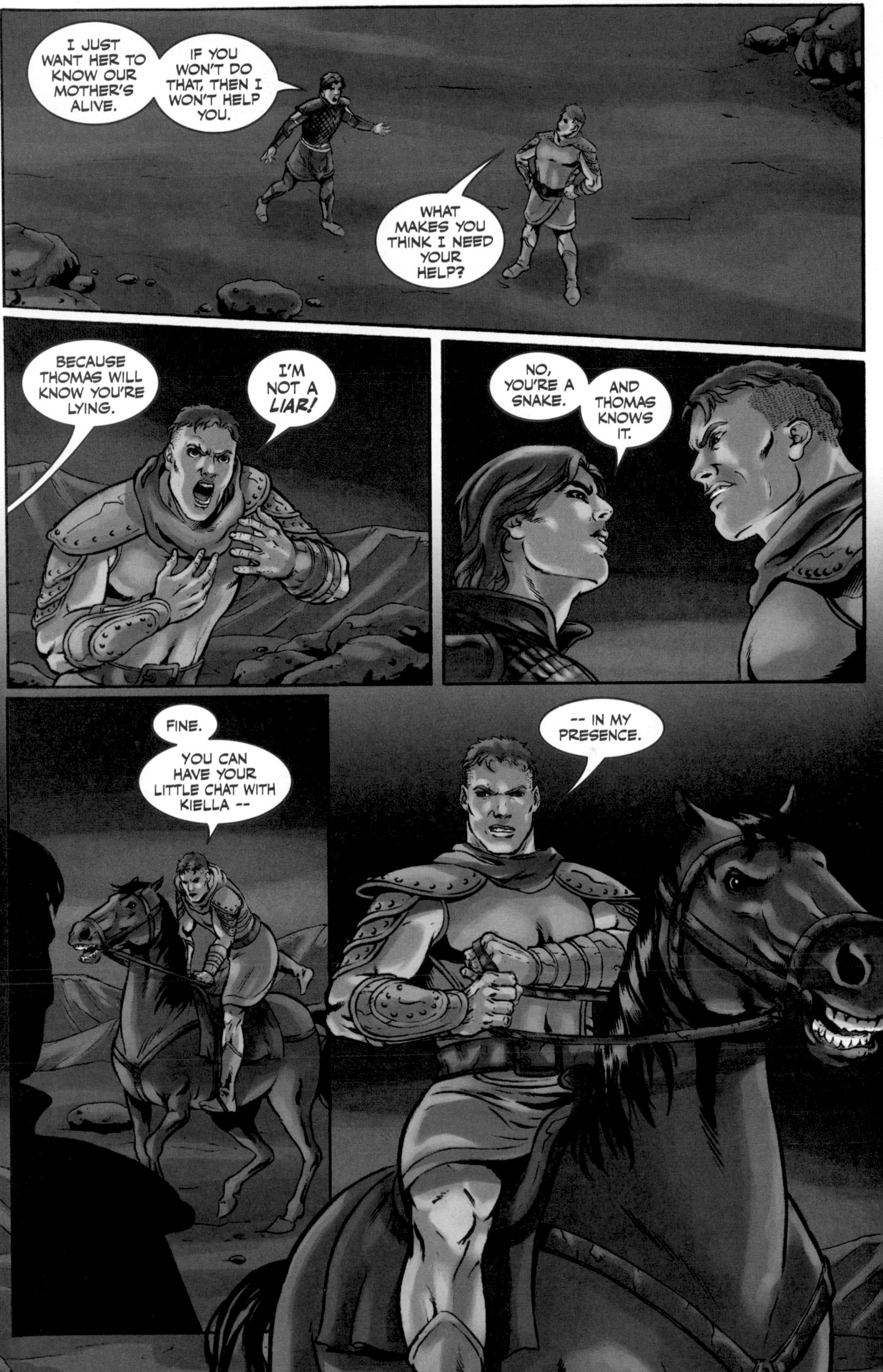
I JUST WANT HER TO KNOW OUR MOTHER'S ALIVE.
IF YOU WON'T DO THAT, THEN I WON'T HELP YOU.
WHAT MAKES YOU THINK I NEED YOUR HELP?
BECAUSE THOMAS WILL KNOW YOU'RE LYING.
I'M NOT A *LIAR!*
NO, YOU'RE A SNAKE.
AND THOMAS KNOWS IT.
FINE.
YOU CAN HAVE YOUR LITTLE CHAT WITH KIELLA --
-- IN MY PRESENCE.

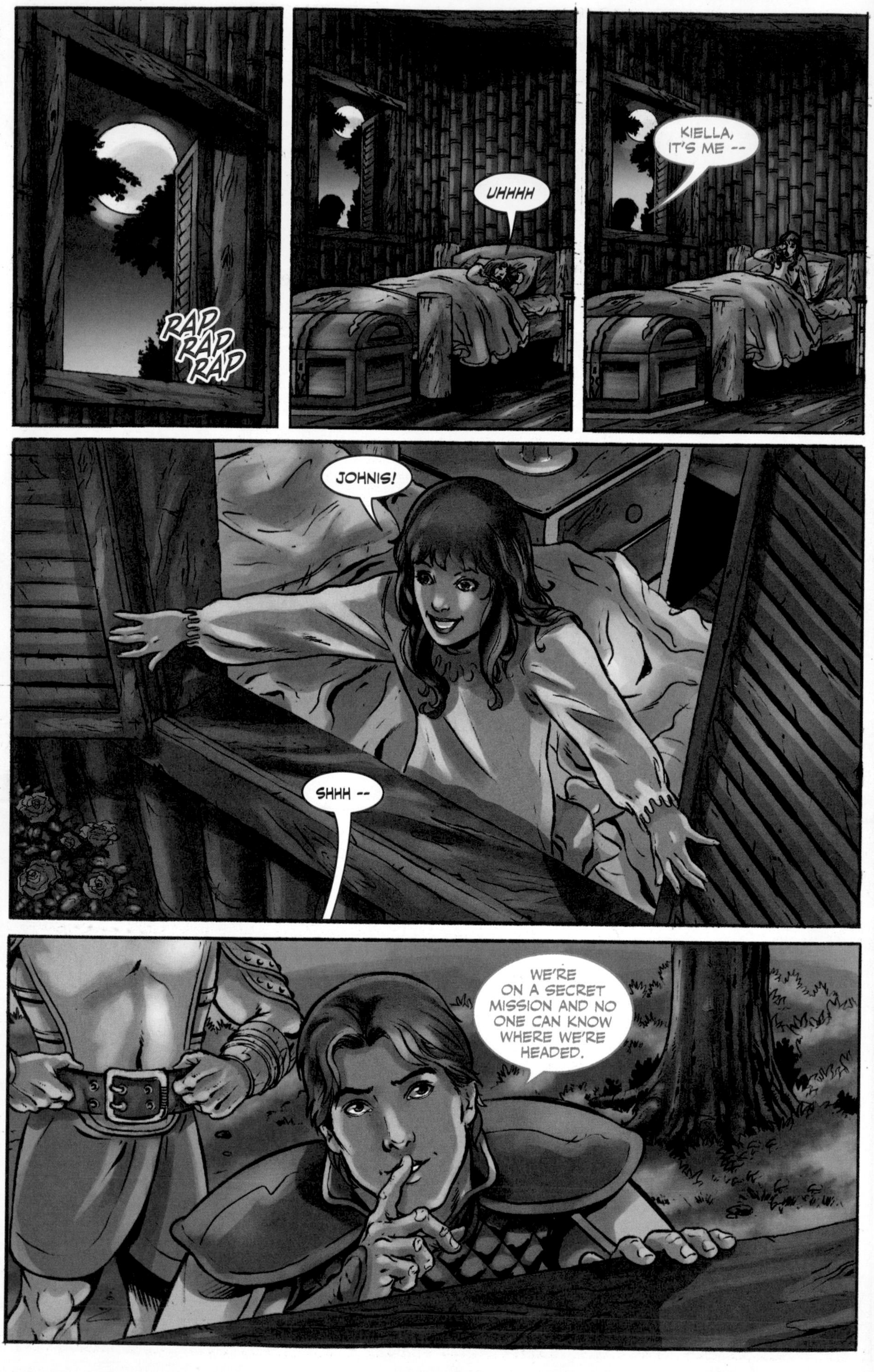
RAP RAP RAP
UHHHH
KIELLA, IT'S ME --
JOHNIS!
SHHH --
WE'RE ON A SECRET MISSION AND NO ONE CAN KNOW WHERE WE'RE HEADED.

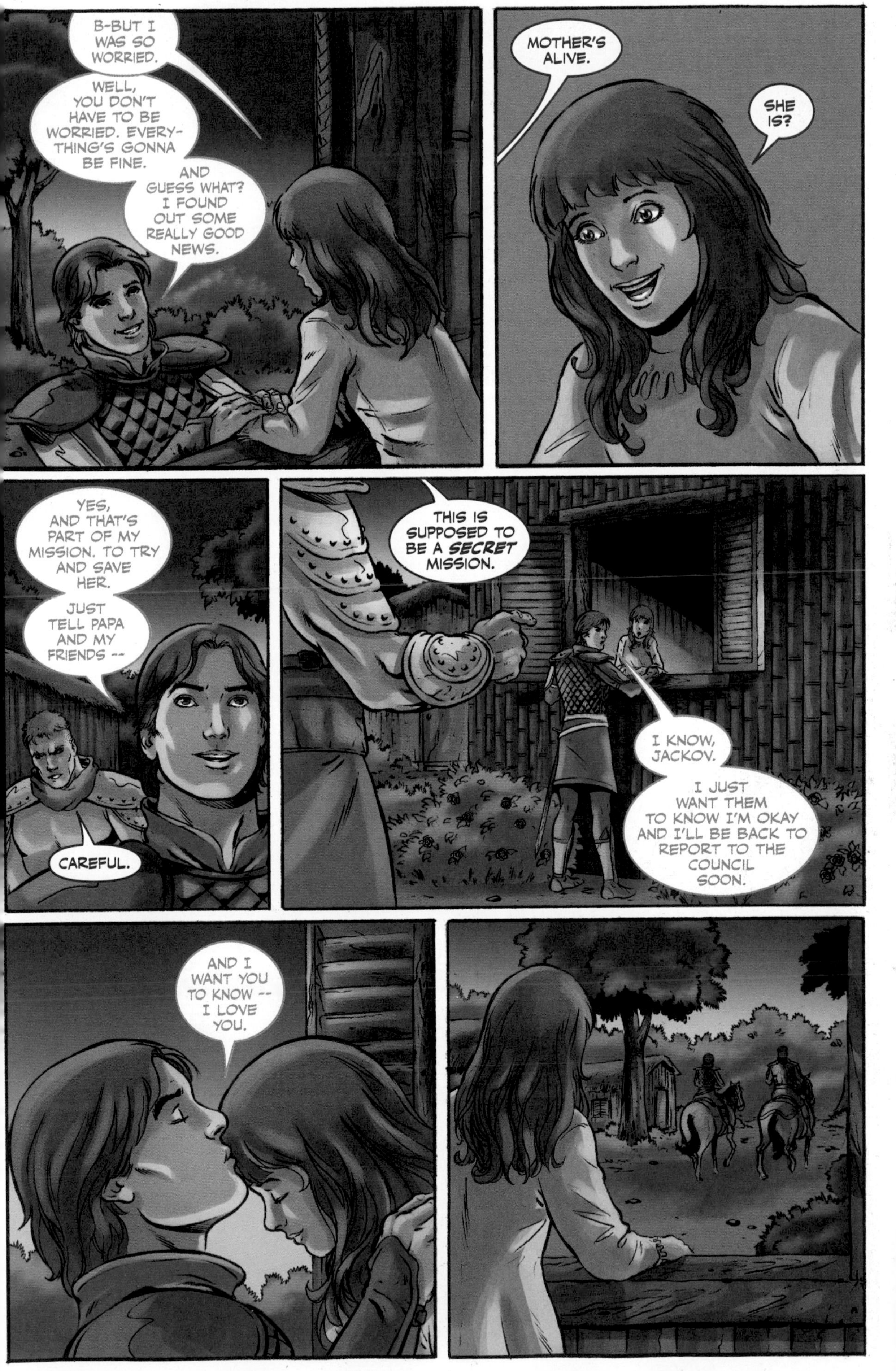
B-BUT I WAS SO WORRIED.
WELL, YOU DON'T HAVE TO BE WORRIED. EVERY-THING'S GONNA BE FINE.
AND GUESS WHAT? I FOUND OUT SOME REALLY GOOD NEWS.
MOTHER'S ALIVE.
SHE IS?
YES, AND THAT'S PART OF MY MISSION. TO TRY AND SAVE HER.
JUST TELL PAPA AND MY FRIENDS --
CAREFUL.
THIS IS SUPPOSED TO BE A *SECRET* MISSION.
I KNOW, JACKOV.
I JUST WANT THEM TO KNOW I'M OKAY AND I'LL BE BACK TO REPORT TO THE COUNCIL SOON.
AND I WANT YOU TO KNOW -- I LOVE YOU.

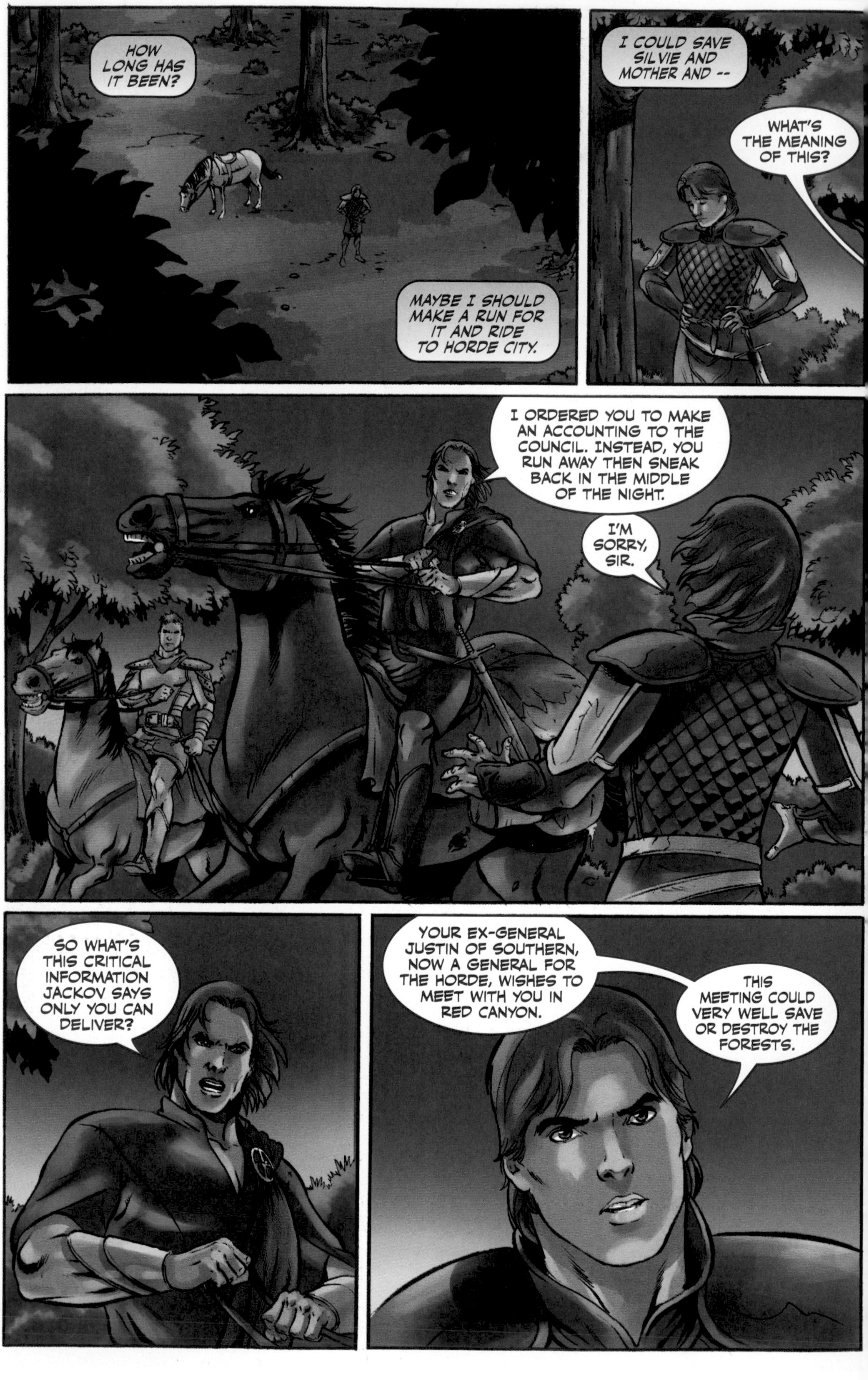
HOW LONG HAS IT BEEN?
MAYBE I SHOULD MAKE A RUN FOR IT AND RIDE TO HORDE CITY.
I COULD SAVE SILVIE AND MOTHER AND --
WHAT'S THE MEANING OF THIS?
I ORDERED YOU TO MAKE AN ACCOUNTING TO THE COUNCIL. INSTEAD, YOU RUN AWAY THEN SNEAK BACK IN THE MIDDLE OF THE NIGHT.
I'M SORRY, SIR.
SO WHAT'S THIS CRITICAL INFORMATION JACKOV SAYS ONLY YOU CAN DELIVER?
YOUR EX-GENERAL JUSTIN OF SOUTHERN, NOW A GENERAL FOR THE HORDE, WISHES TO MEET WITH YOU IN RED CANYON.
THIS MEETING COULD VERY WELL SAVE OR DESTROY THE FORESTS.

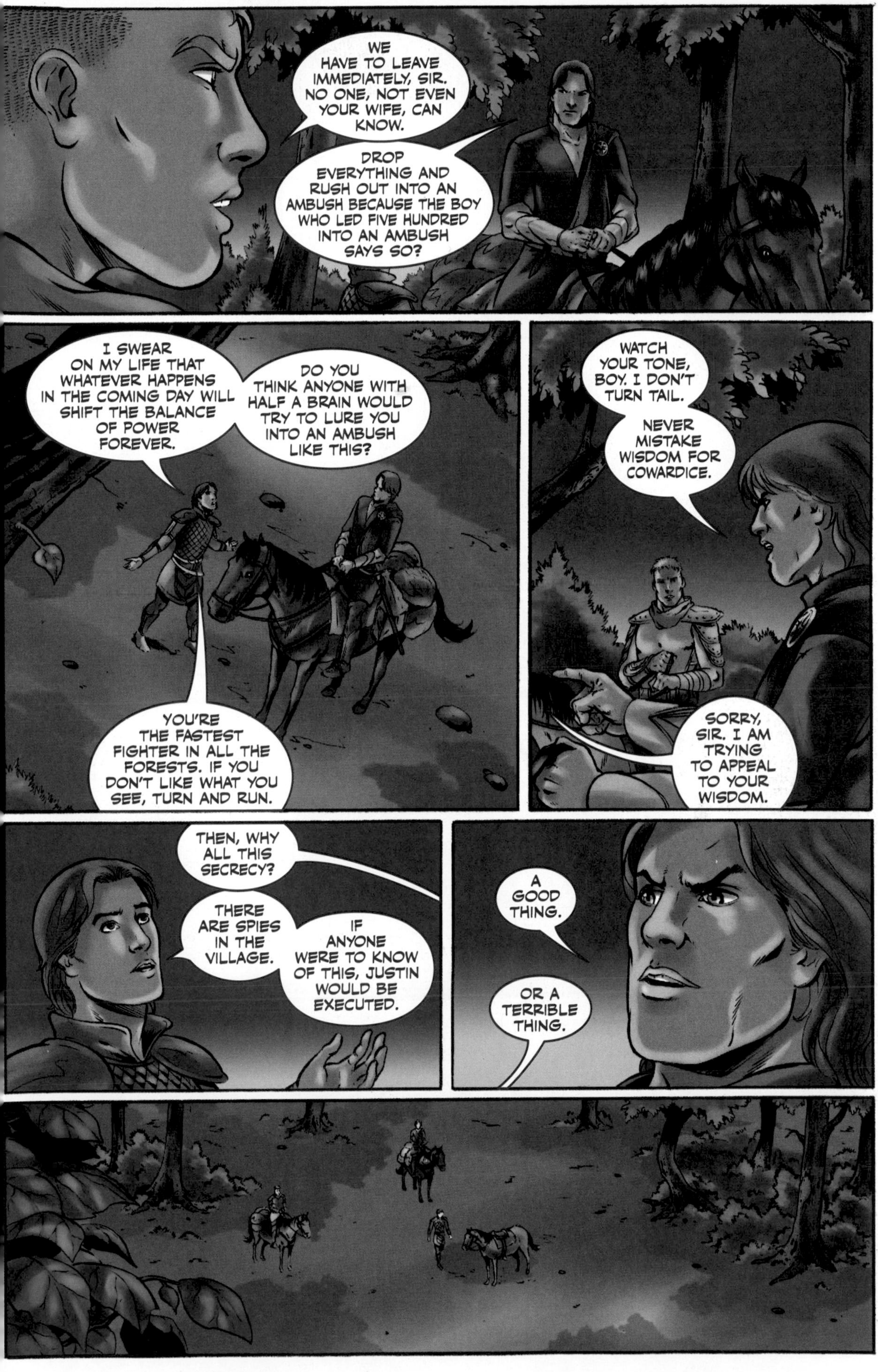
WE HAVE TO LEAVE IMMEDIATELY, SIR. NO ONE, NOT EVEN YOUR WIFE, CAN KNOW.
DROP EVERYTHING AND RUSH OUT INTO AN AMBUSH BECAUSE THE BOY WHO LED FIVE HUNDRED INTO AN AMBUSH SAYS SO?
I SWEAR ON MY LIFE THAT WHATEVER HAPPENS IN THE COMING DAY WILL SHIFT THE BALANCE OF POWER FOREVER.
DO YOU THINK ANYONE WITH HALF A BRAIN WOULD TRY TO LURE YOU INTO AN AMBUSH LIKE THIS?
YOU'RE THE FASTEST FIGHTER IN ALL THE FORESTS. IF YOU DON'T LIKE WHAT YOU SEE, TURN AND RUN.
WATCH YOUR TONE, BOY. I DON'T TURN TAIL.
NEVER MISTAKE WISDOM FOR COWARDICE.
SORRY, SIR. I AM TRYING TO APPEAL TO YOUR WISDOM.
THEN, WHY ALL THIS SECRECY?
THERE ARE SPIES IN THE VILLAGE.
IF ANYONE WERE TO KNOW OF THIS, JUSTIN WOULD BE EXECUTED.
A GOOD THING.
OR A TERRIBLE THING.

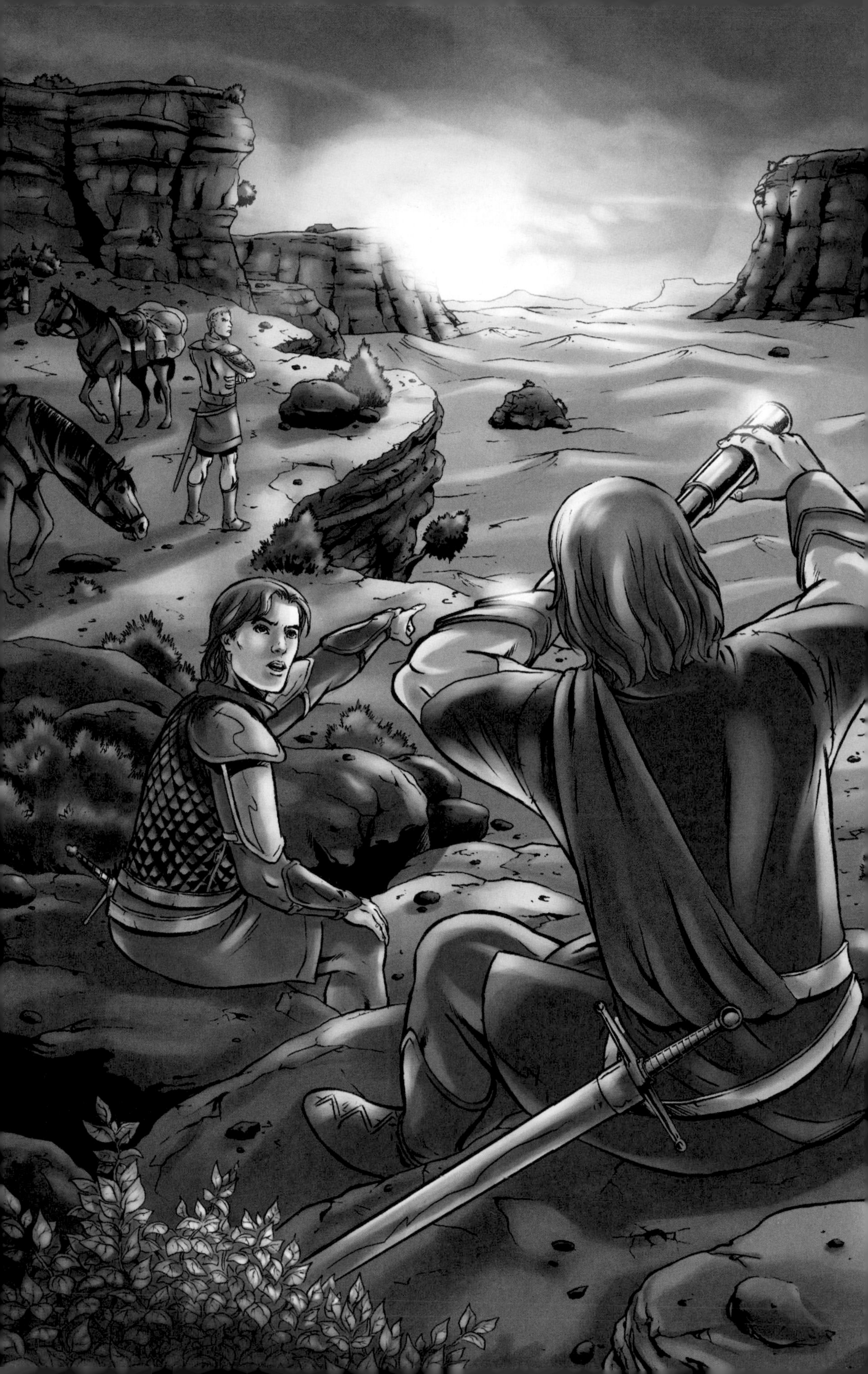

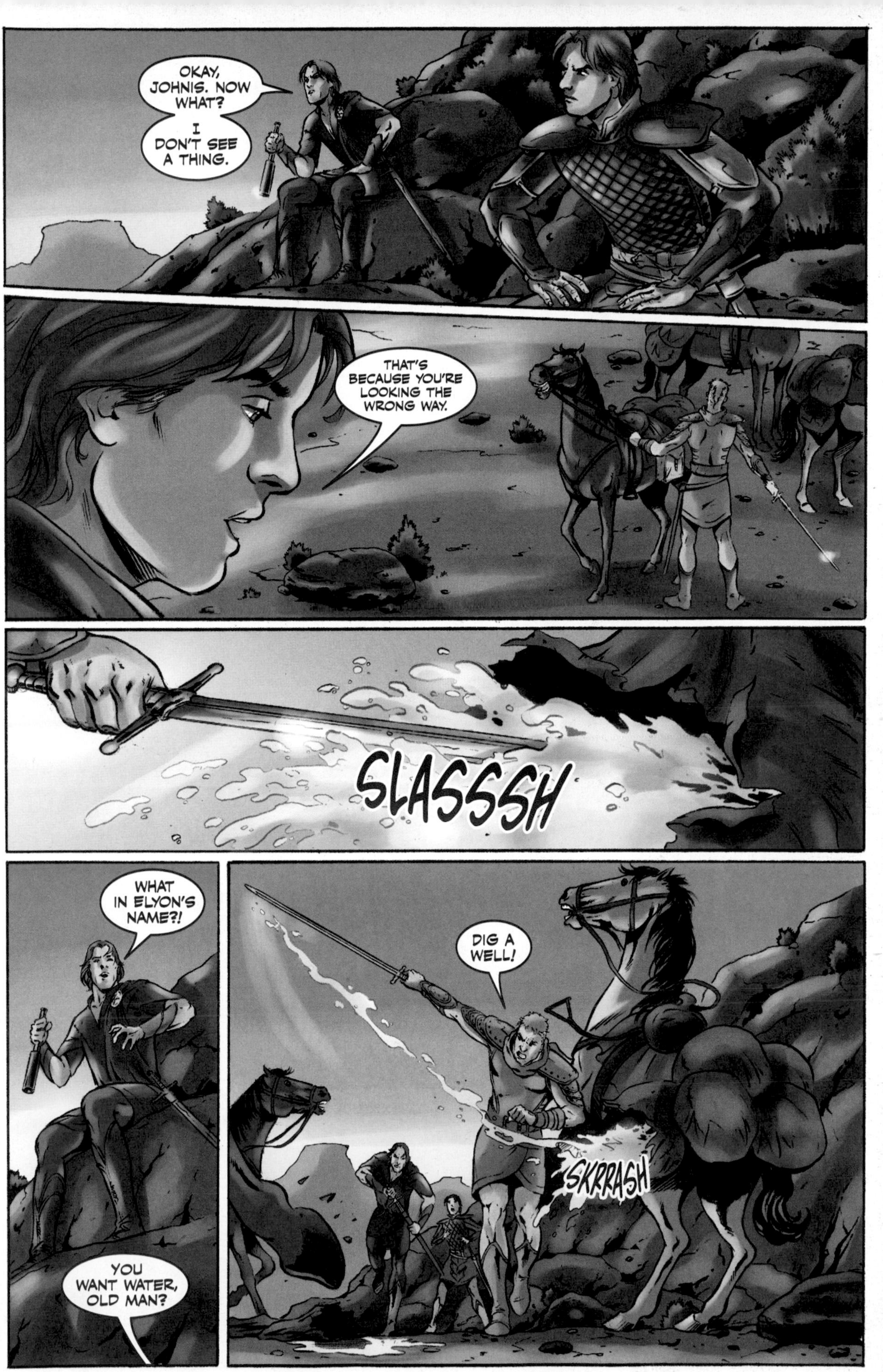
OKAY, JOHNIS. NOW WHAT?
I DON'T SEE A THING.
THAT'S BECAUSE YOU'RE LOOKING THE WRONG WAY.
SLASSSH
WHAT IN ELYON'S NAME?!
YOU WANT WATER, OLD MAN?
DIG A WELL!
SKRRASH

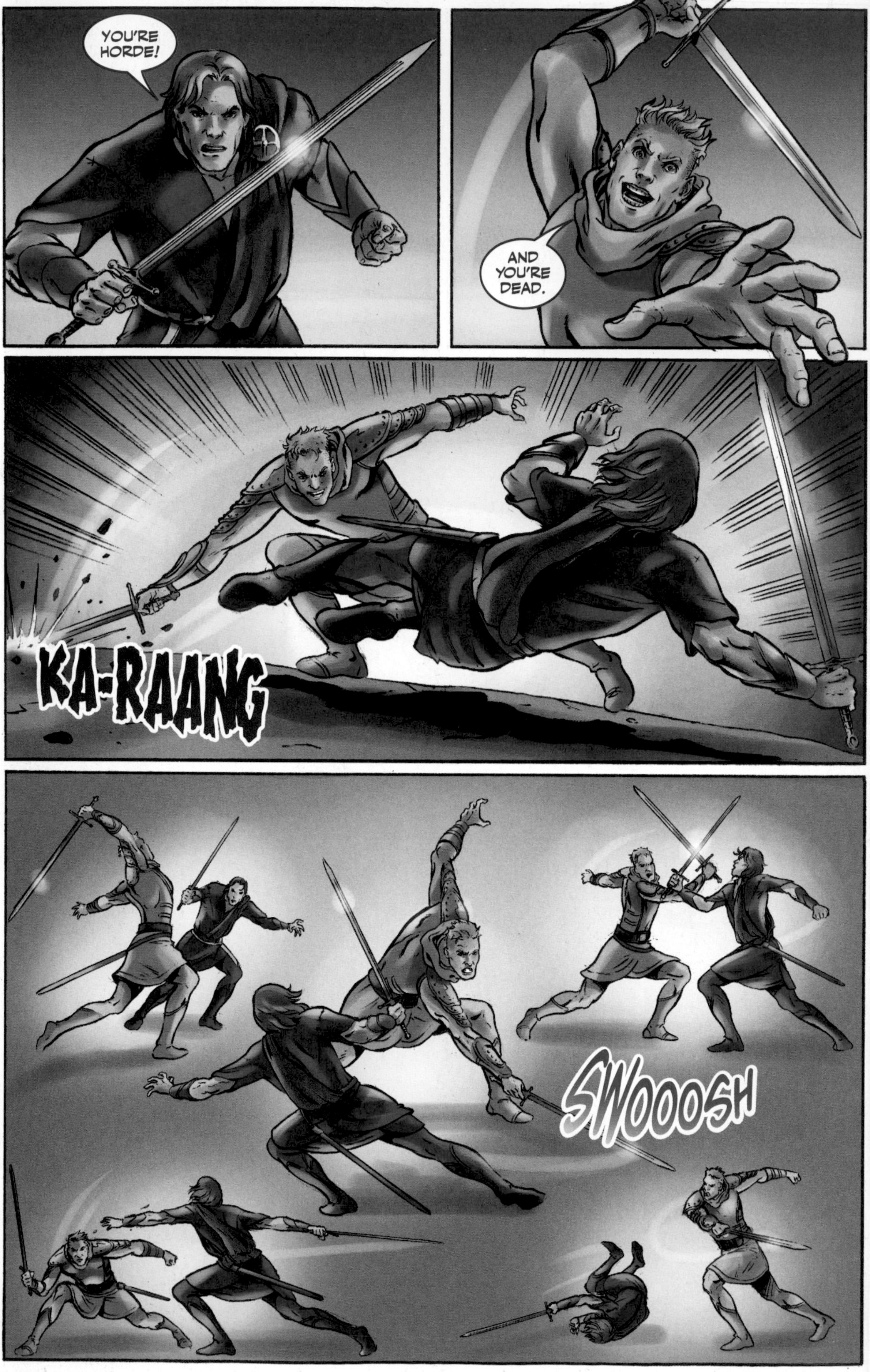
YOU'RE HORDE!
AND YOU'RE DEAD.
KA-RAANG
SWOOOSH

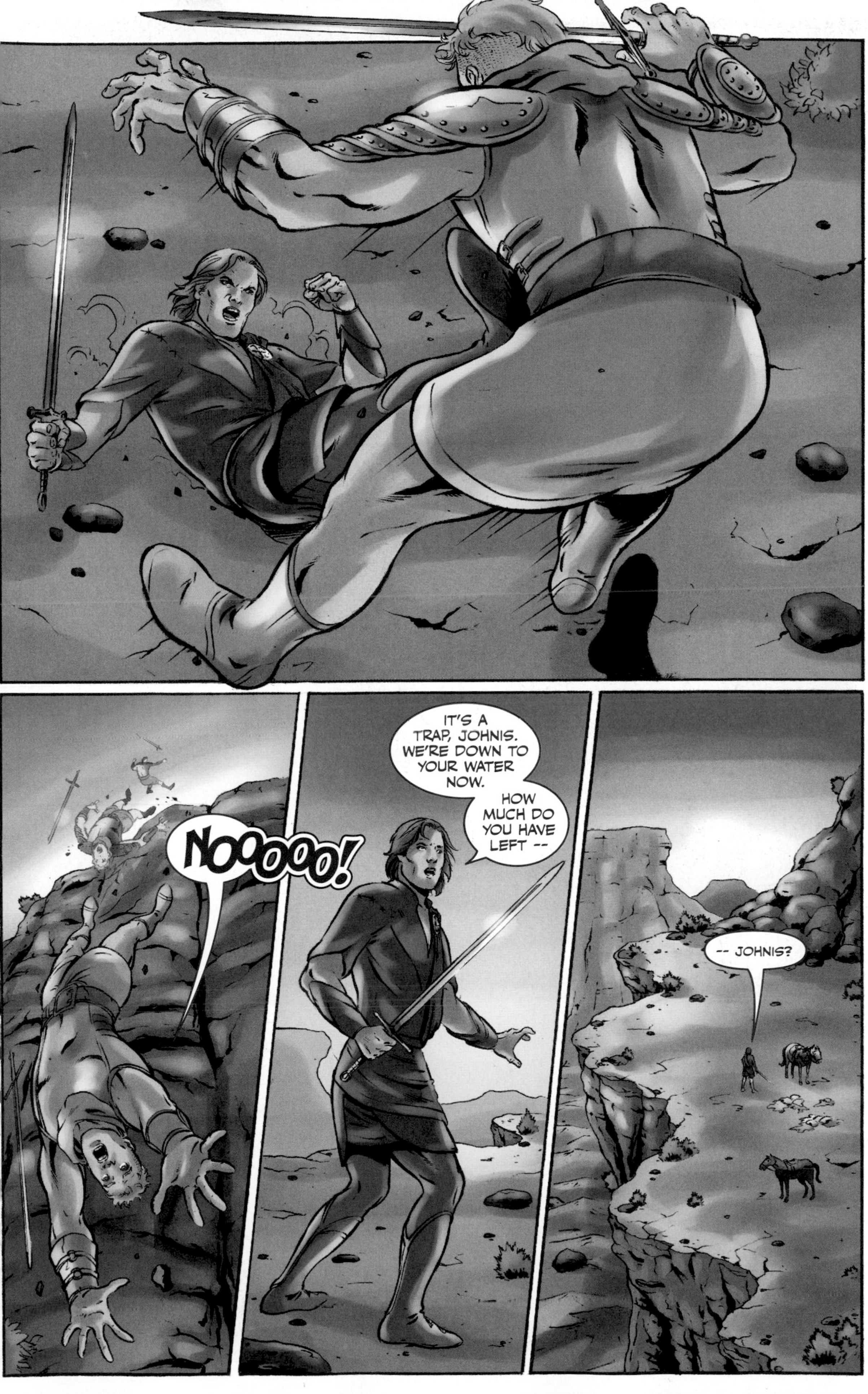
NOOOOO!
IT'S A TRAP, JOHNIS. WE'RE DOWN TO YOUR WATER NOW.
HOW MUCH DO YOU HAVE LEFT --
-- JOHNIS?

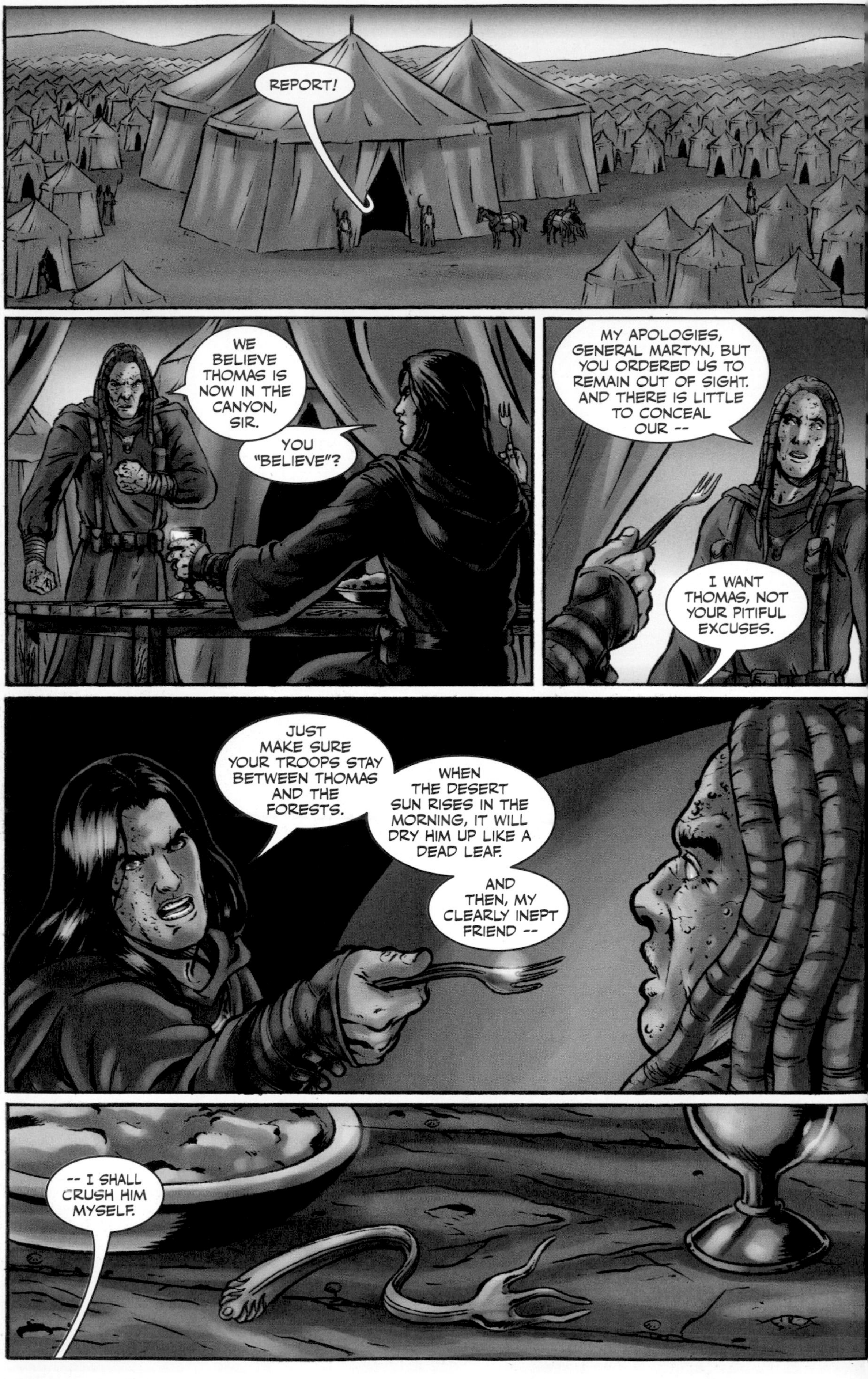
REPORT!
WE BELIEVE THOMAS IS NOW IN THE CANYON, SIR.
YOU "BELIEVE"?
MY APOLOGIES, GENERAL MARTYN, BUT YOU ORDERED US TO REMAIN OUT OF SIGHT. AND THERE IS LITTLE TO CONCEAL OUR --
I WANT THOMAS, NOT YOUR PITIFUL EXCUSES.
JUST MAKE SURE YOUR TROOPS STAY BETWEEN THOMAS AND THE FORESTS.
WHEN THE DESERT SUN RISES IN THE MORNING, IT WILL DRY HIM UP LIKE A DEAD LEAF.
AND THEN, MY CLEARLY INEPT FRIEND --
-- I SHALL CRUSH HIM MYSELF.

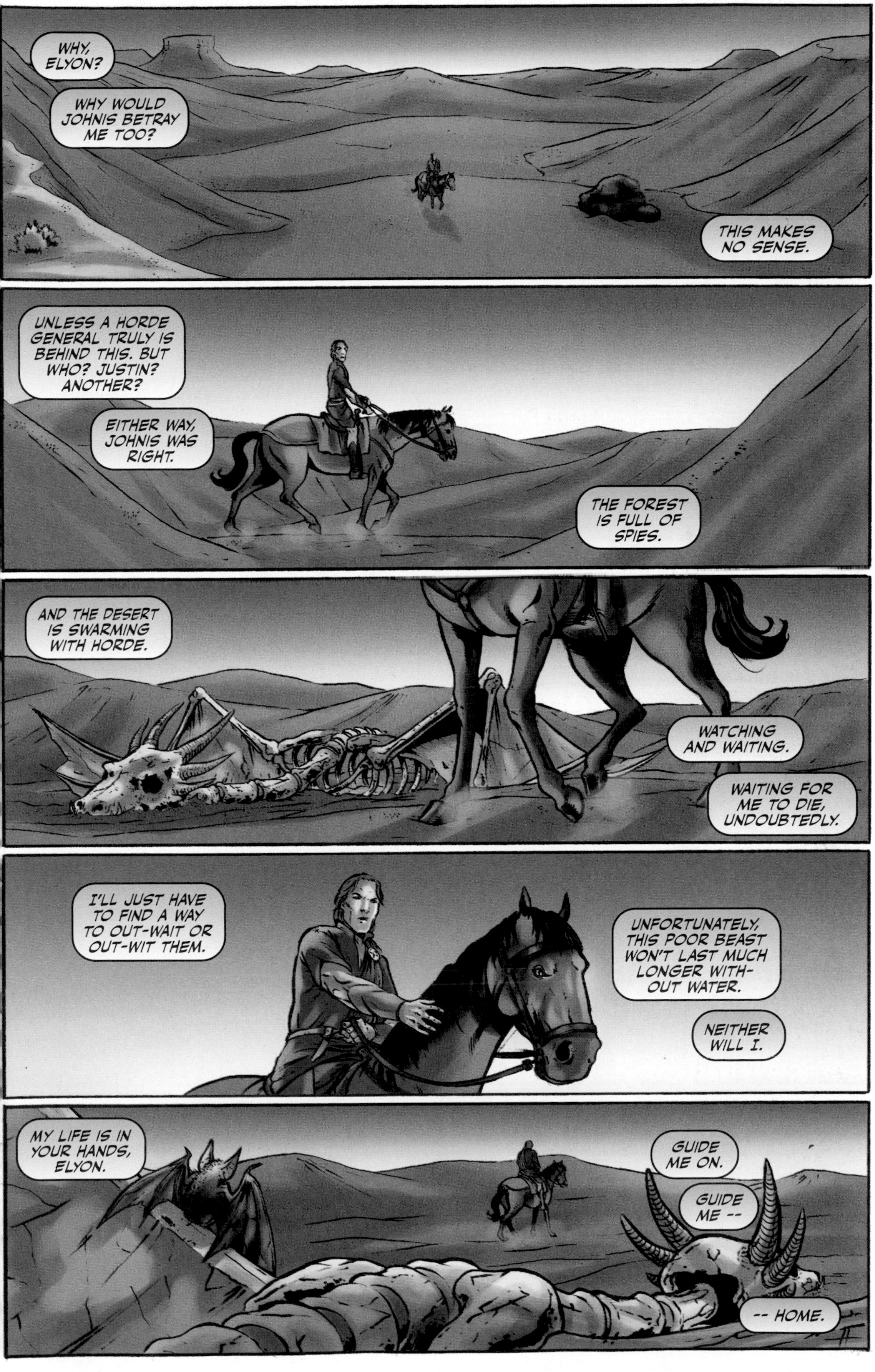
WHY, ELYON?
WHY WOULD JOHNIS BETRAY ME TOO?
THIS MAKES NO SENSE.
UNLESS A HORDE GENERAL TRULY IS BEHIND THIS. BUT WHO? JUSTIN? ANOTHER?
EITHER WAY, JOHNIS WAS RIGHT.
THE FOREST IS FULL OF SPIES.
AND THE DESERT IS SWARMING WITH HORDE.
WATCHING AND WAITING.
WAITING FOR ME TO DIE, UNDOUBTEDLY.
I'LL JUST HAVE TO FIND A WAY TO OUT-WAIT OR OUT-WIT THEM.
UNFORTUNATELY, THIS POOR BEAST WON'T LAST MUCH LONGER WITH-OUT WATER.
NEITHER WILL I.
MY LIFE IS IN YOUR HANDS, ELYON.
GUIDE ME ON.
GUIDE ME --
-- HOME.

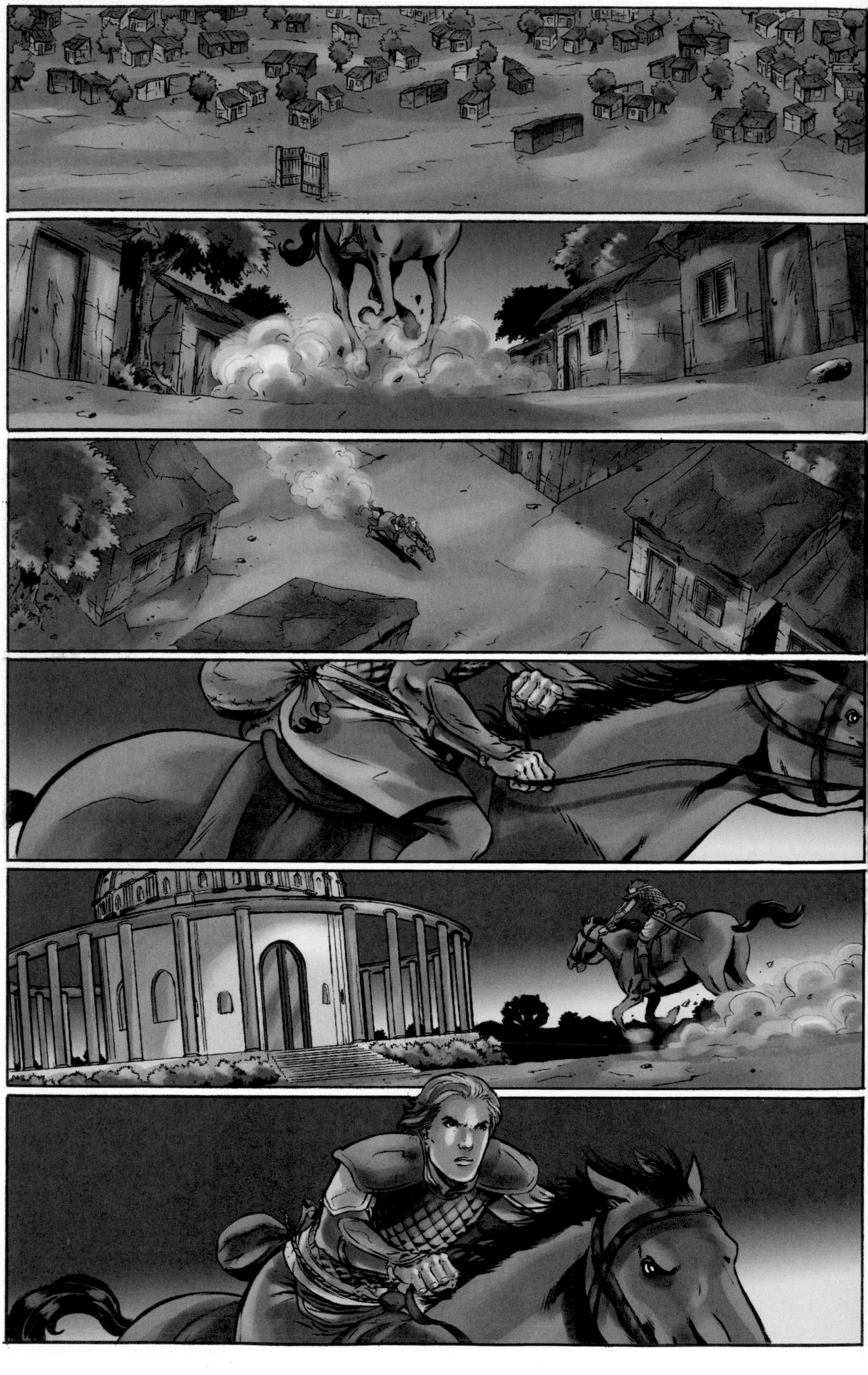

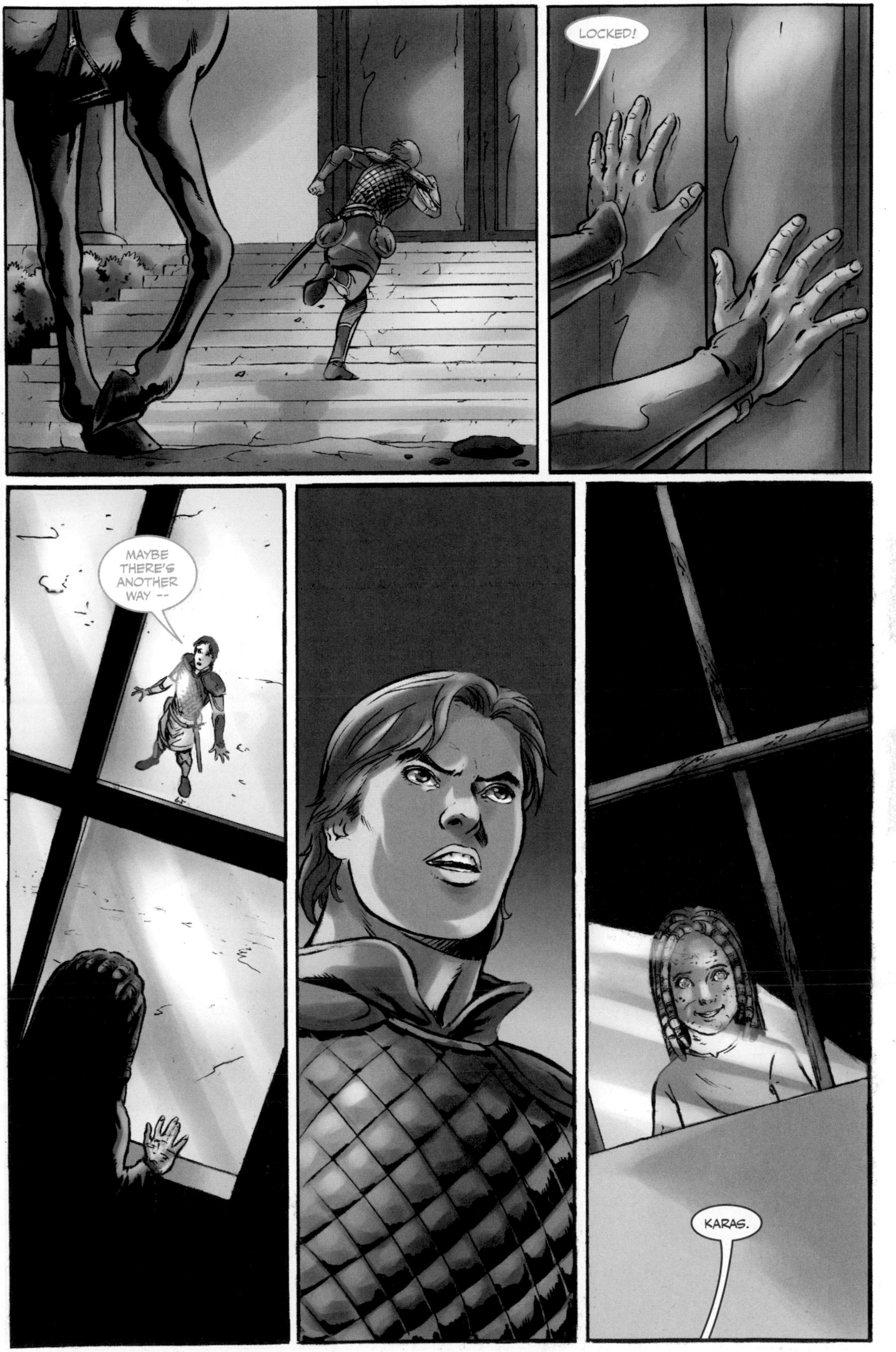
LOCKED!
MAYBE THERE'S ANOTHER WAY --
KARAS.

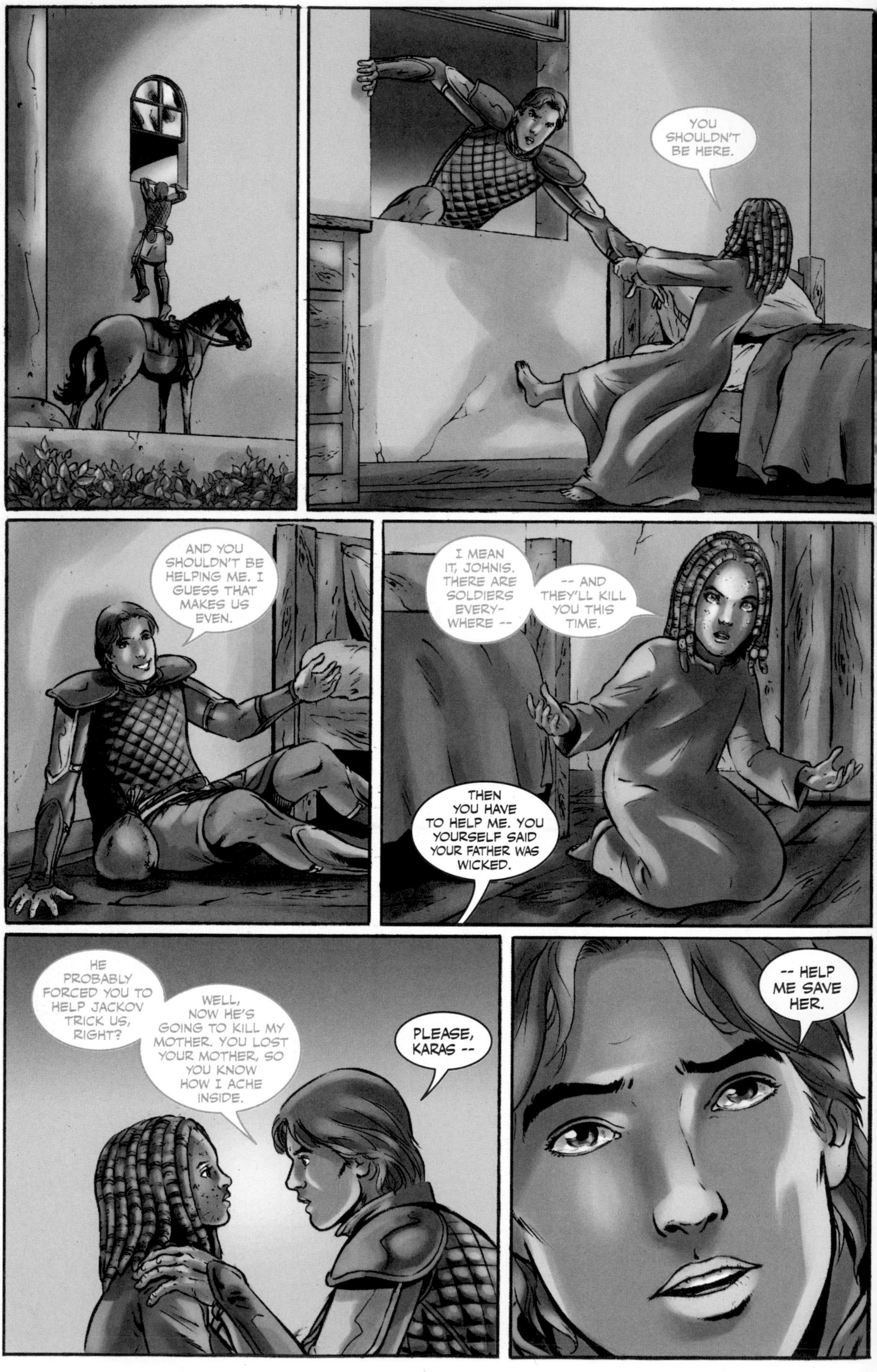
YOU SHOULDN'T BE HERE.
AND YOU SHOULDN'T BE HELPING ME. I GUESS THAT MAKES US EVEN.
I MEAN IT, JOHNIS. THERE ARE SOLDIERS EVERY-WHERE --
-- AND THEY'LL KILL YOU THIS TIME.
THEN YOU HAVE TO HELP ME. YOU YOURSELF SAID YOUR FATHER WAS WICKED.
HE PROBABLY FORCED YOU TO HELP JACKOV TRICK US, RIGHT?
WELL, NOW HE'S GOING TO KILL MY MOTHER. YOU LOST YOUR MOTHER, SO YOU KNOW HOW I ACHE INSIDE.
PLEASE, KARAS --
-- HELP ME SAVE HER.

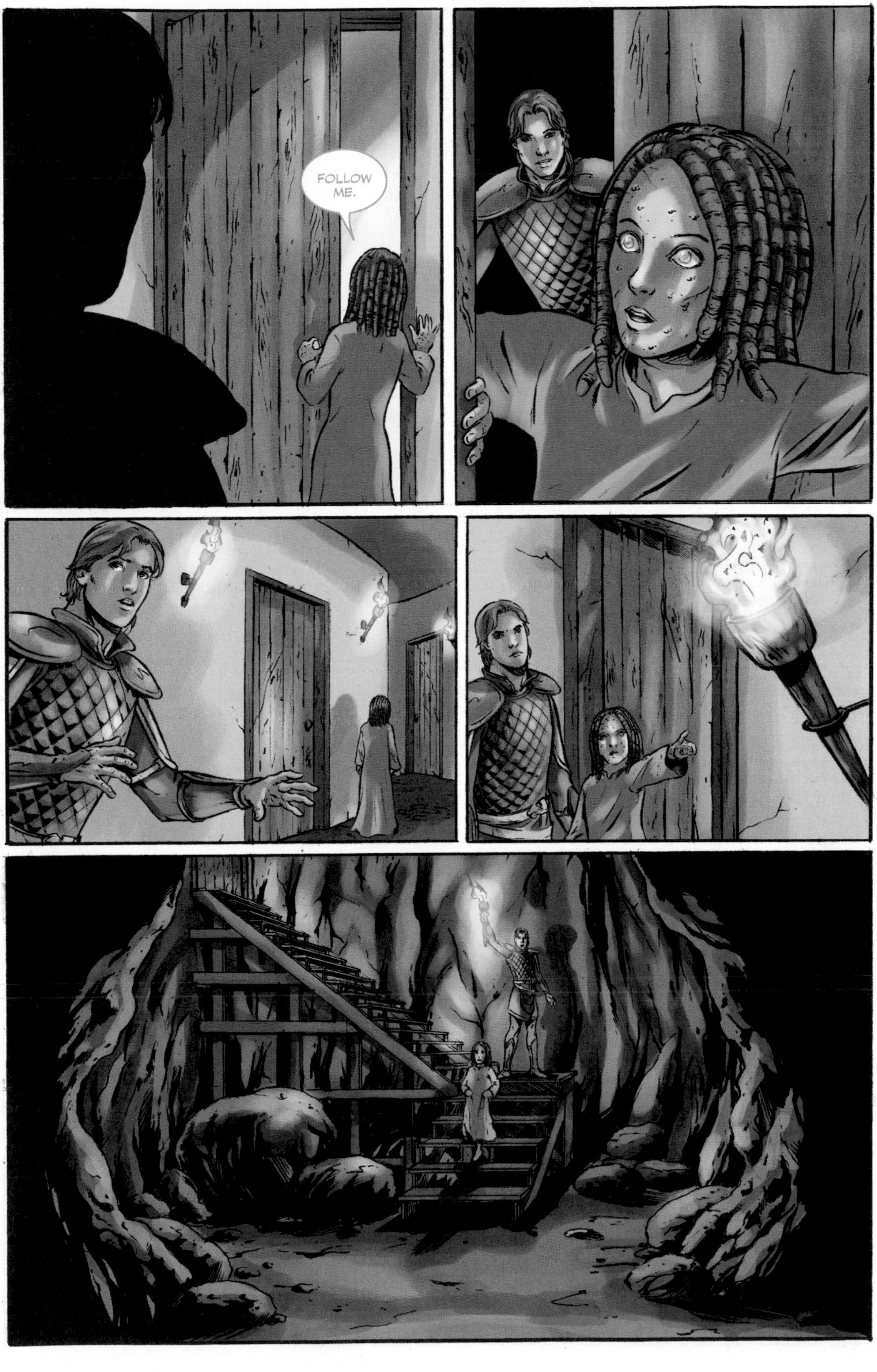
FOLLOW ME.

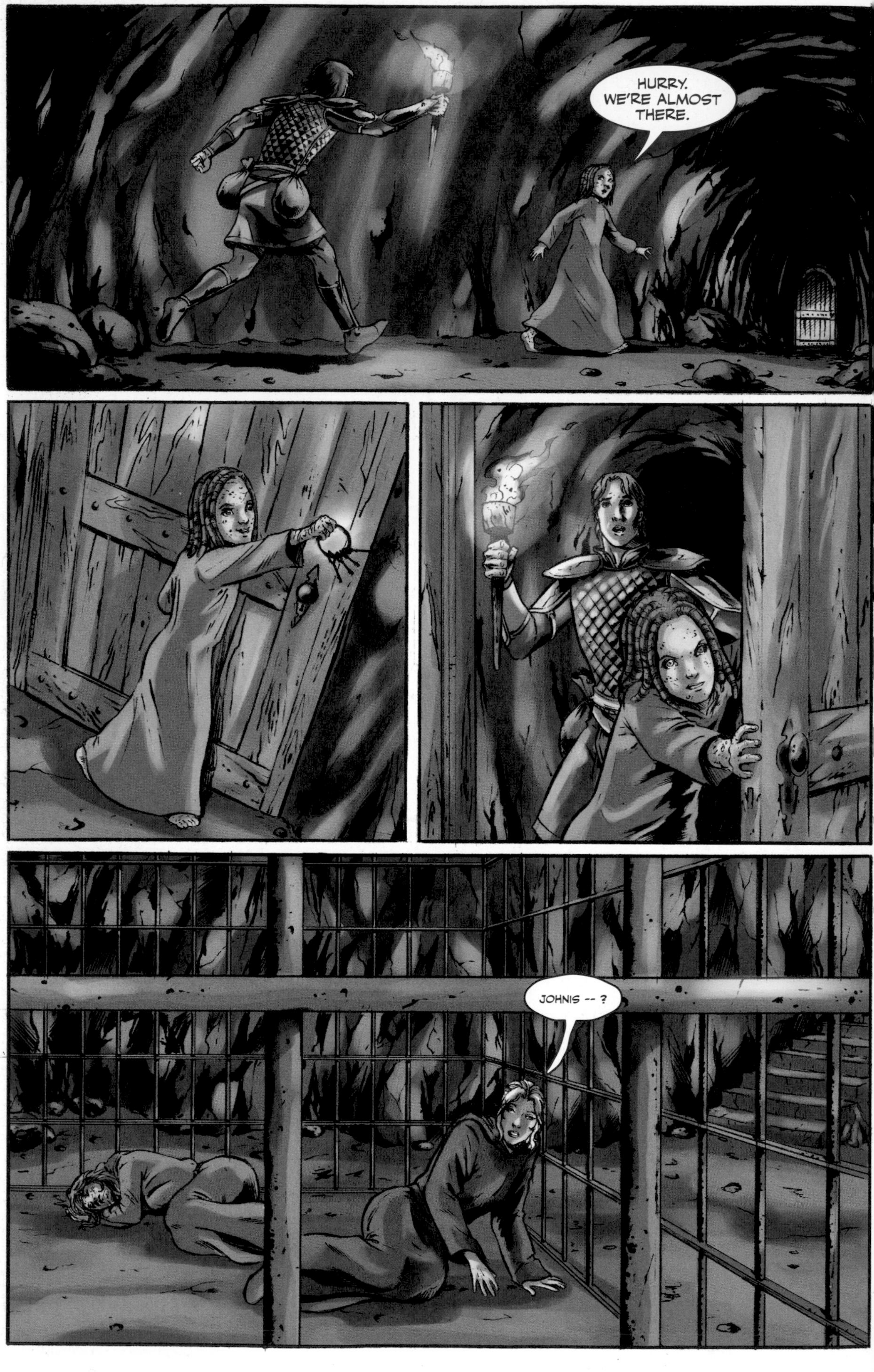
HURRY. WE'RE ALMOST THERE.
JOHNIS -- ?

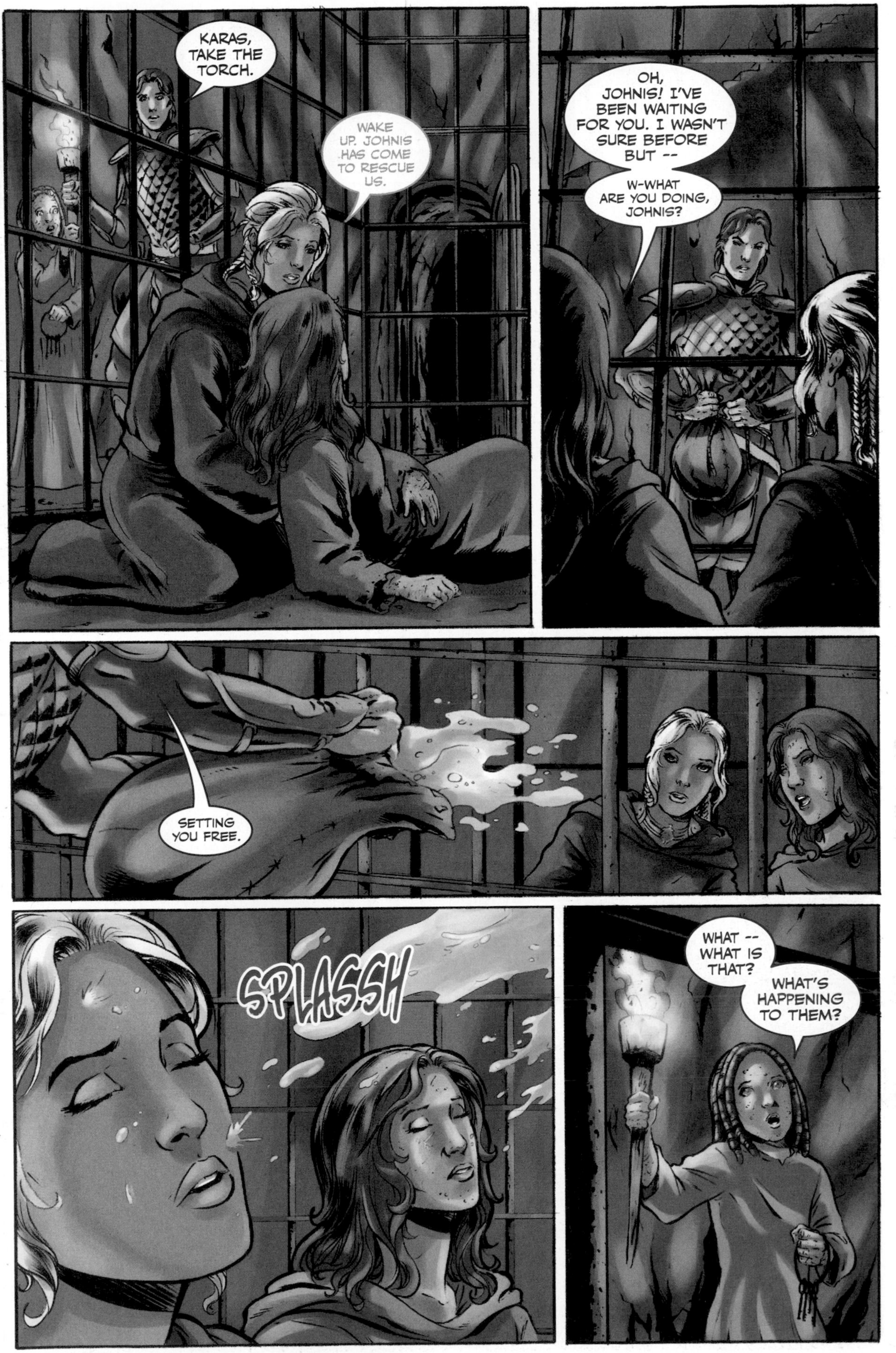
KARAS, TAKE THE TORCH.
WAKE UP. JOHNIS HAS COME TO RESCUE US.
OH, JOHNIS! I'VE BEEN WAITING FOR YOU. I WASN'T SURE BEFORE BUT --
W-WHAT ARE YOU DOING, JOHNIS?
SETTING YOU FREE.
SPLASSH
WHAT -- WHAT IS THAT?
WHAT'S HAPPENING TO THEM?

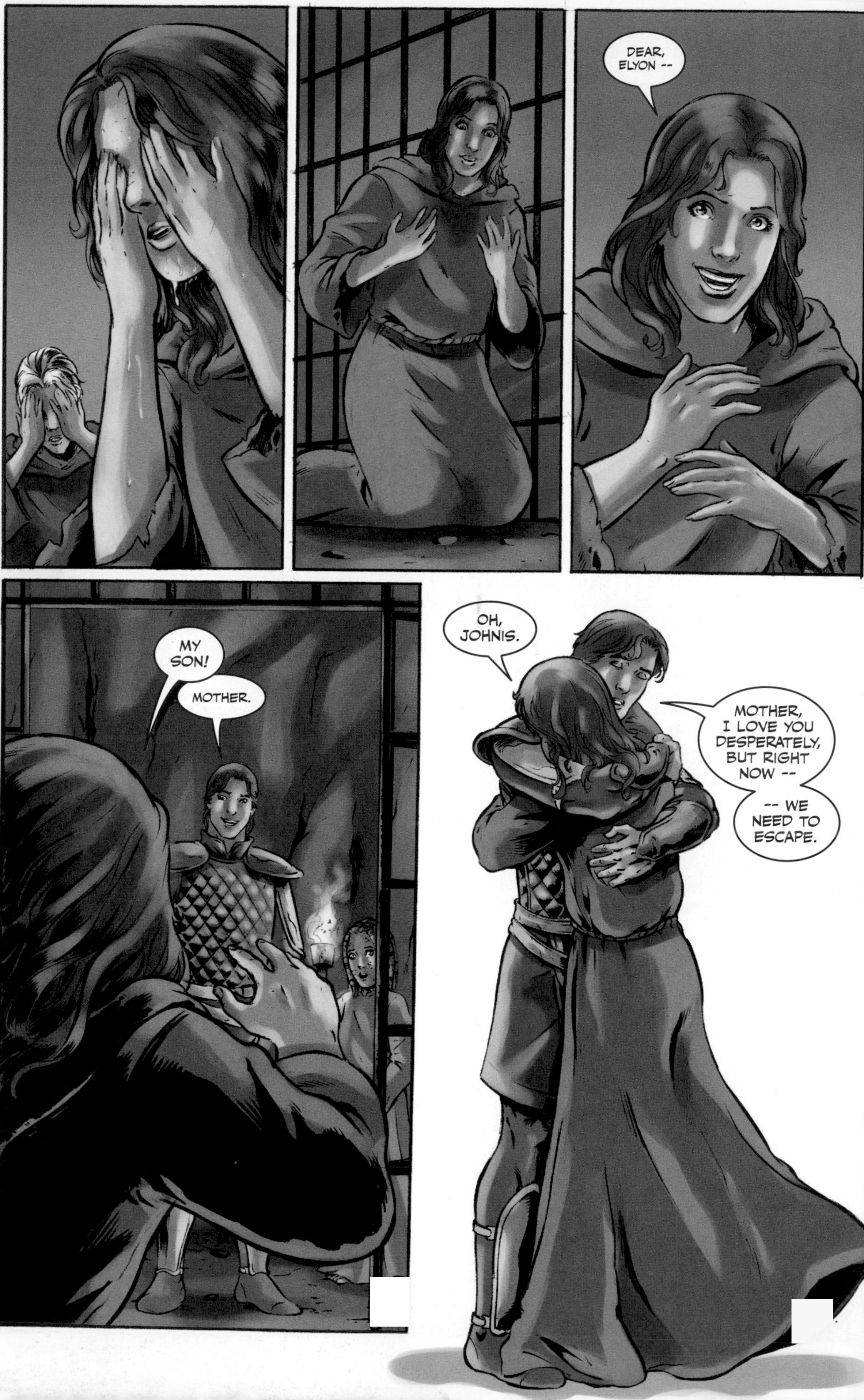
DEAR, ELYON --
MY SON!
MOTHER.
OH, JOHNIS.
MOTHER, I LOVE YOU DESPERATELY, BUT RIGHT NOW --
-- WE NEED TO ESCAPE.

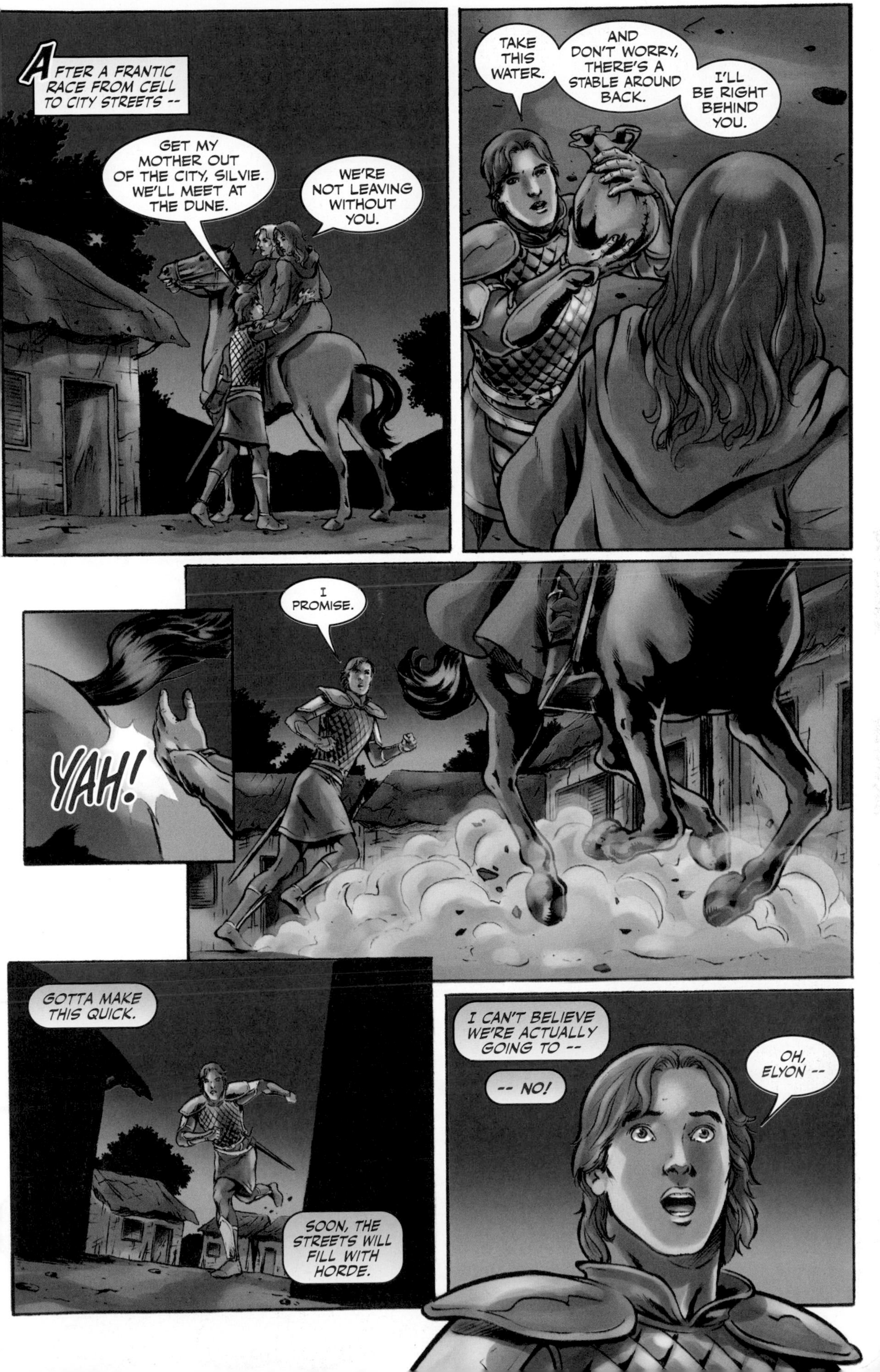
AFTER A FRANTIC RACE FROM CELL TO CITY STREETS --
GET MY MOTHER OUT OF THE CITY, SILVIE. WE'LL MEET AT THE DUNE.
WE'RE NOT LEAVING WITHOUT YOU.
TAKE THIS WATER.
AND DON'T WORRY, THERE'S A STABLE AROUND BACK.
I'LL BE RIGHT BEHIND YOU.
YAH!
I PROMISE.
GOTTA MAKE THIS QUICK.
SOON, THE STREETS WILL FILL WITH HORDE.
I CAN'T BELIEVE WE'RE ACTUALLY GOING TO --
-- NO!
OH, ELYON --

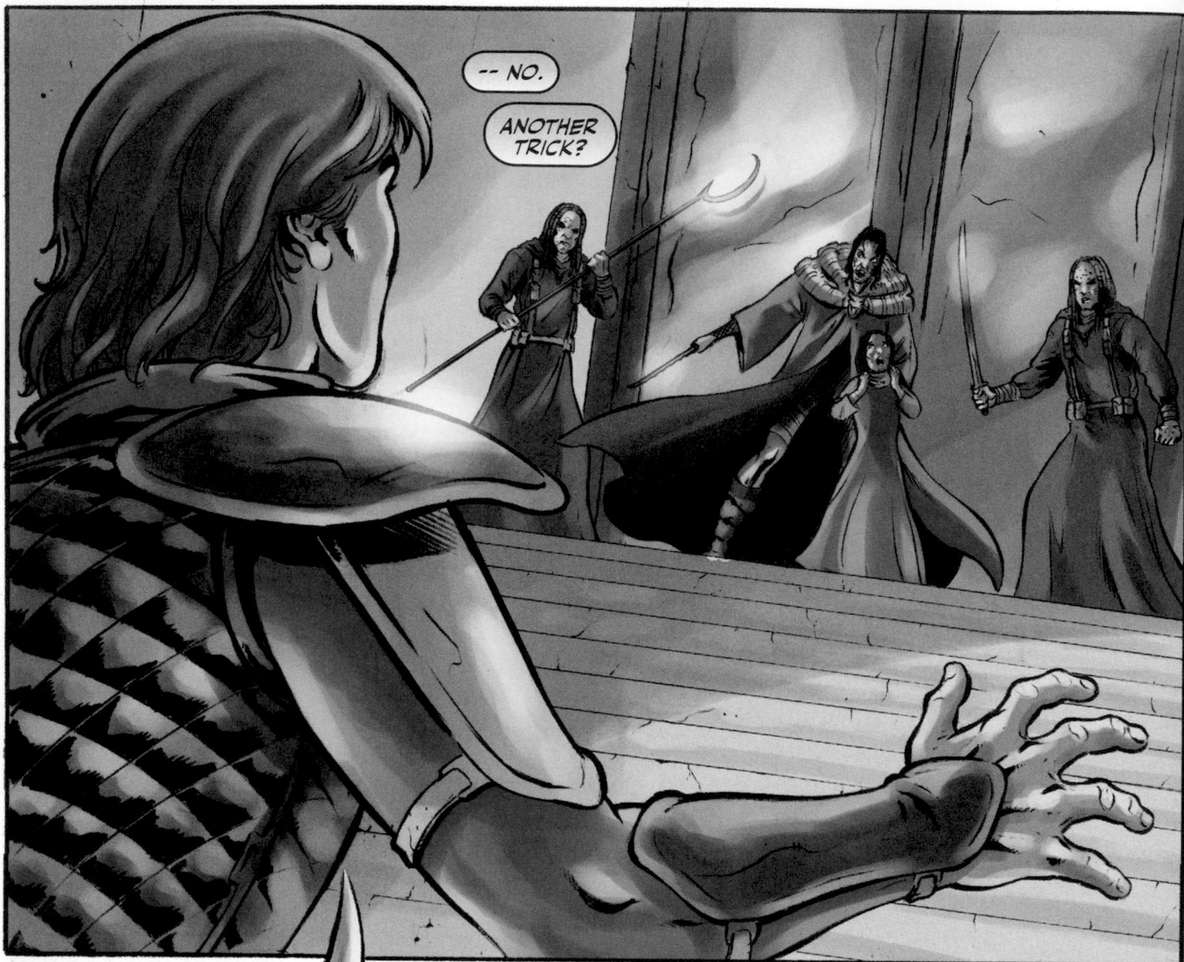
-- NO.
ANOTHER TRICK?
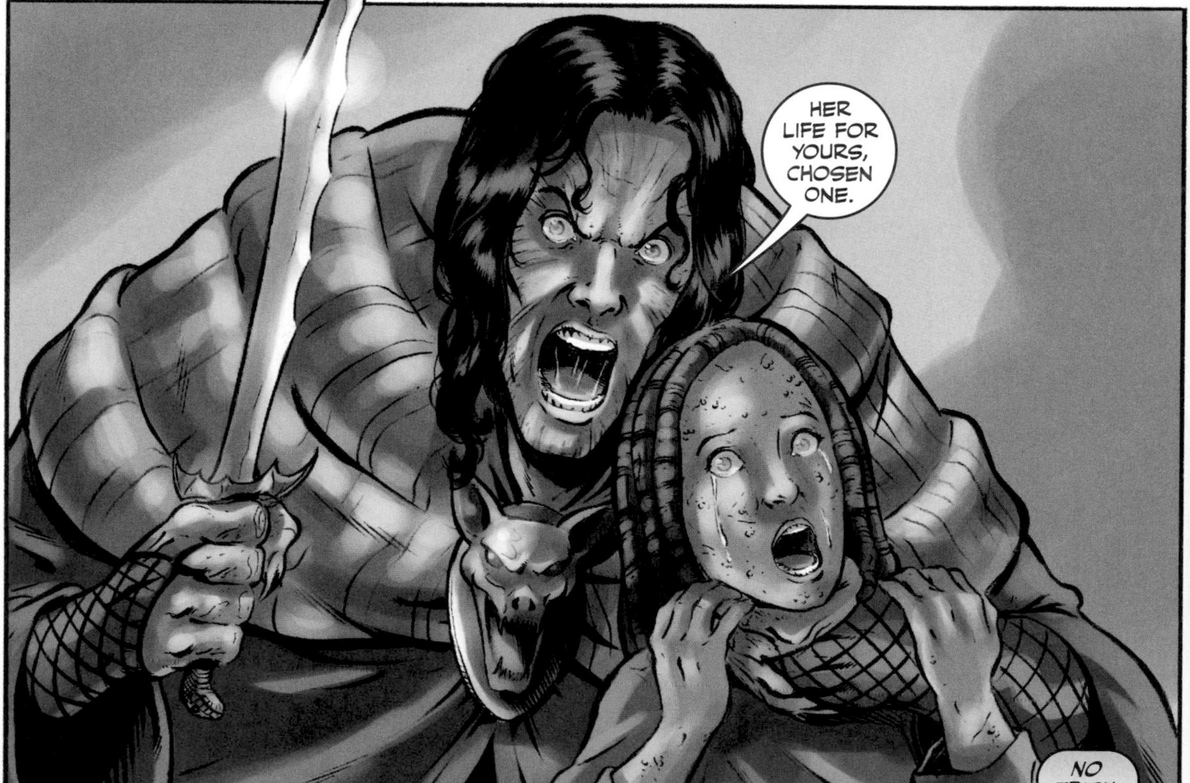
HER LIFE FOR YOURS, CHOSEN ONE.
NO TRICK.

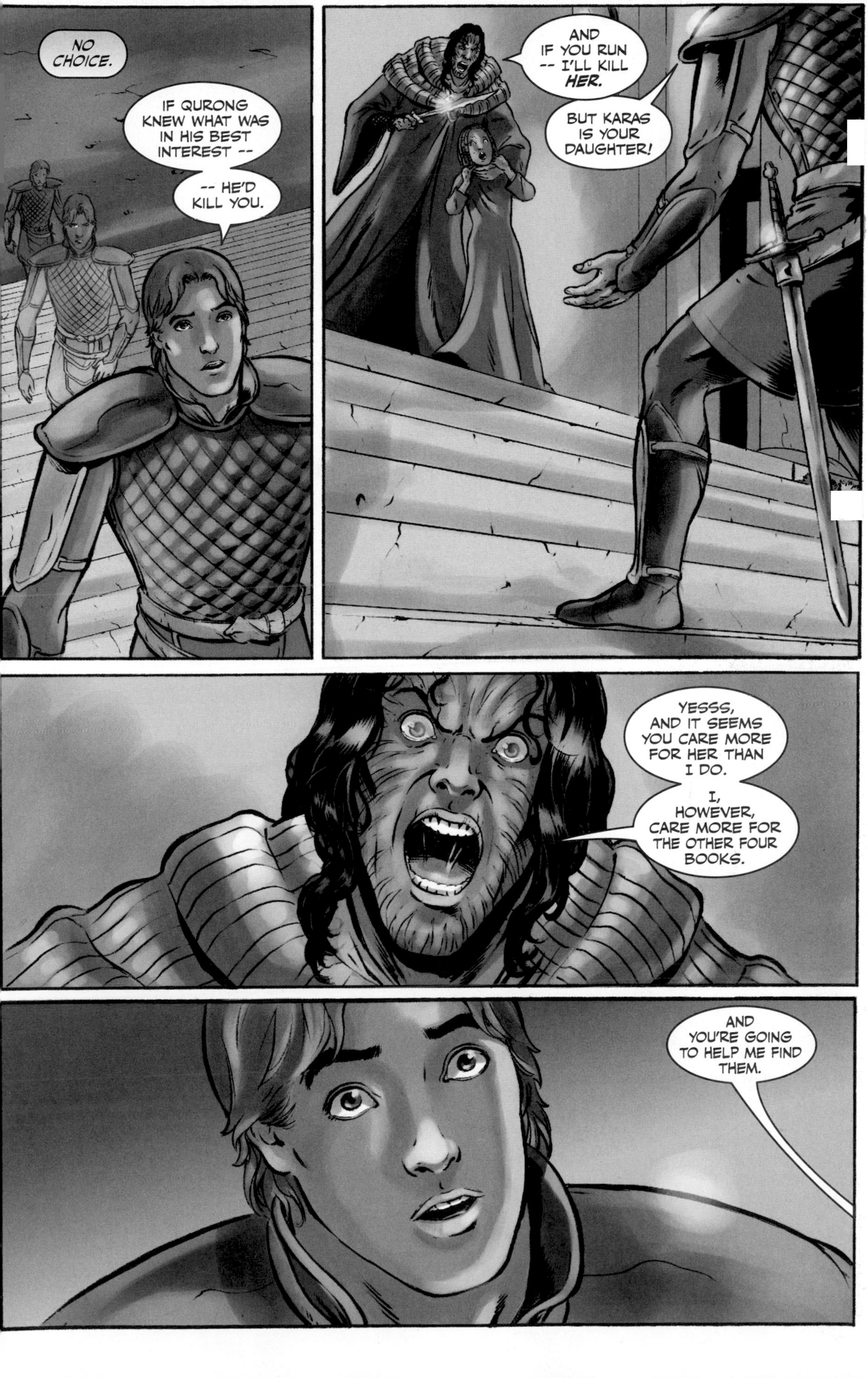

NO CHOICE.
IF QURONG KNEW WHAT WAS IN HIS BEST INTEREST --
-- HE'D KILL YOU.
AND IF YOU RUN -- I'LL KILL HER.
BUT KARAS IS YOUR DAUGHTER!
YESSS, AND IT SEEMS YOU CARE MORE FOR HER THAN I DO.
I, HOWEVER, CARE MORE FOR THE OTHER FOUR BOOKS.
AND YOU'RE GOING TO HELP ME FIND THEM.

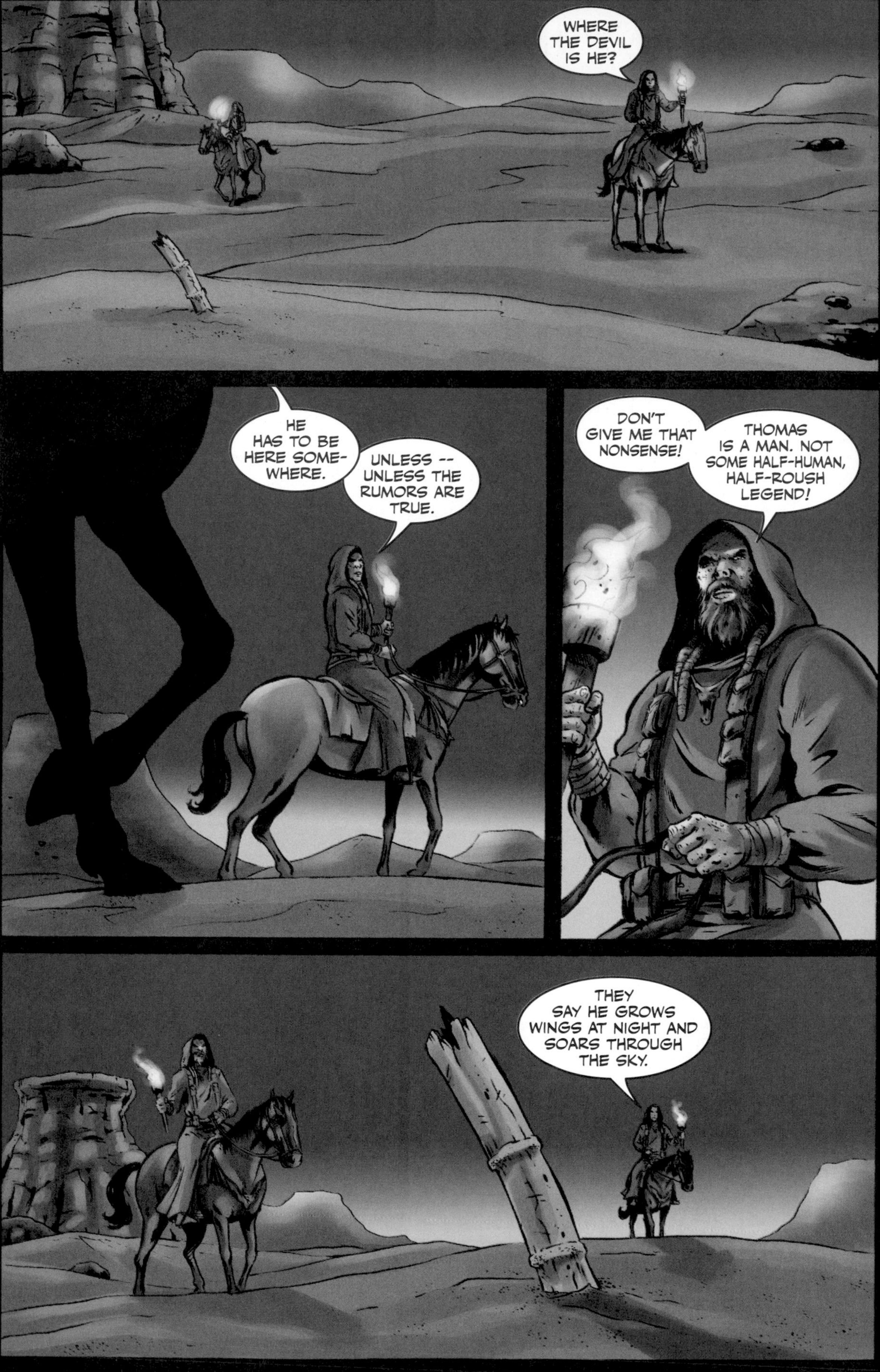
WHERE THE DEVIL IS HE?
HE HAS TO BE HERE SOME-WHERE.
UNLESS -- UNLESS THE RUMORS ARE TRUE.
DON'T GIVE ME THAT NONSENSE!
THOMAS IS A MAN. NOT SOME HALF-HUMAN, HALF-ROUSH LEGEND!
THEY SAY HE GROWS WINGS AT NIGHT AND SOARS THROUGH THE SKY.

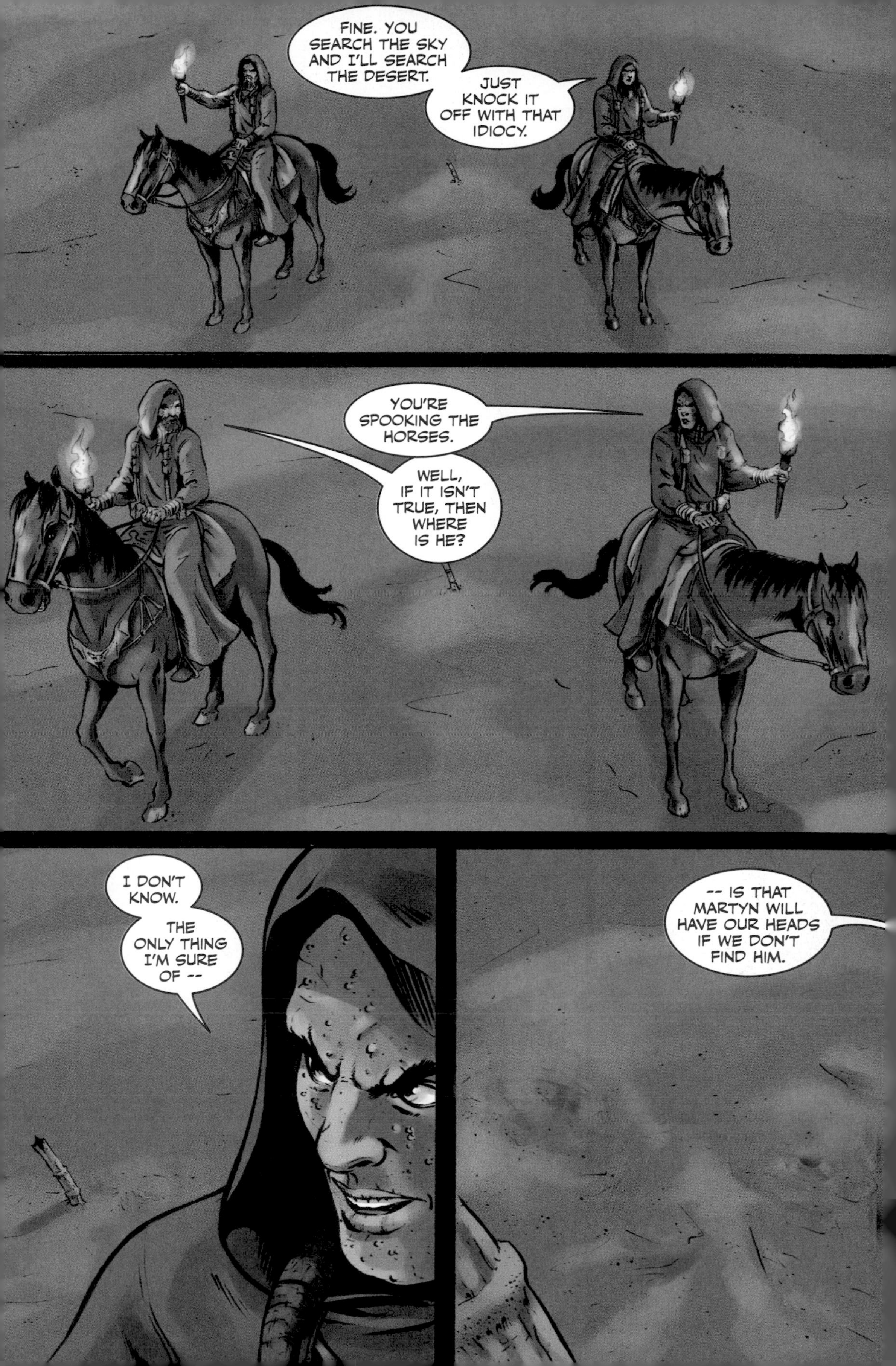
FINE. YOU SEARCH THE SKY AND I'LL SEARCH THE DESERT.
JUST KNOCK IT OFF WITH THAT IDIOCY.
YOU'RE SPOOKING THE HORSES.
WELL, IF IT ISN'T TRUE, THEN WHERE IS HE?
I DON'T KNOW.
THE ONLY THING I'M SURE OF --
-- IS THAT MARTYN WILL HAVE OUR HEADS IF WE DON'T FIND HIM.

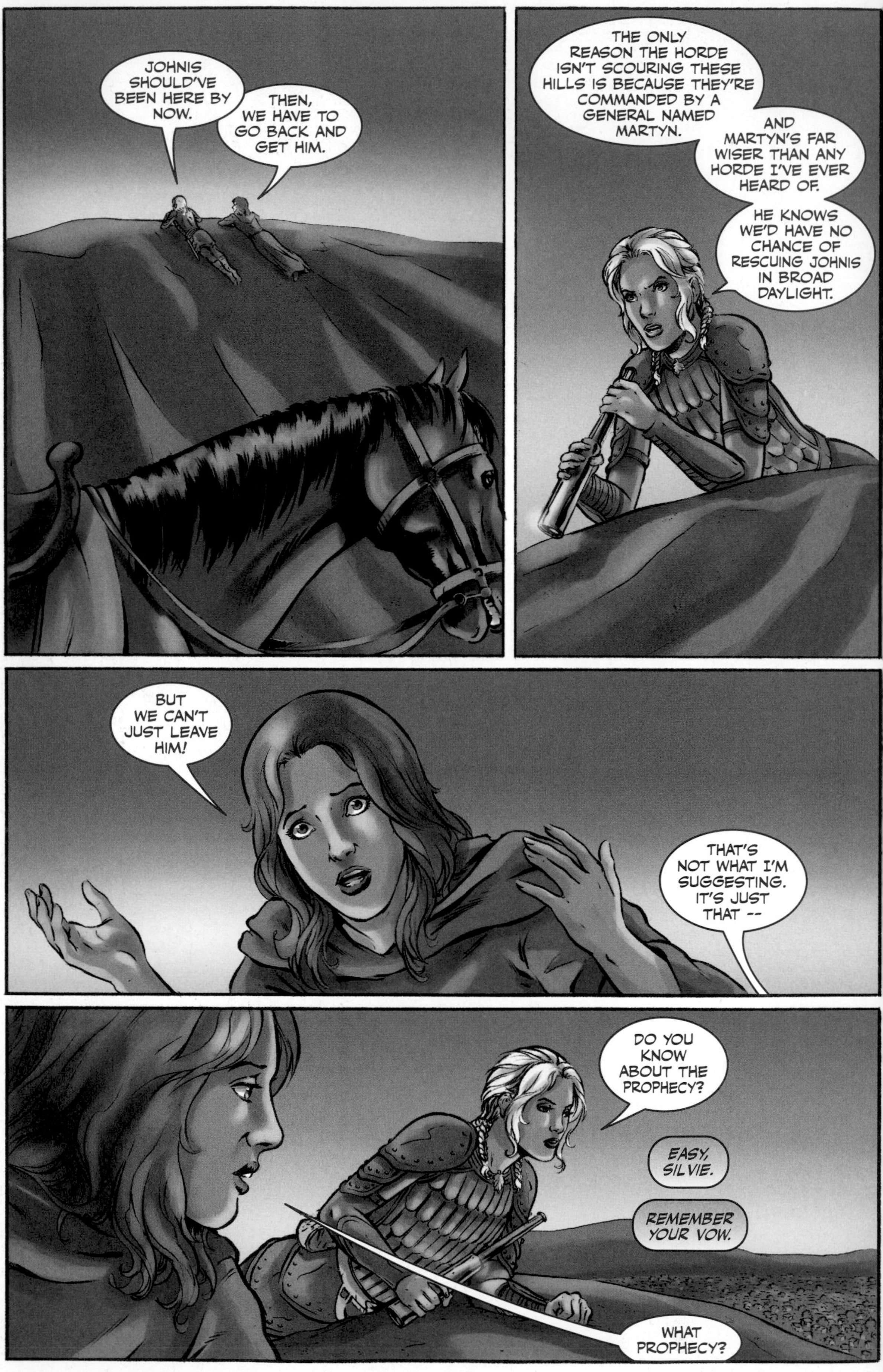
JOHNIS SHOULD'VE BEEN HERE BY NOW.
THEN, WE HAVE TO GO BACK AND GET HIM.
THE ONLY REASON THE HORDE ISN'T SCOURING THESE HILLS IS BECAUSE THEY'RE COMMANDED BY A GENERAL NAMED MARTYN.
AND MARTYN'S FAR WISER THAN ANY HORDE I'VE EVER HEARD OF.
HE KNOWS WE'D HAVE NO CHANCE OF RESCUING JOHNIS IN BROAD DAYLIGHT.
BUT WE CAN'T JUST LEAVE HIM!
THAT'S NOT WHAT I'M SUGGESTING. IT'S JUST THAT --
DO YOU KNOW ABOUT THE PROPHECY?
EASY, SILVIE.
REMEMBER YOUR VOW.
WHAT PROPHECY?

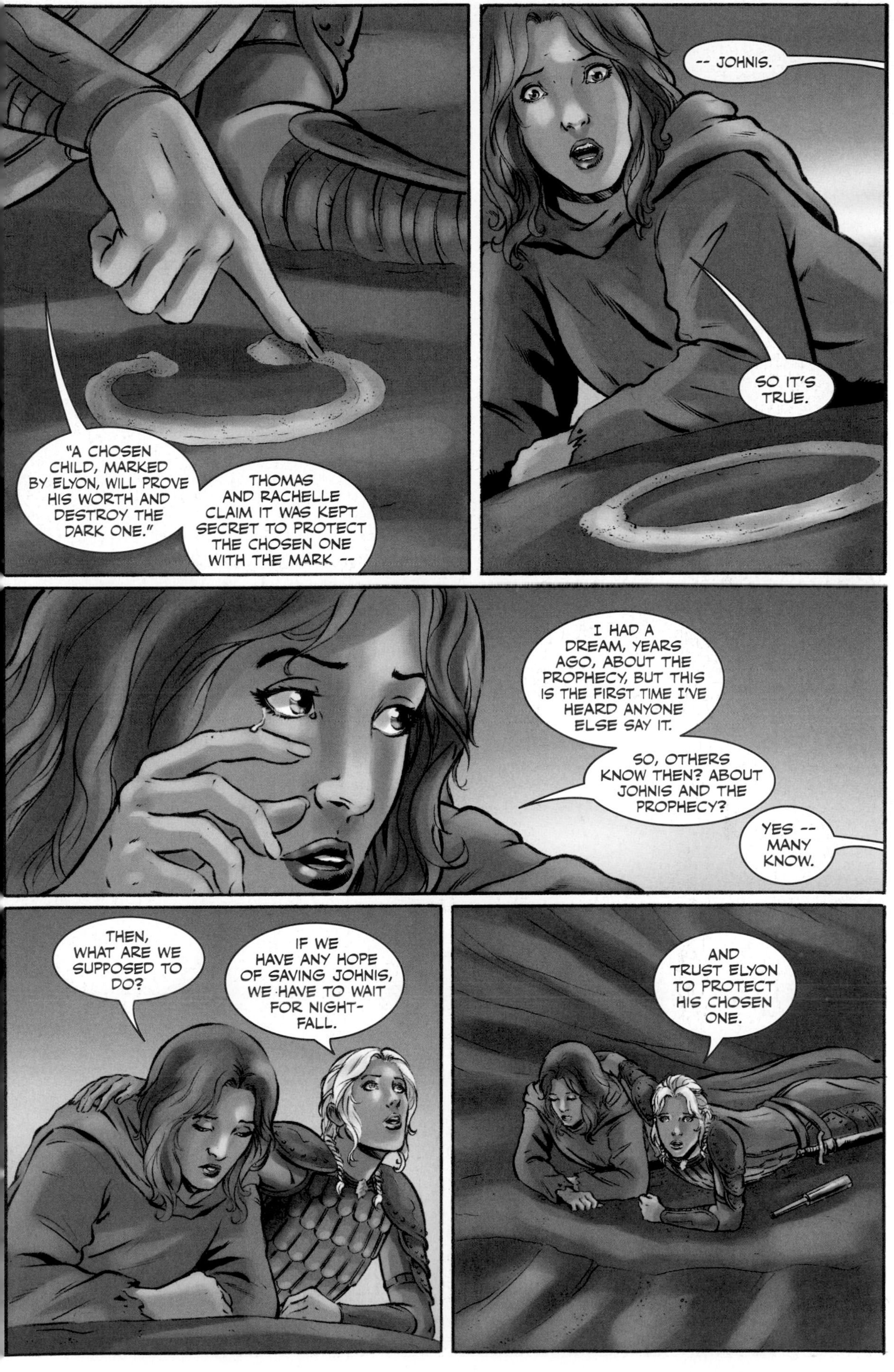
"A CHOSEN CHILD, MARKED BY ELYON, WILL PROVE HIS WORTH AND DESTROY THE DARK ONE."
THOMAS AND RACHELLE CLAIM IT WAS KEPT SECRET TO PROTECT THE CHOSEN ONE WITH THE MARK --
-- JOHNIS.
SO IT'S TRUE.
I HAD A DREAM, YEARS AGO, ABOUT THE PROPHECY, BUT THIS IS THE FIRST TIME I'VE HEARD ANYONE ELSE SAY IT.
SO, OTHERS KNOW THEN? ABOUT JOHNIS AND THE PROPHECY?
YES -- MANY KNOW.
THEN, WHAT ARE WE SUPPOSED TO DO?
IF WE HAVE ANY HOPE OF SAVING JOHNIS, WE HAVE TO WAIT FOR NIGHT-FALL.
AND TRUST ELYON TO PROTECT HIS CHOSEN ONE.

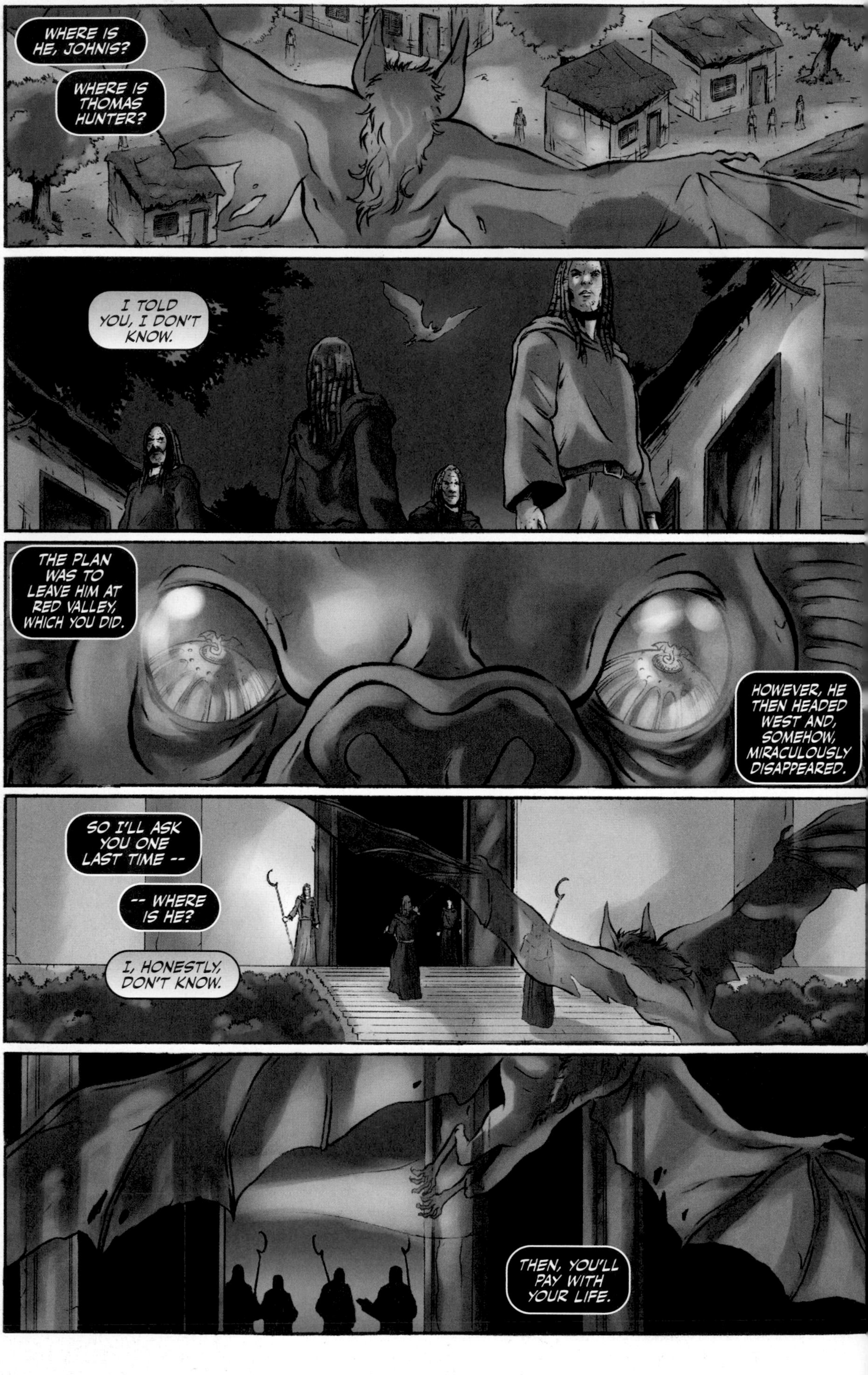
WHERE IS HE, JOHNIS?
WHERE IS THOMAS HUNTER?
I TOLD YOU, I DON'T KNOW.
THE PLAN WAS TO LEAVE HIM AT RED VALLEY, WHICH YOU DID.
HOWEVER, HE THEN HEADED WEST AND, SOMEHOW, MIRACULOUSLY DISAPPEARED.
SO I'LL ASK YOU ONE LAST TIME --
-- WHERE IS HE?
I, HONESTLY, DON'T KNOW.
THEN, YOU'LL PAY WITH YOUR LIFE.

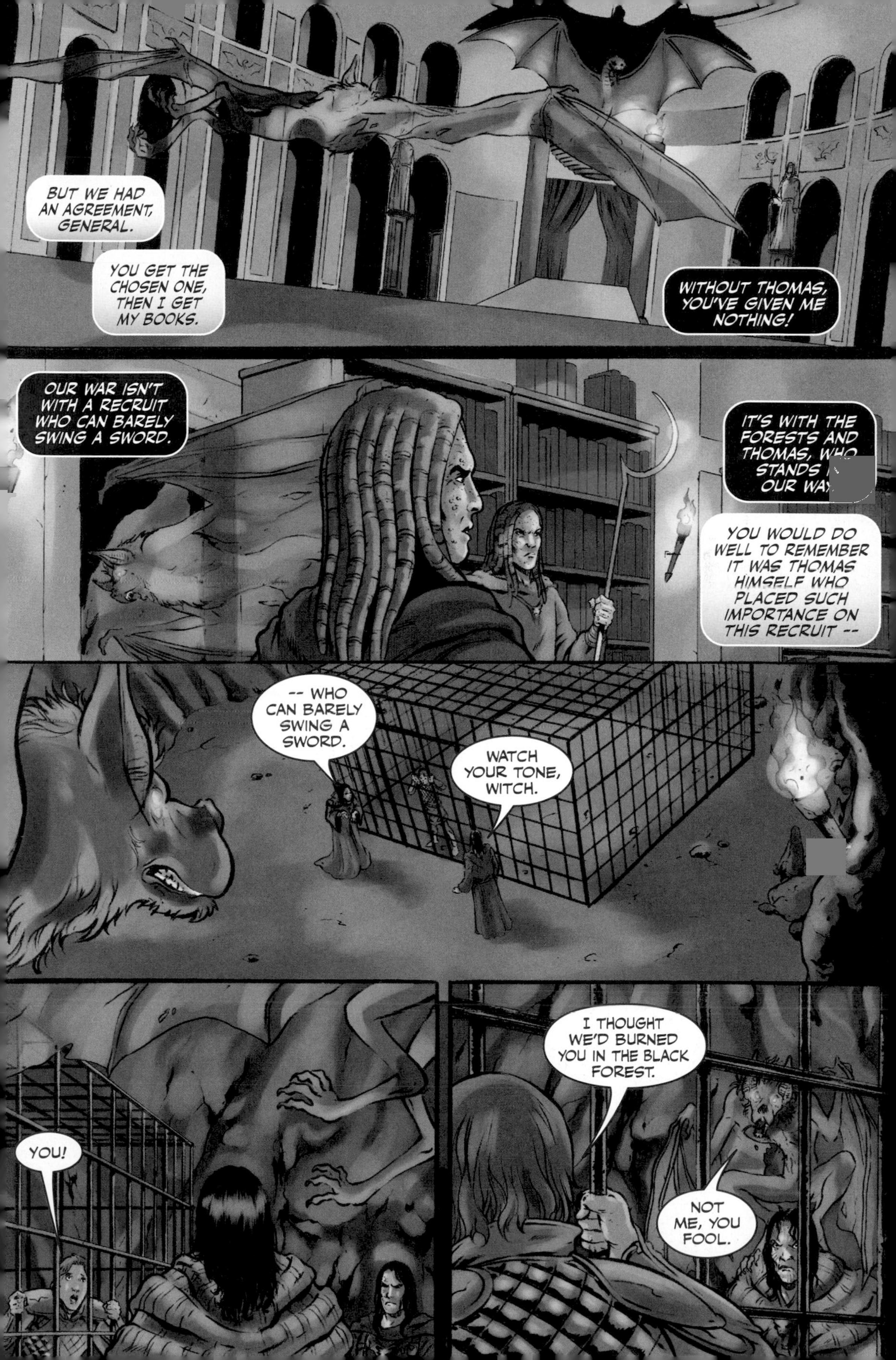
BUT WE HAD AN AGREEMENT, GENERAL.
YOU GET THE CHOSEN ONE, THEN I GET MY BOOKS.
WITHOUT THOMAS, YOU'VE GIVEN ME NOTHING!
OUR WAR ISN'T WITH A RECRUIT WHO CAN BARELY SWING A SWORD.
IT'S WITH THE FORESTS AND THOMAS, WHO STANDS I OUR WA
YOU WOULD DO WELL TO REMEMBER IT WAS THOMAS HIMSELF WHO PLACED SUCH IMPORTANCE ON THIS RECRUIT --
-- WHO CAN BARELY SWING A SWORD.
WATCH YOUR TONE, WITCH.
YOU!
I THOUGHT WE'D BURNED YOU IN THE BLACK FOREST.
NOT ME, YOU FOOL.

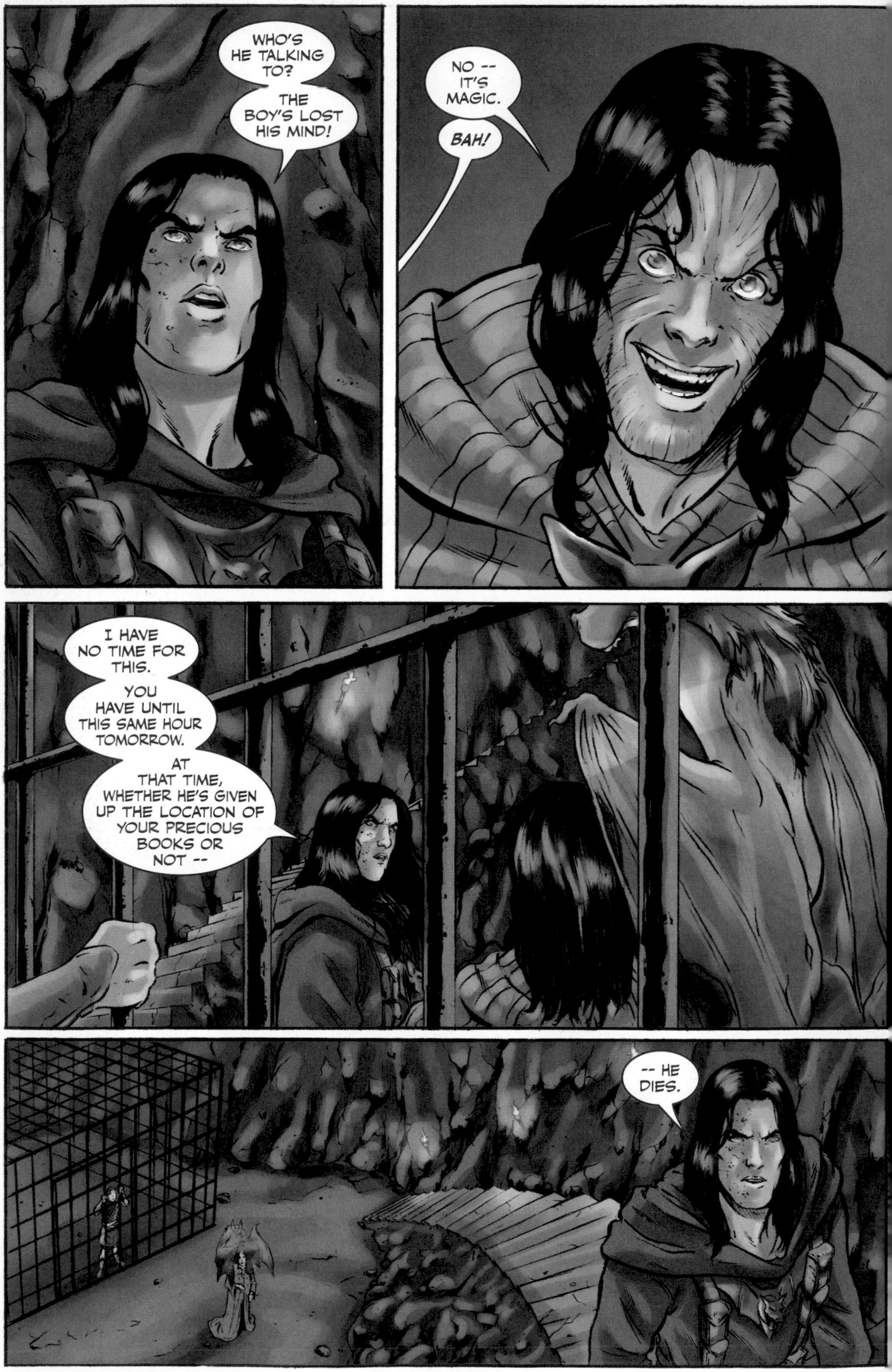
WHO'S HE TALKING TO?
THE BOY'S LOST HIS MIND!
NO -- IT'S MAGIC.
BAH!
I HAVE NO TIME FOR THIS.
YOU HAVE UNTIL THIS SAME HOUR TOMORROW.
AT THAT TIME, WHETHER HE'S GIVEN UP THE LOCATION OF YOUR PRECIOUS BOOKS OR NOT --
-- HE DIES.

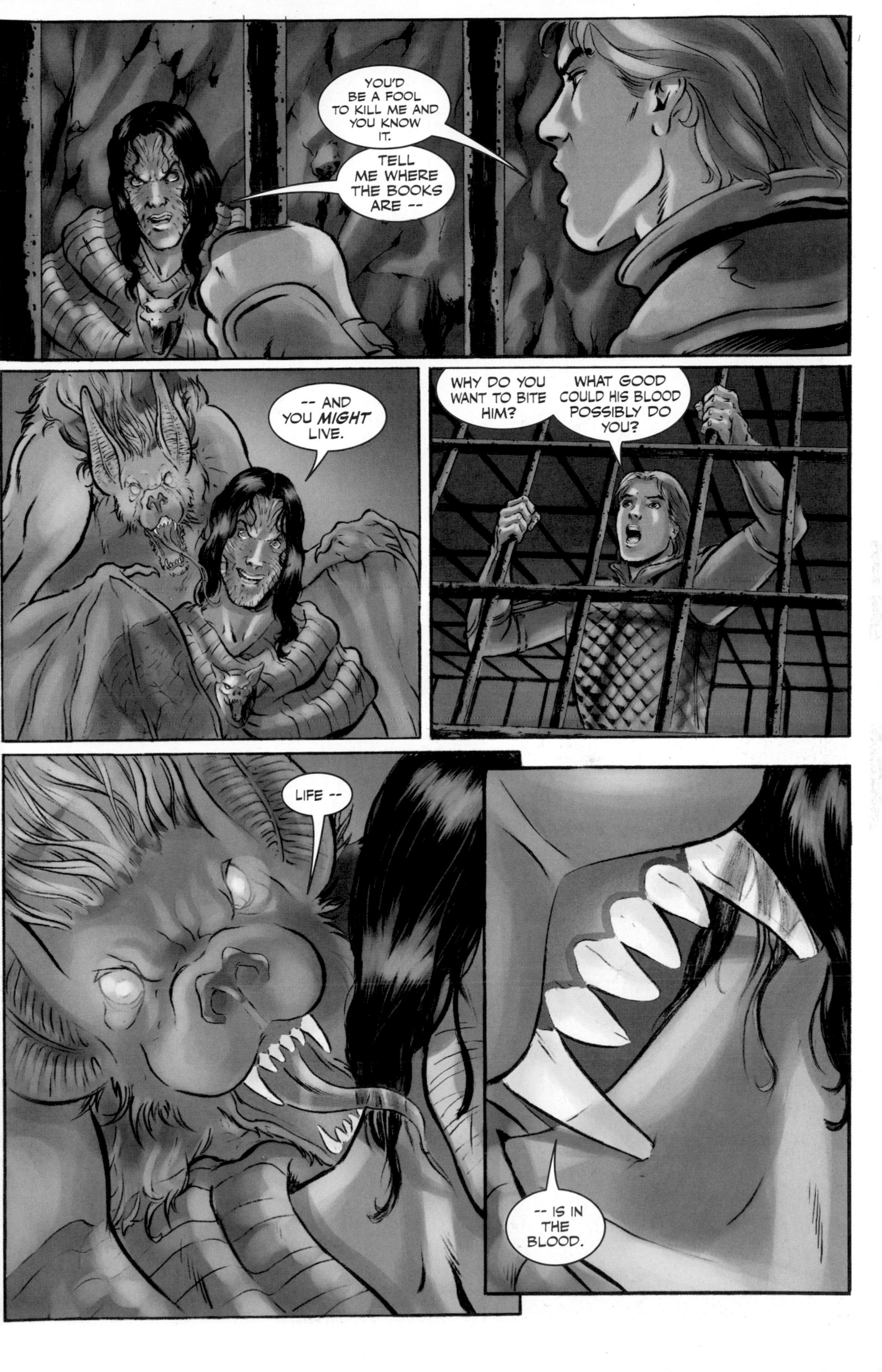
YOU'D BE A FOOL TO KILL ME AND YOU KNOW IT.
TELL ME WHERE THE BOOKS ARE --
-- AND YOU *MIGHT* LIVE.
WHY DO YOU WANT TO BITE HIM?
WHAT GOOD COULD HIS BLOOD POSSIBLY DO YOU?
LIFE --
-- IS IN THE BLOOD.

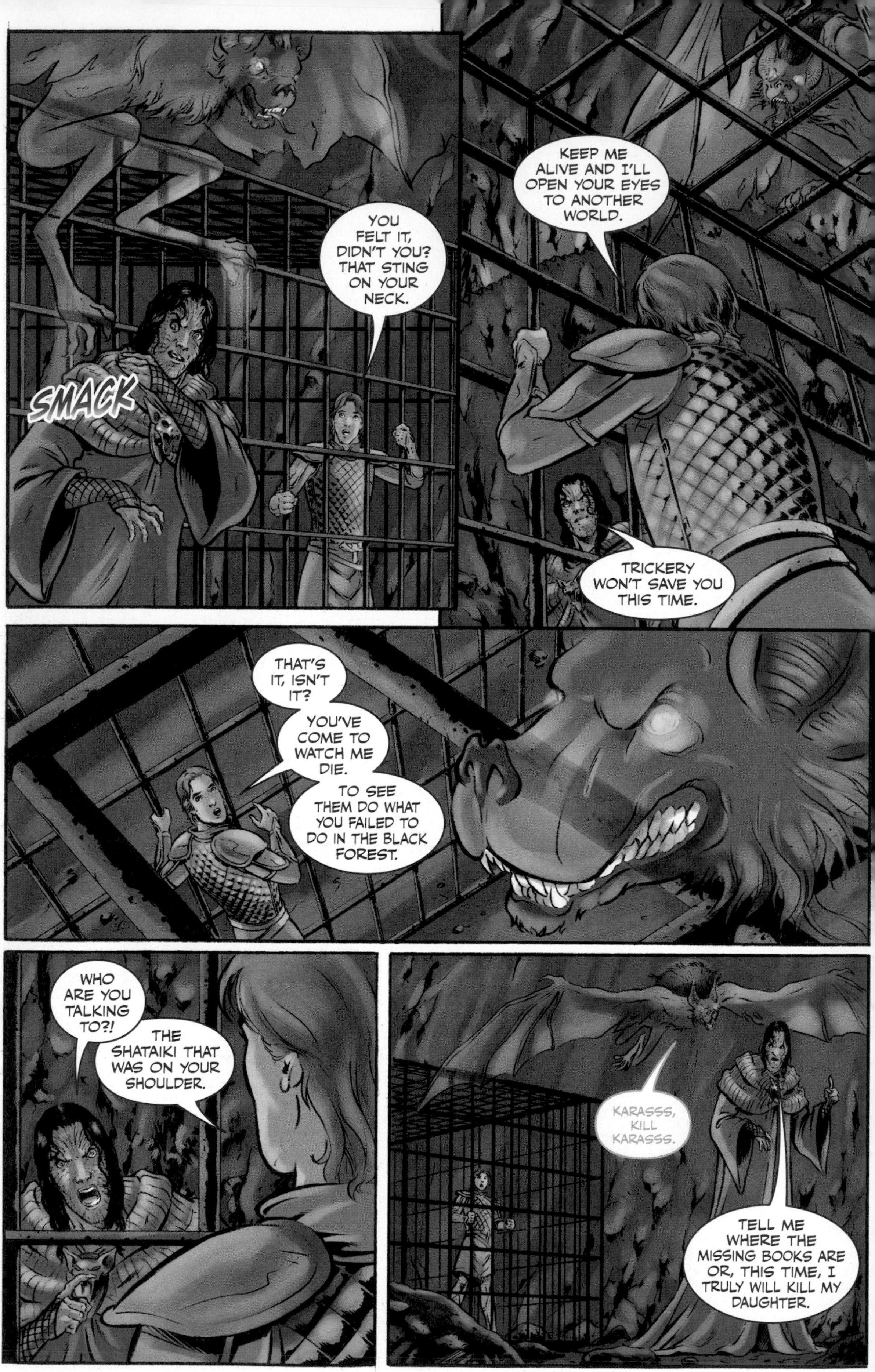
YOU FELT IT, DIDN'T YOU? THAT STING ON YOUR NECK.
SMACK
KEEP ME ALIVE AND I'LL OPEN YOUR EYES TO ANOTHER WORLD.
TRICKERY WON'T SAVE YOU THIS TIME.
THAT'S IT, ISN'T IT?
YOU'VE COME TO WATCH ME DIE.
TO SEE THEM DO WHAT YOU FAILED TO DO IN THE BLACK FOREST.
WHO ARE YOU TALKING TO?!
THE SHATAIKI THAT WAS ON YOUR SHOULDER.
KARASSS, KILL KARASSS.
TELL ME WHERE THE MISSING BOOKS ARE OR, THIS TIME, I TRULY WILL KILL MY DAUGHTER.

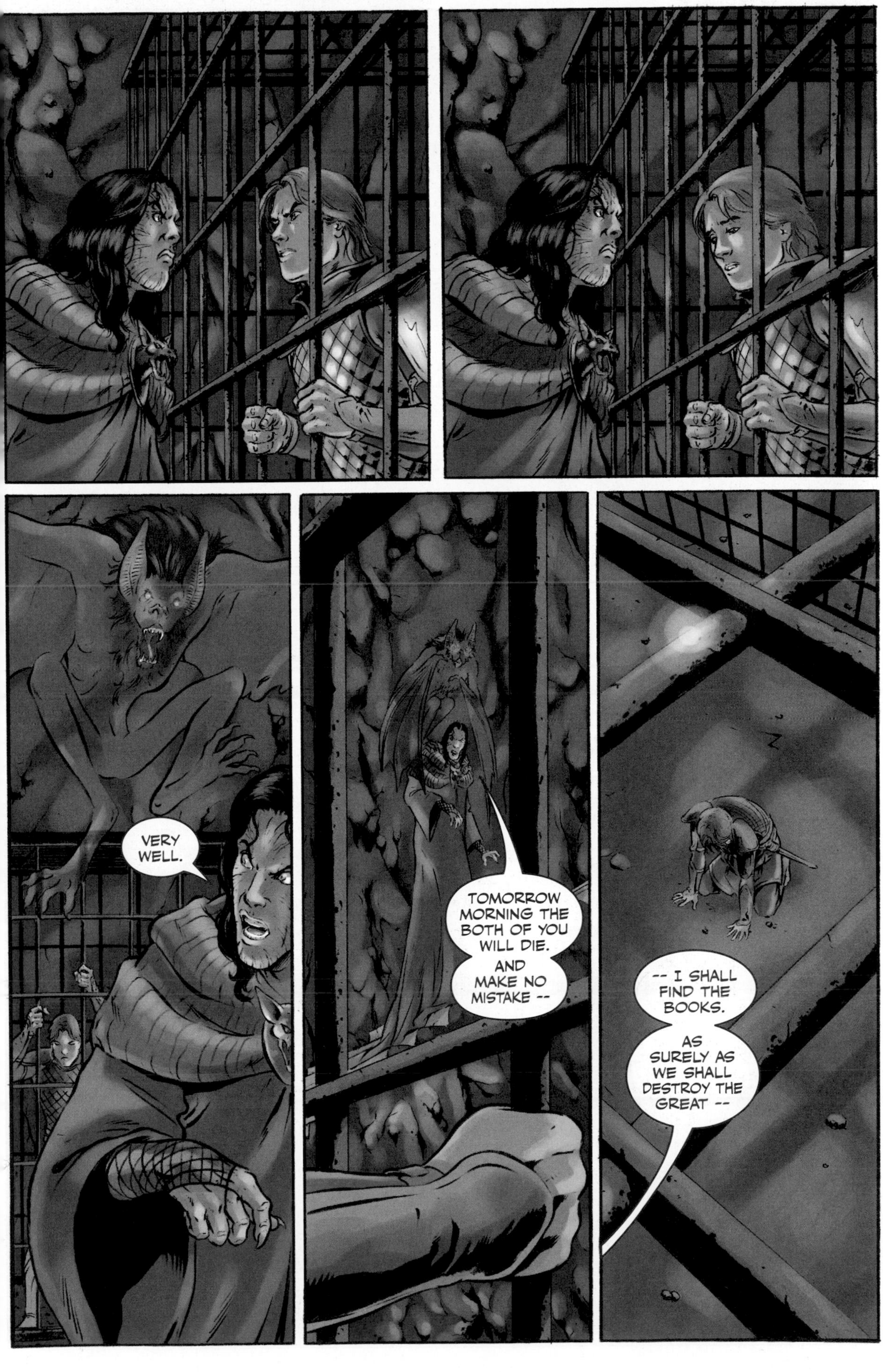
VERY WELL.
TOMORROW MORNING THE BOTH OF YOU WILL DIE.
AND MAKE NO MISTAKE --
-- I SHALL FIND THE BOOKS.
AS SURELY AS WE SHALL DESTROY THE GREAT --

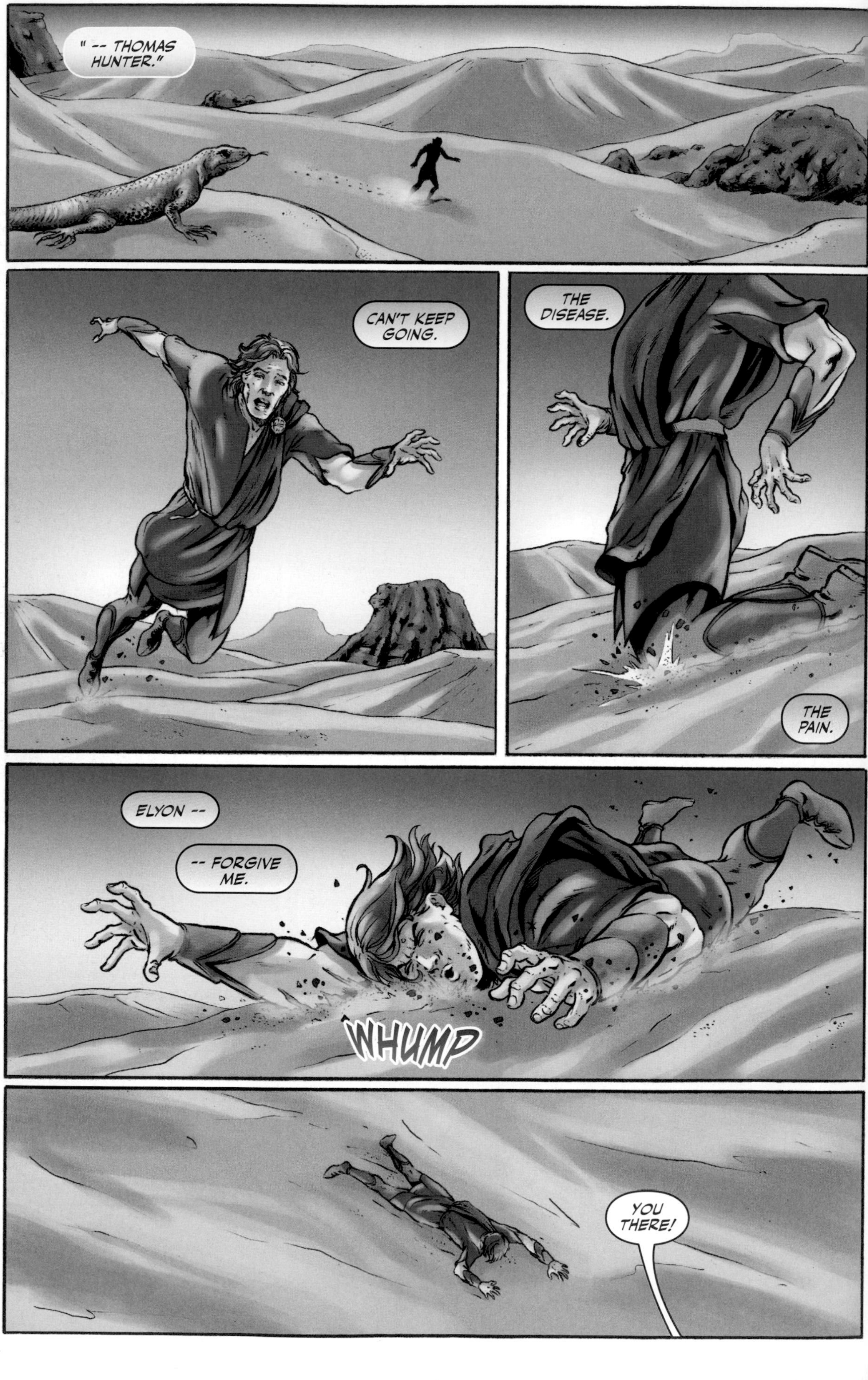
" -- THOMAS HUNTER."
CAN'T KEEP GOING.
THE DISEASE.
THE PAIN.
ELYON --
-- FORGIVE ME.
WHUMP
YOU THERE!

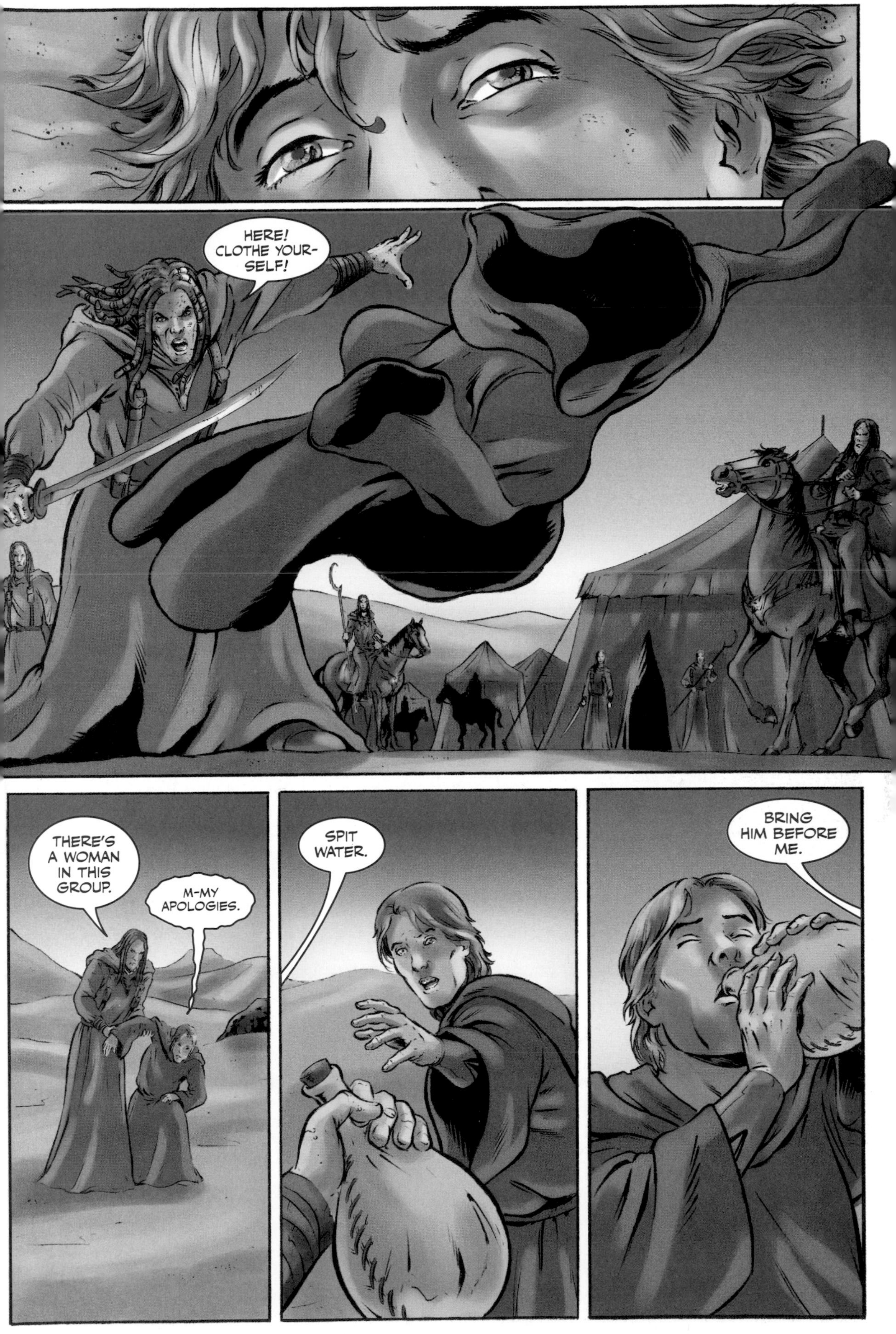
HERE! CLOTHE YOUR-SELF!
THERE'S A WOMAN IN THIS GROUP.
M-MY APOLOGIES.
SPIT WATER.
BRING HIM BEFORE ME.

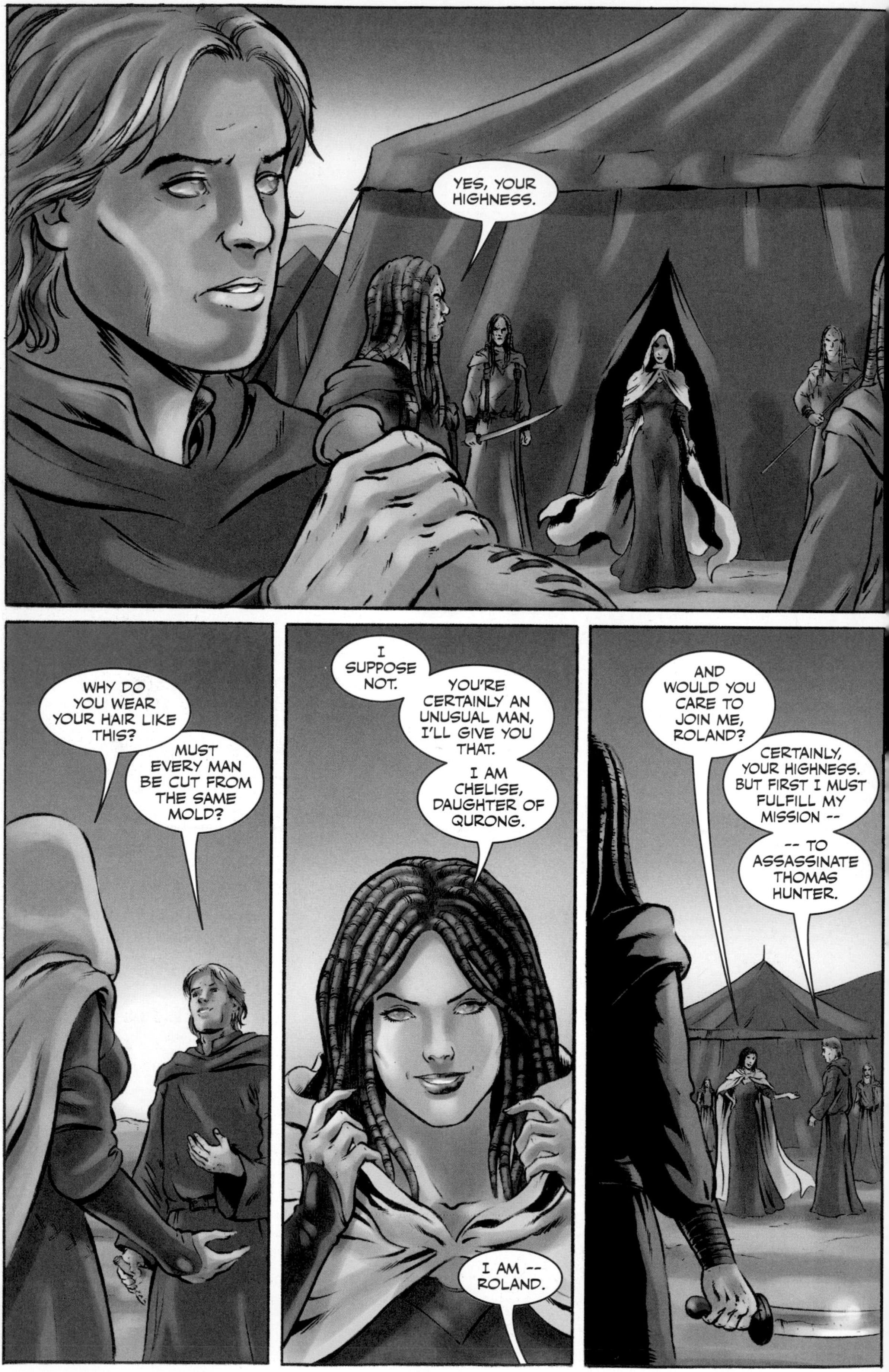
YES, YOUR HIGHNESS.
WHY DO YOU WEAR YOUR HAIR LIKE THIS?
MUST EVERY MAN BE CUT FROM THE SAME MOLD?
I SUPPOSE NOT.
YOU'RE CERTAINLY AN UNUSUAL MAN, I'LL GIVE YOU THAT.
I AM CHELISE, DAUGHTER OF QURONG.
I AM -- ROLAND.
AND WOULD YOU CARE TO JOIN ME, ROLAND?
CERTAINLY, YOUR HIGHNESS. BUT FIRST I MUST FULFILL MY MISSION --
-- TO ASSASSINATE THOMAS HUNTER.

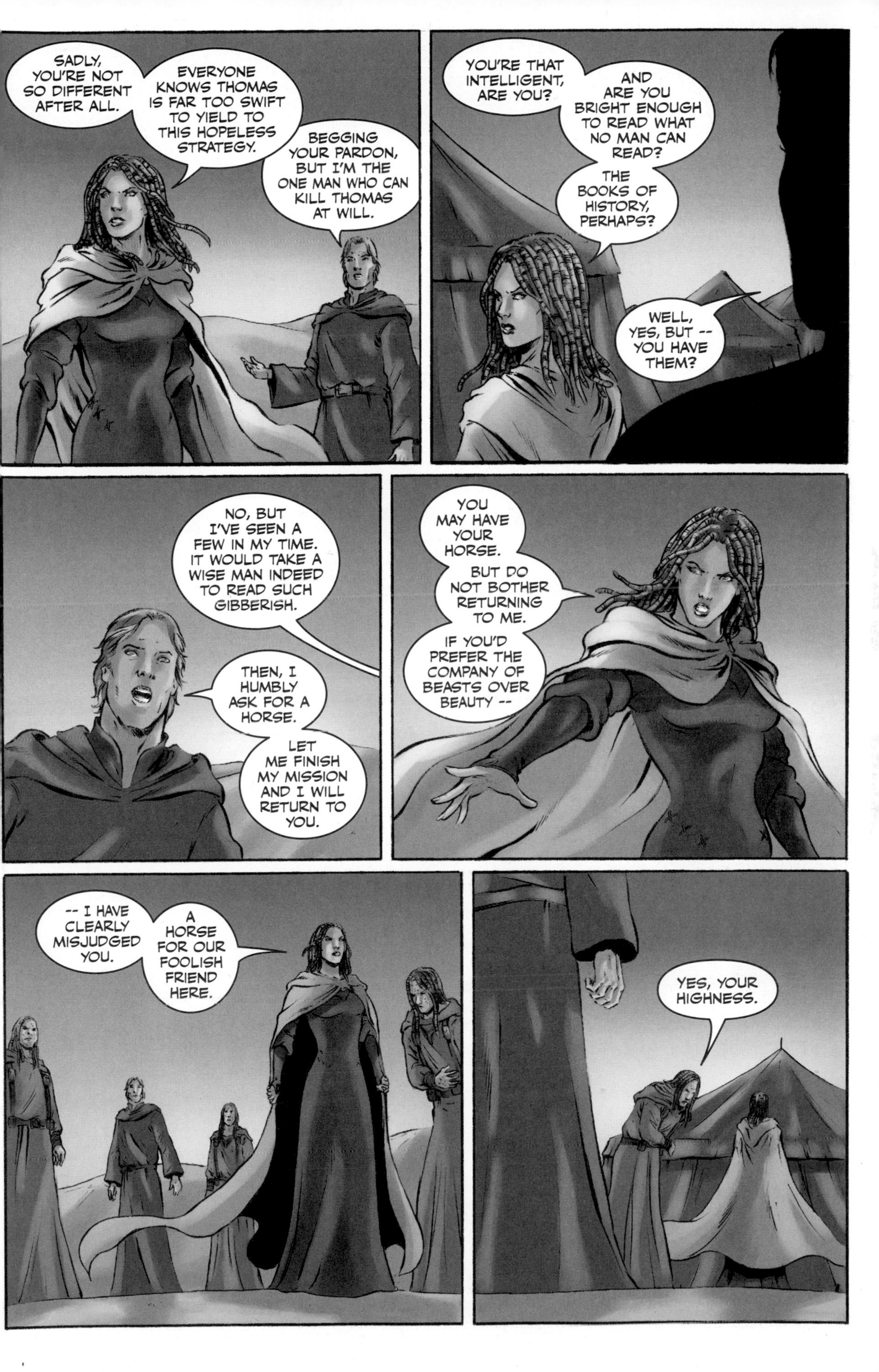
SADLY, YOU'RE NOT SO DIFFERENT AFTER ALL.
EVERYONE KNOWS THOMAS IS FAR TOO SWIFT TO YIELD TO THIS HOPELESS STRATEGY.
BEGGING YOUR PARDON, BUT I'M THE ONE MAN WHO CAN KILL THOMAS AT WILL.
YOU'RE THAT INTELLIGENT, ARE YOU?
AND ARE YOU BRIGHT ENOUGH TO READ WHAT NO MAN CAN READ?
THE BOOKS OF HISTORY, PERHAPS?
WELL, YES, BUT -- YOU HAVE THEM?
NO, BUT I'VE SEEN A FEW IN MY TIME. IT WOULD TAKE A WISE MAN INDEED TO READ SUCH GIBBERISH.
THEN, I HUMBLY ASK FOR A HORSE.
LET ME FINISH MY MISSION AND I WILL RETURN TO YOU.
YOU MAY HAVE YOUR HORSE.
BUT DO NOT BOTHER RETURNING TO ME.
IF YOU'D PREFER THE COMPANY OF BEASTS OVER BEAUTY --
-- I HAVE CLEARLY MISJUDGED YOU.
A HORSE FOR OUR FOOLISH FRIEND HERE.
YES, YOUR HIGHNESS.

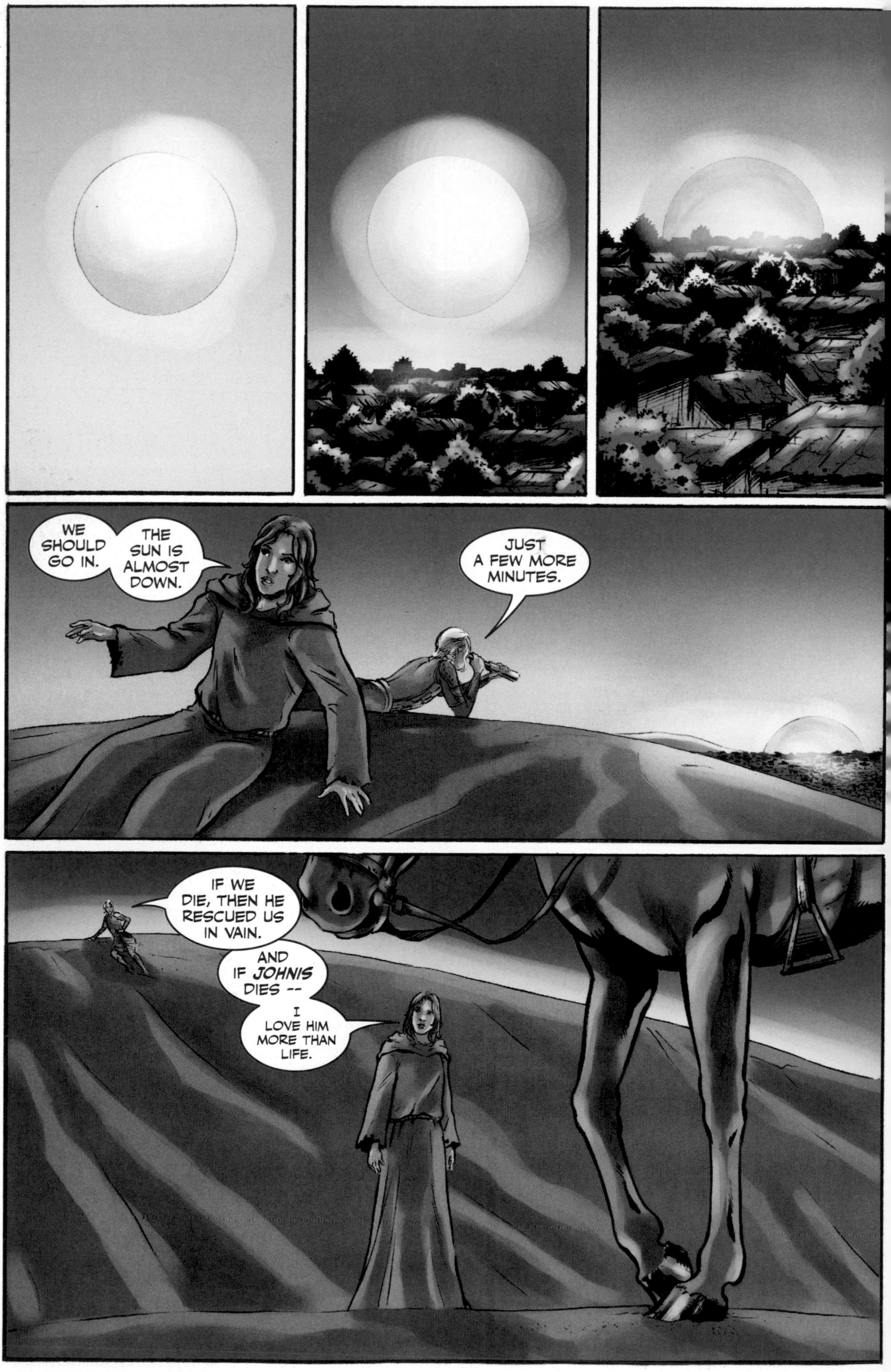
WE SHOULD GO IN.
THE SUN IS ALMOST DOWN.
JUST A FEW MORE MINUTES.
IF WE DIE, THEN HE RESCUED US IN VAIN.
AND IF *JOHNIS* DIES --
I LOVE HIM MORE THAN LIFE.

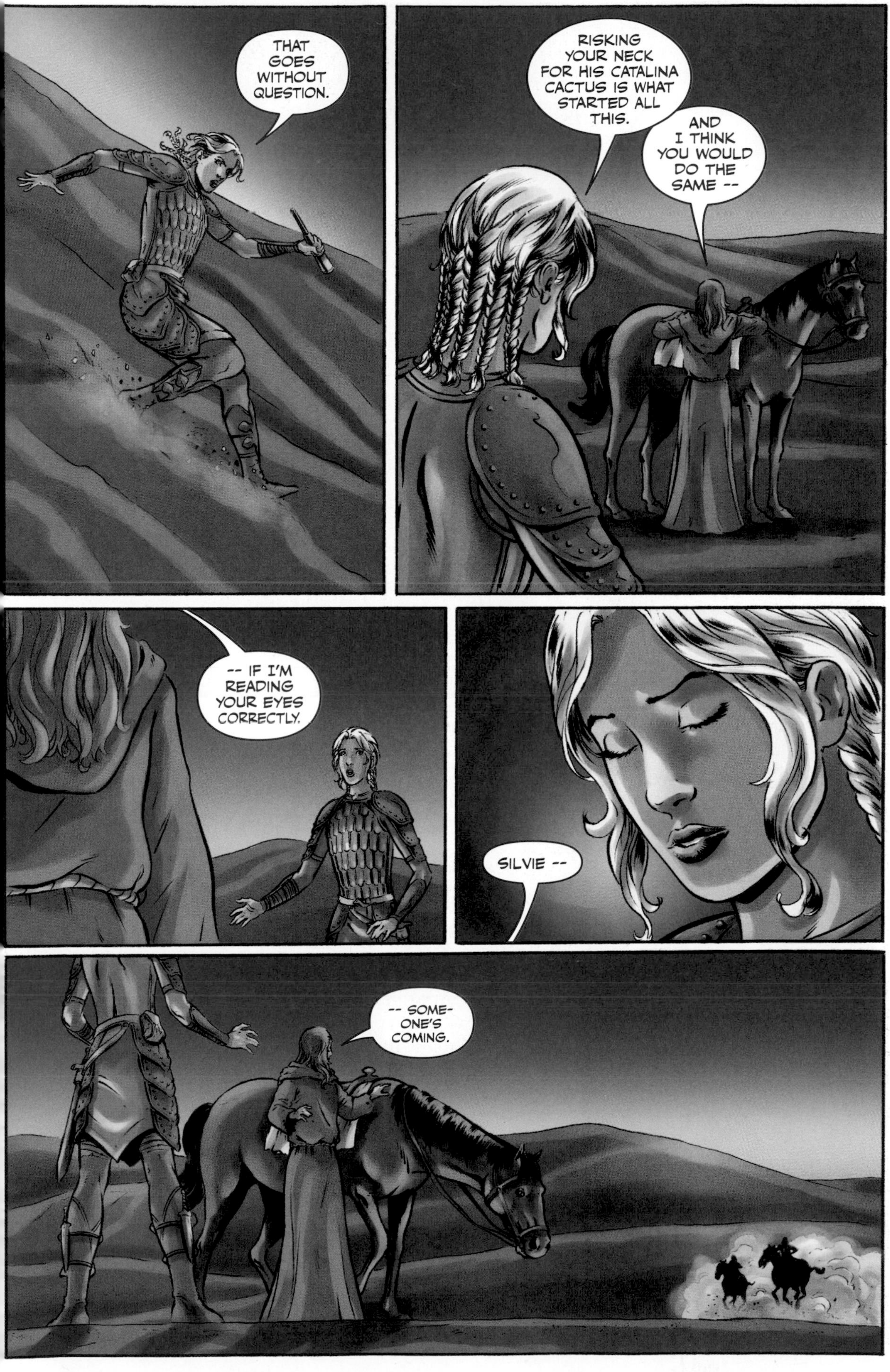
THAT GOES WITHOUT QUESTION.
RISKING YOUR NECK FOR HIS CATALINA CACTUS IS WHAT STARTED ALL THIS.
AND I THINK YOU WOULD DO THE SAME --
-- IF I'M READING YOUR EYES CORRECTLY.
SILVIE --
-- SOME-ONE'S COMING.

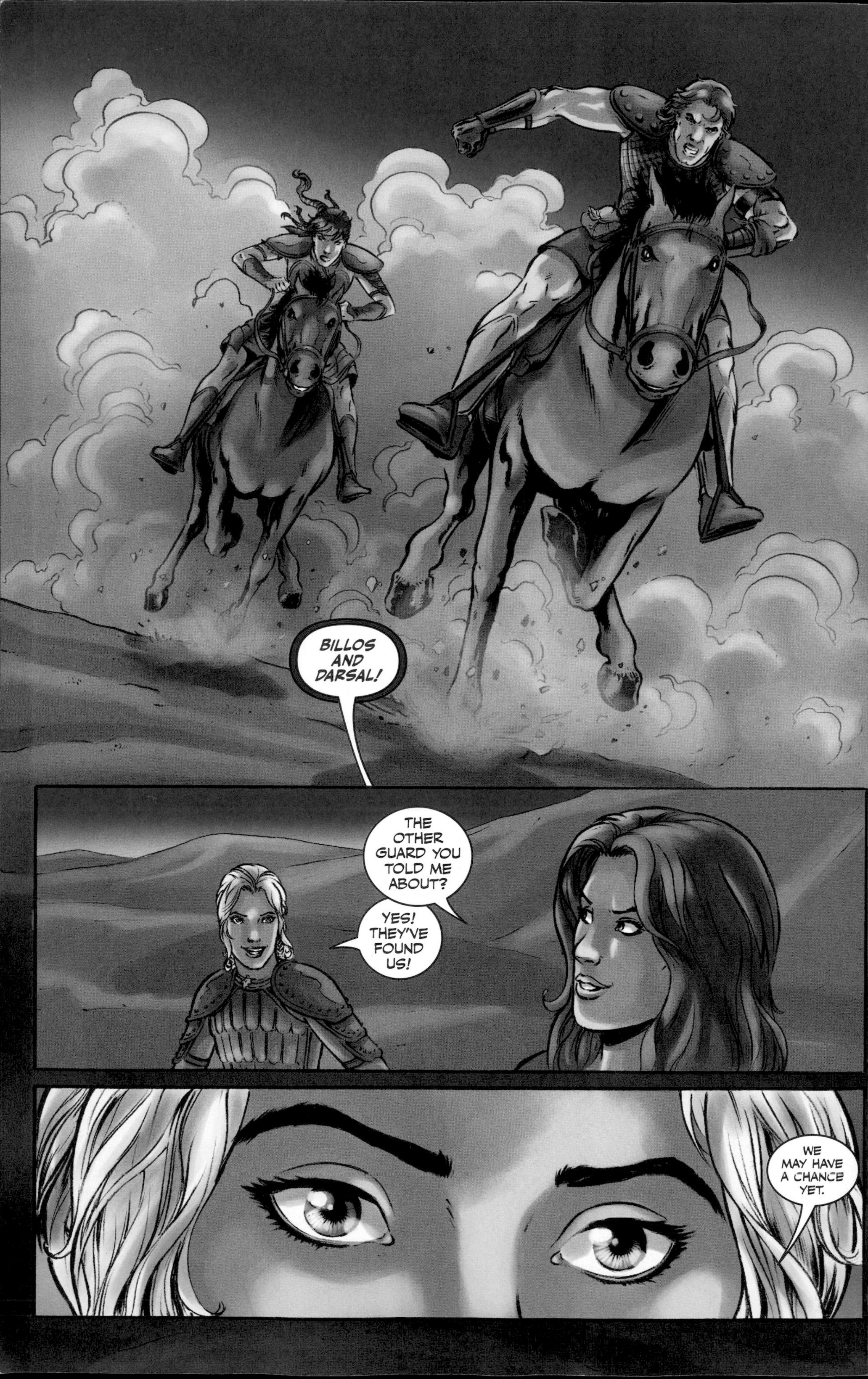
BILLOS AND DARSAL!
THE OTHER GUARD YOU TOLD ME ABOUT?
YES! THEY'VE FOUND US!
WE MAY HAVE A CHANCE YET.

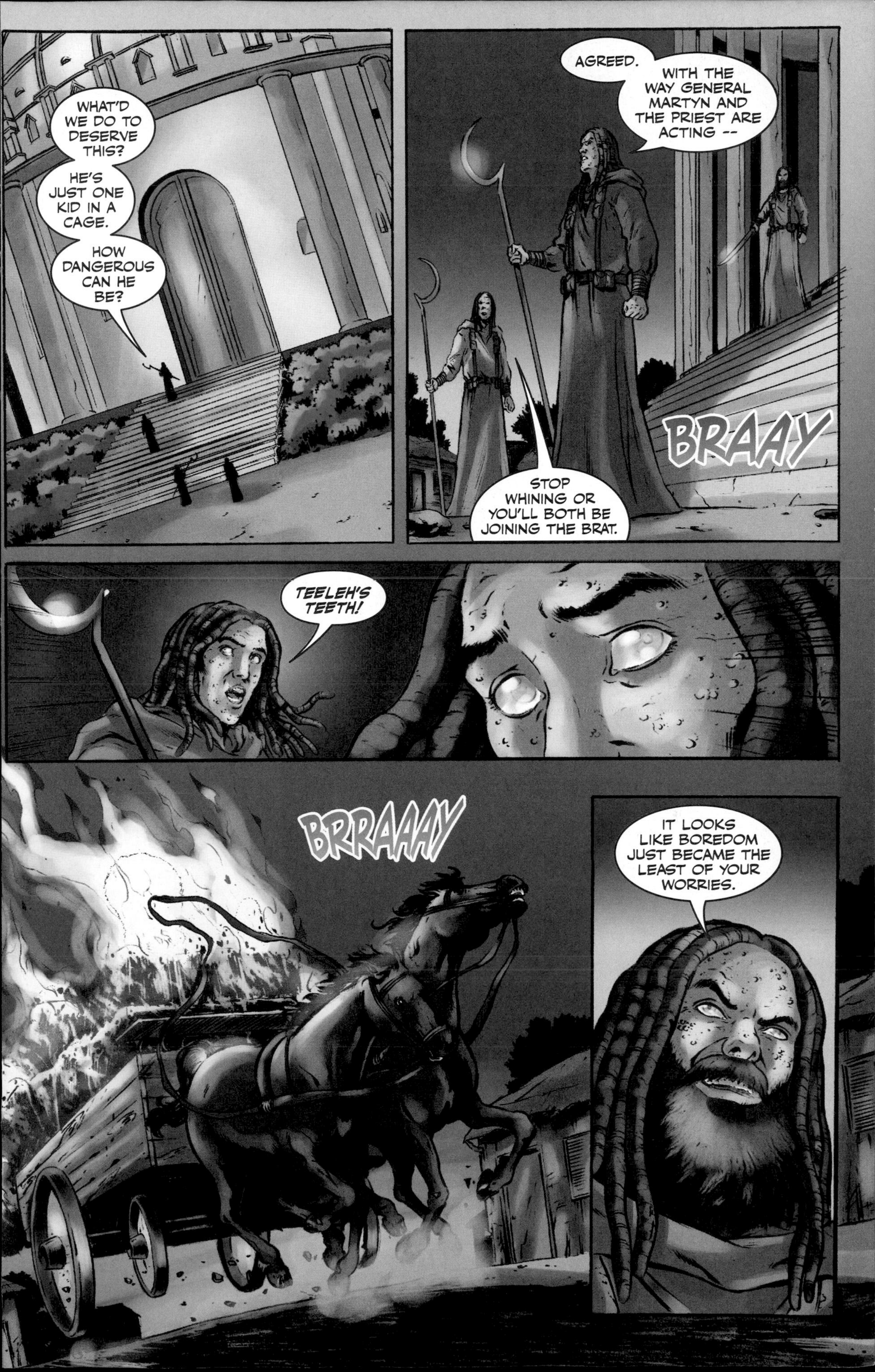
WHAT'D WE DO TO DESERVE THIS?
HE'S JUST ONE KID IN A CAGE.
HOW DANGEROUS CAN HE BE?
AGREED.
WITH THE WAY GENERAL MARTYN AND THE PRIEST ARE ACTING --
BRAAY
STOP WHINING OR YOU'LL BOTH BE JOINING THE BRAT.
TEELEH'S TEETH!
BRRAAAY
IT LOOKS LIKE BOREDOM JUST BECAME THE LEAST OF YOUR WORRIES.

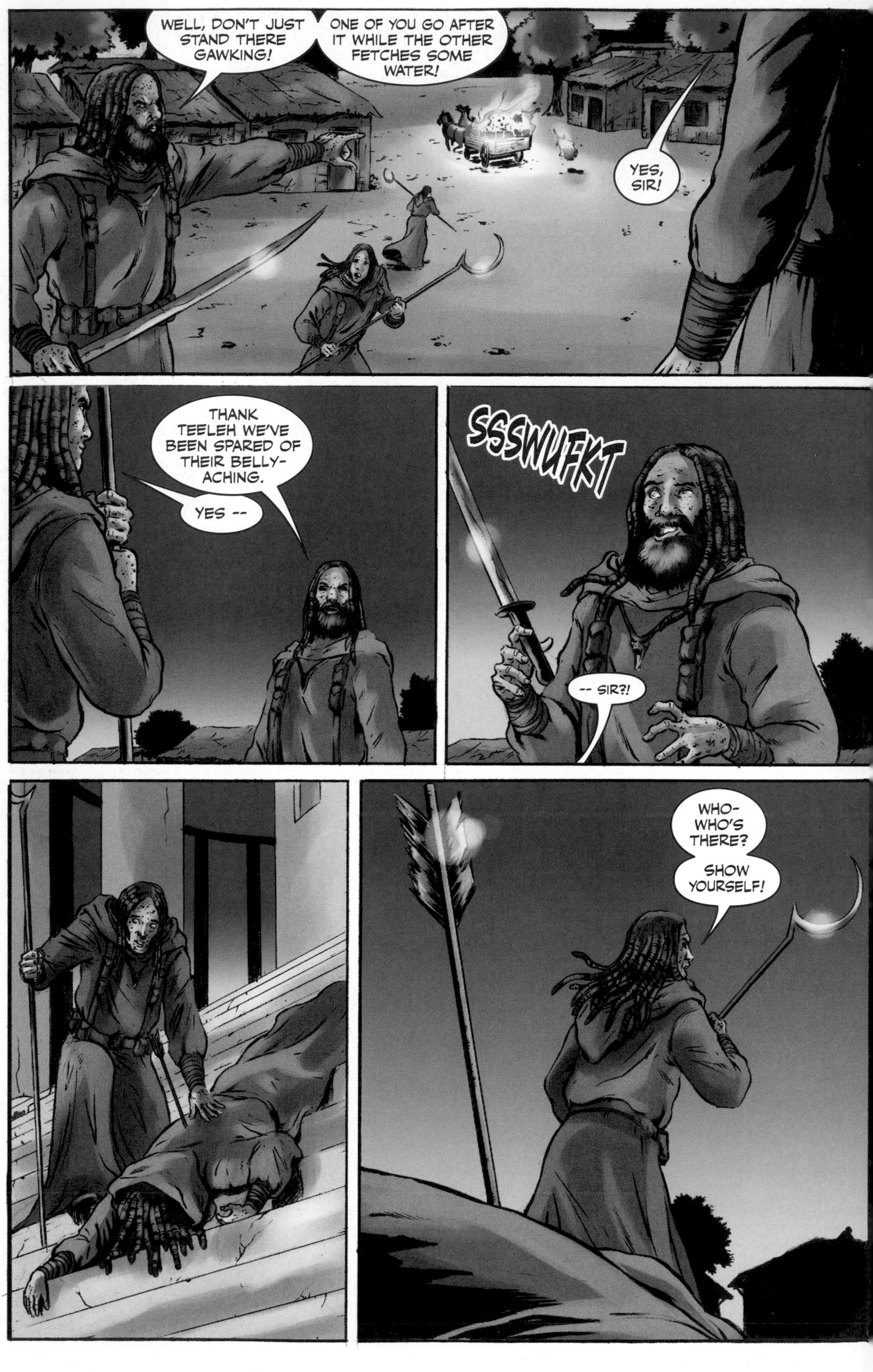
WELL, DON'T JUST STAND THERE GAWKING!
ONE OF YOU GO AFTER IT WHILE THE OTHER FETCHES SOME WATER!
YES, SIR!
THANK TEELEH WE'VE BEEN SPARED OF THEIR BELLY-ACHING.
YES --
SSSWUFKT
-- SIR?!
WHO-WHO'S THERE?
SHOW YOURSELF!

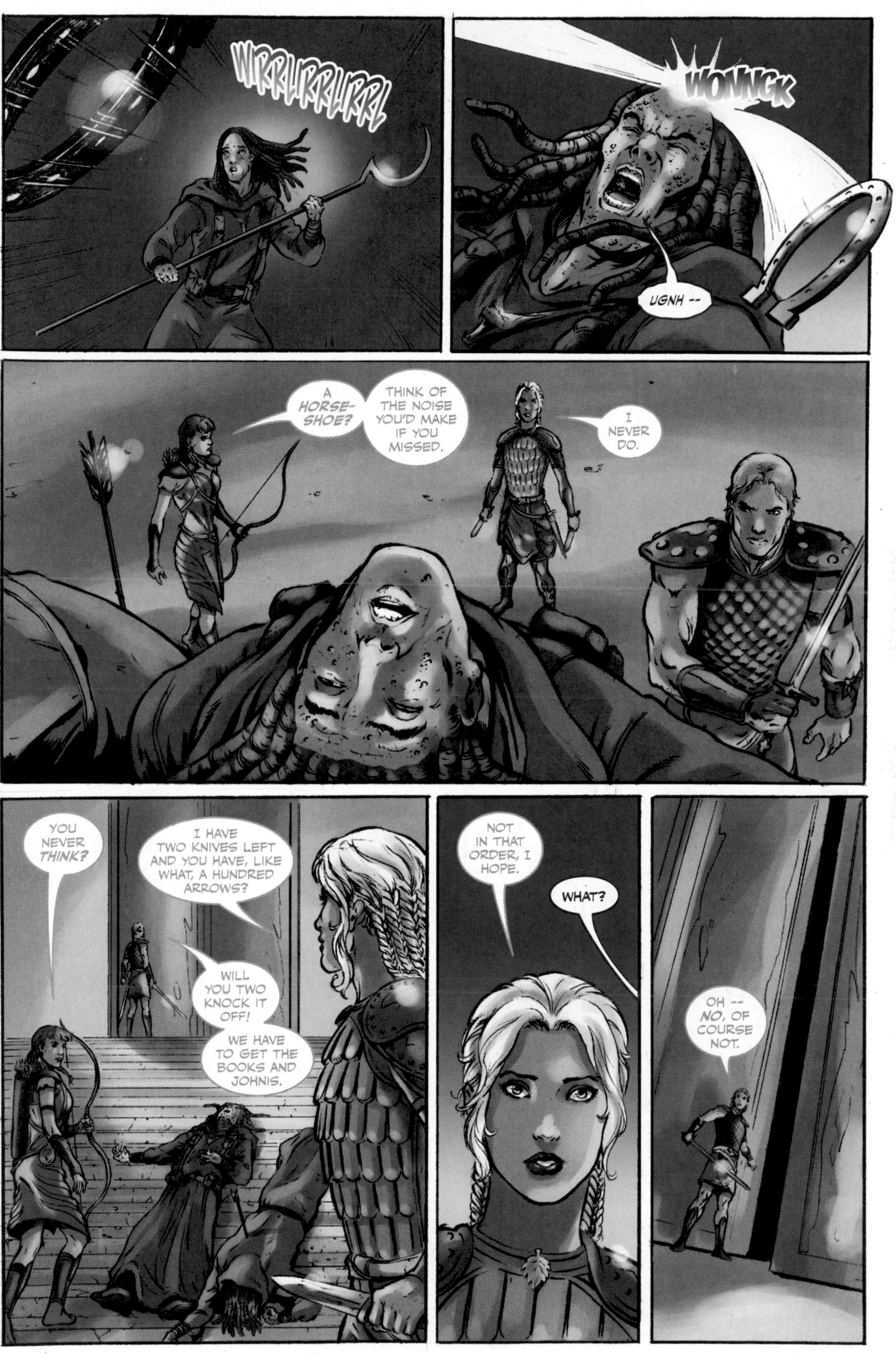
WIRRLIRRLIRRL
WONNGK
UGNH --
A HORSE-SHOE?
THINK OF THE NOISE YOU'D MAKE IF YOU MISSED.
I NEVER DO.
YOU NEVER THINK?
I HAVE TWO KNIVES LEFT AND YOU HAVE, LIKE WHAT, A HUNDRED ARROWS?
WILL YOU TWO KNOCK IT OFF!
WE HAVE TO GET THE BOOKS AND JOHNIS.
NOT IN THAT ORDER, I HOPE.
WHAT?
OH -- NO, OF COURSE NOT.

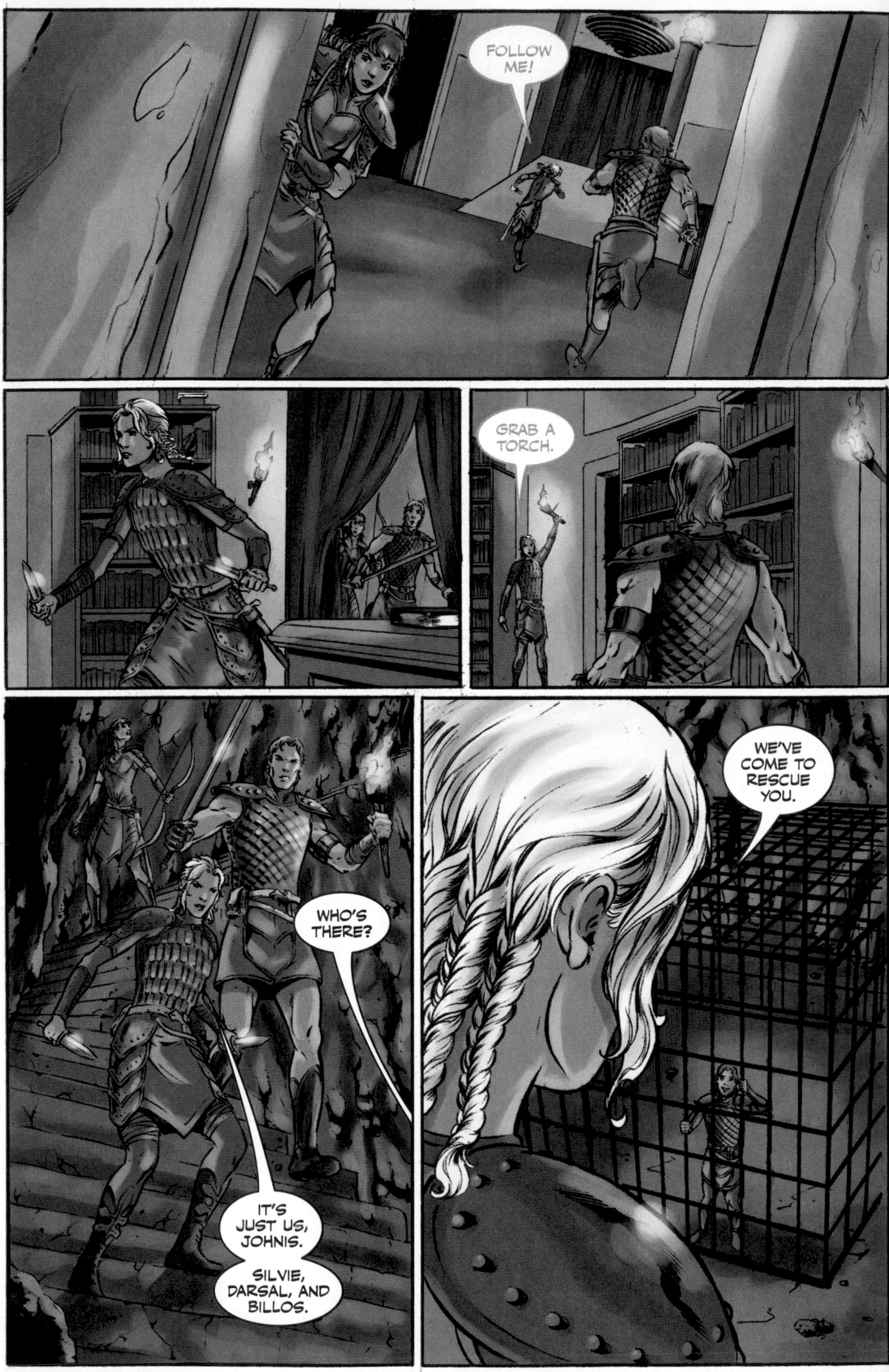
FOLLOW ME!
GRAB A TORCH.
WHO'S THERE?
IT'S JUST US, JOHNIS.
SILVIE, DARSAL, AND BILLOS.
WE'VE COME TO RESCUE YOU.

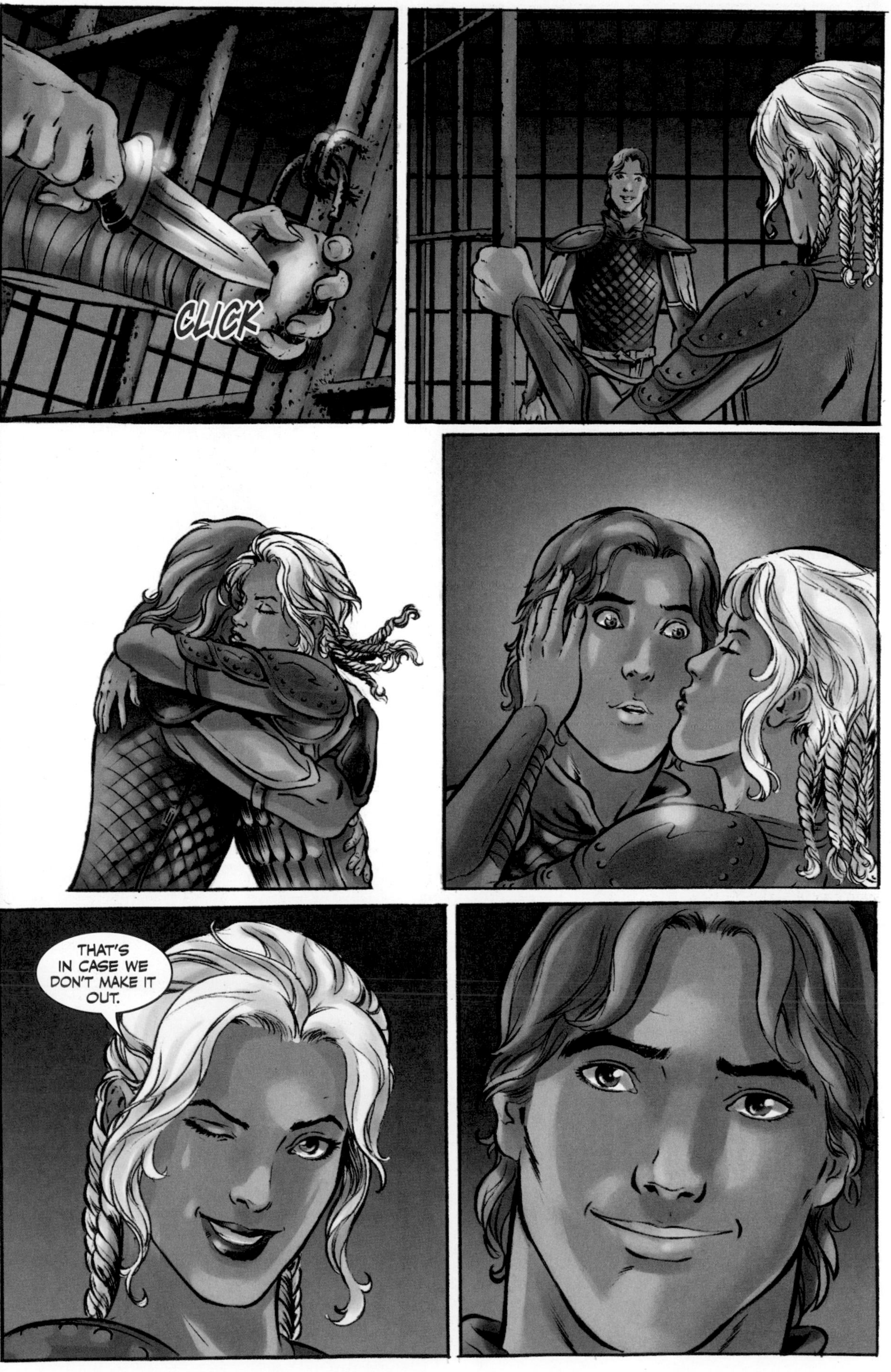
CLICK
THAT'S IN CASE WE DON'T MAKE IT OUT.

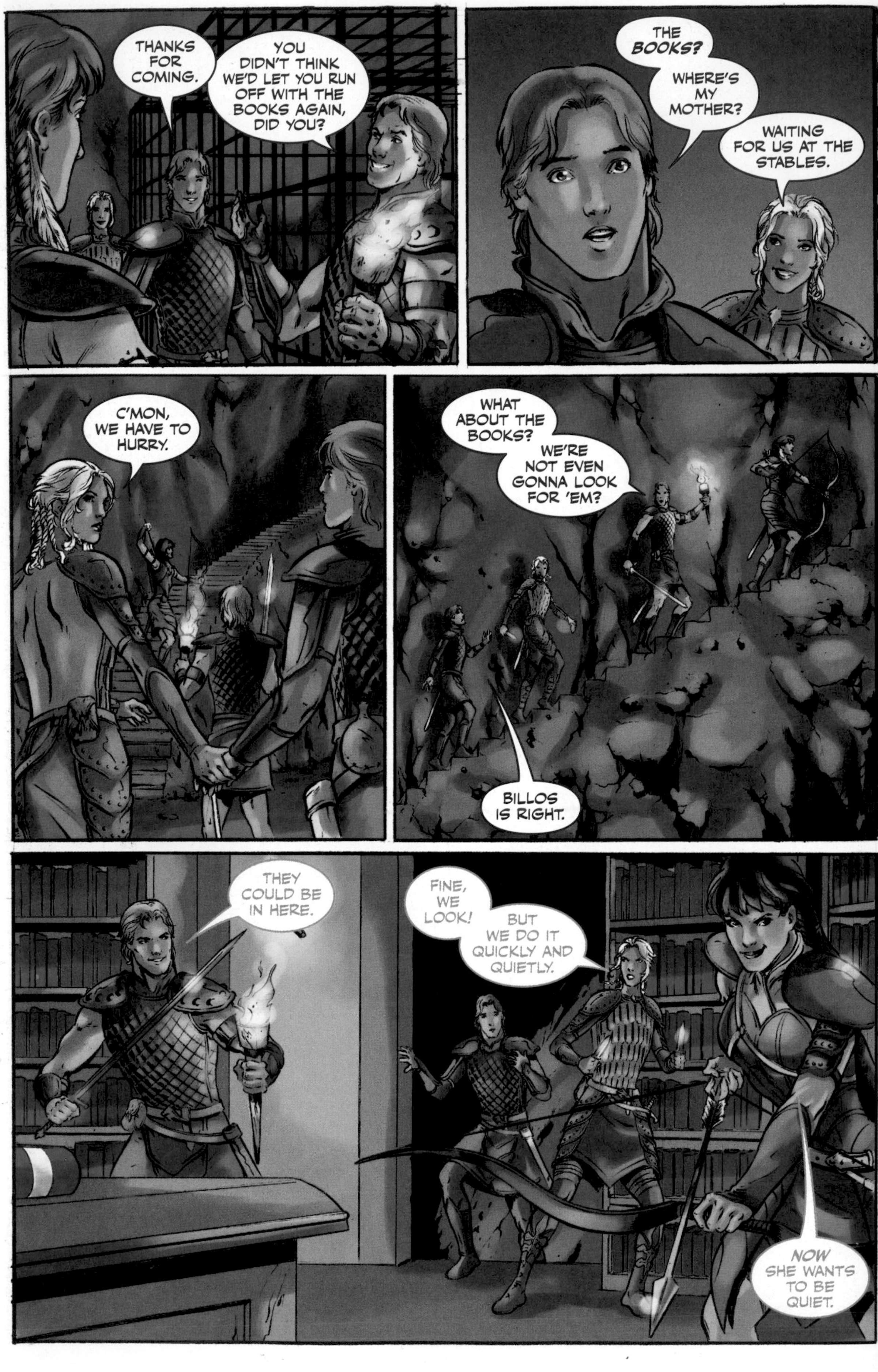

THANKS FOR COMING.
YOU DIDN'T THINK WE'D LET YOU RUN OFF WITH THE BOOKS AGAIN, DID YOU?
THE *BOOKS?*
WHERE'S MY MOTHER?
WAITING FOR US AT THE STABLES.
C'MON, WE HAVE TO HURRY.
WHAT ABOUT THE BOOKS?
WE'RE NOT EVEN GONNA LOOK FOR 'EM?
BILLOS IS RIGHT.
THEY COULD BE IN HERE.
FINE, WE LOOK!
BUT WE DO IT QUICKLY AND QUIETLY.
NOW SHE WANTS TO BE QUIET.

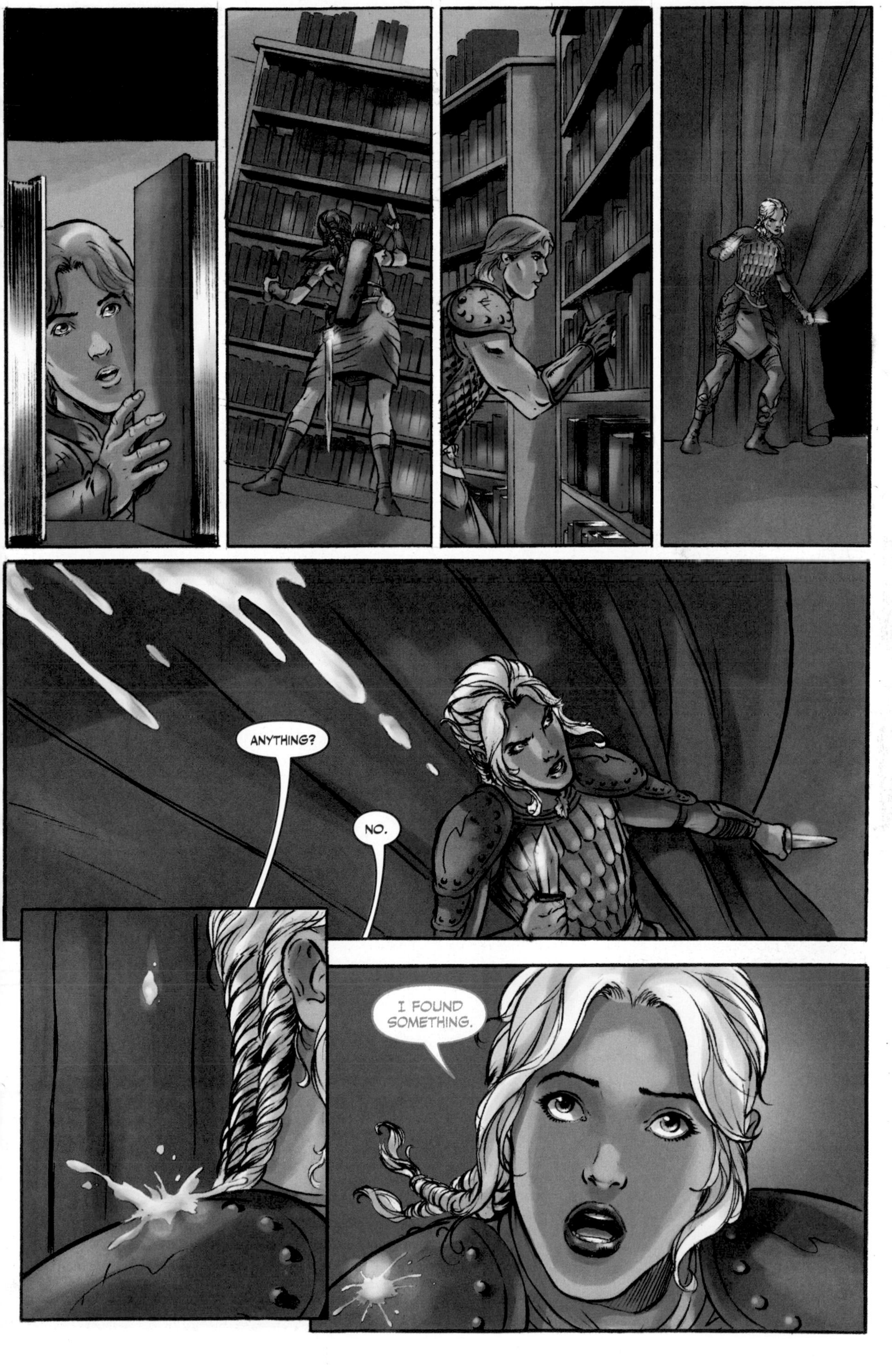
ANYTHING?
NO.
I FOUND SOMETHING.

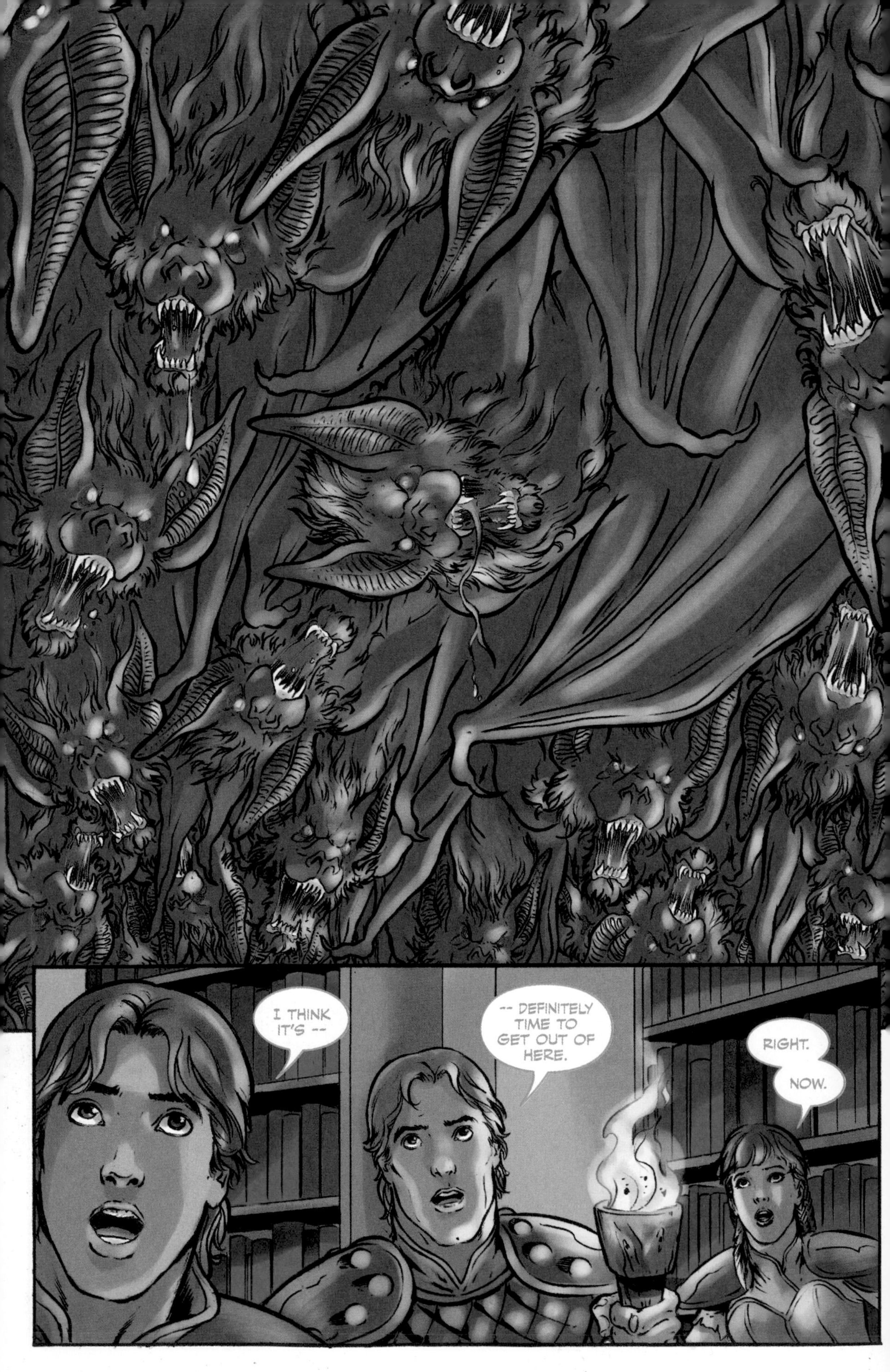
I THINK IT'S --
-- DEFINITELY TIME TO GET OUT OF HERE.
RIGHT.
NOW.

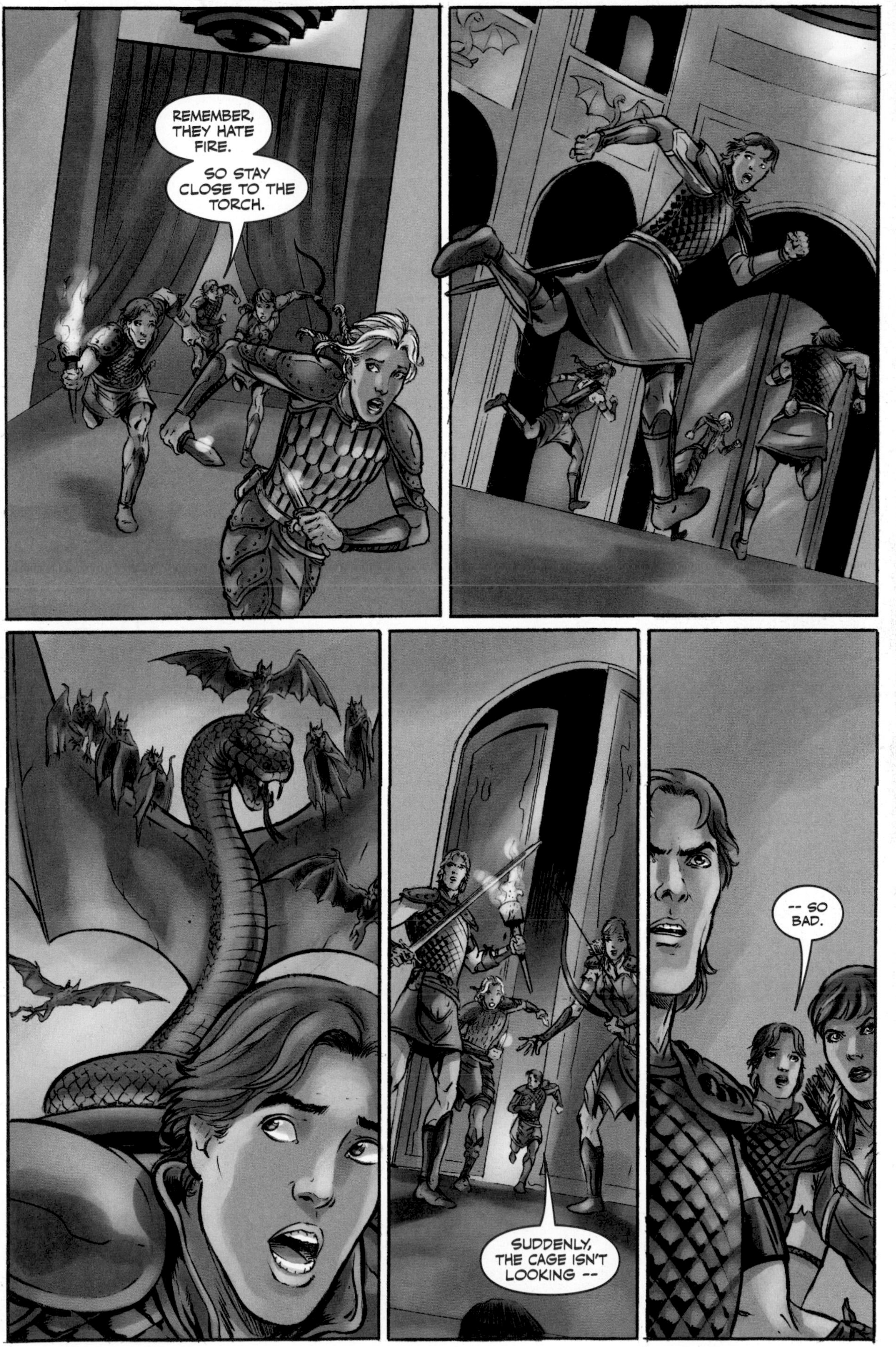
REMEMBER, THEY HATE FIRE.
SO STAY CLOSE TO THE TORCH.
SUDDENLY, THE CAGE ISN'T LOOKING --
-- SO BAD.

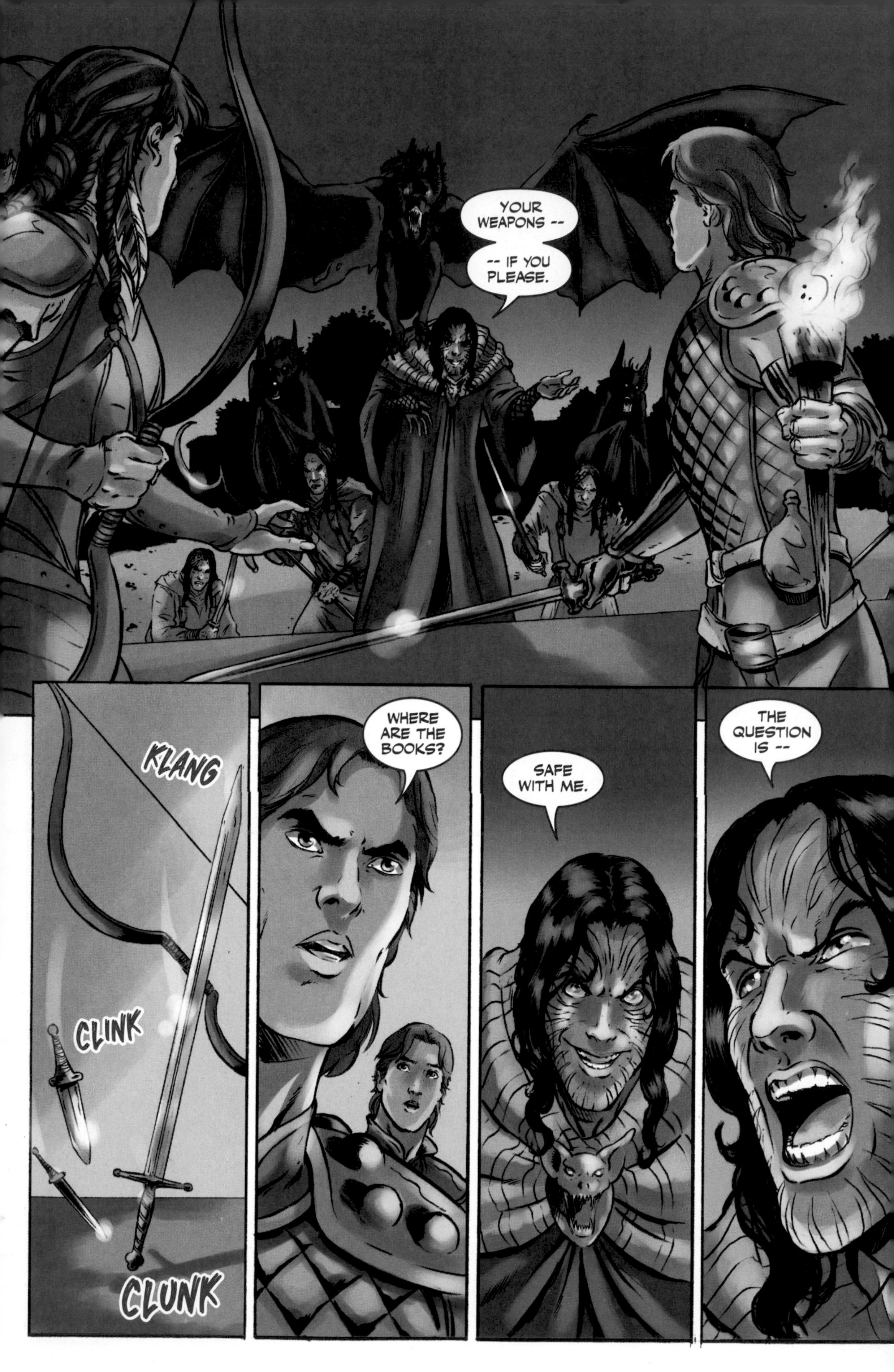
YOUR WEAPONS --
-- IF YOU PLEASE.
KLANG
CLINK
CLUNK
WHERE ARE THE BOOKS?
SAFE WITH ME.
THE QUESTION IS --

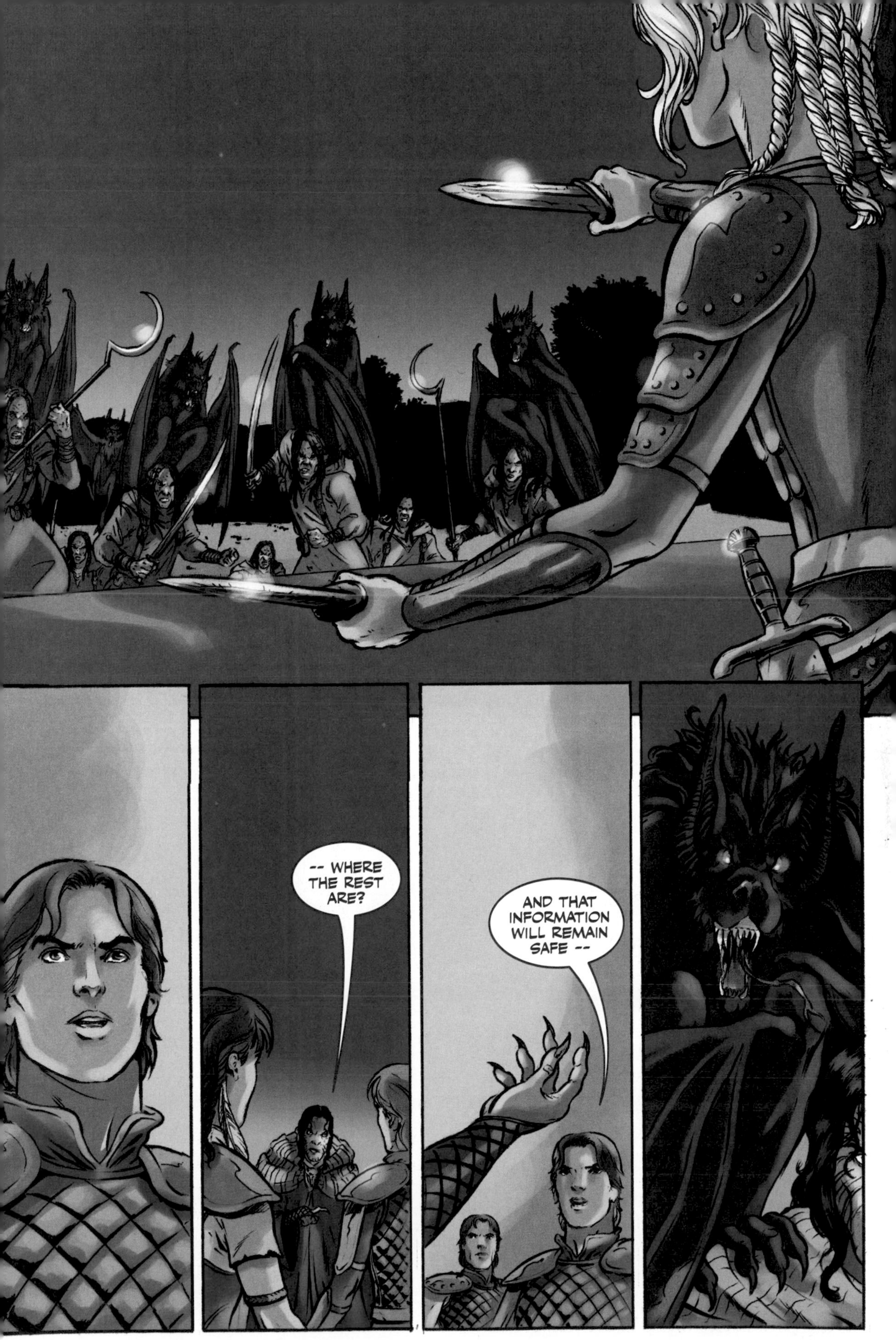
-- WHERE THE REST ARE?
AND THAT INFORMATION WILL REMAIN SAFE --

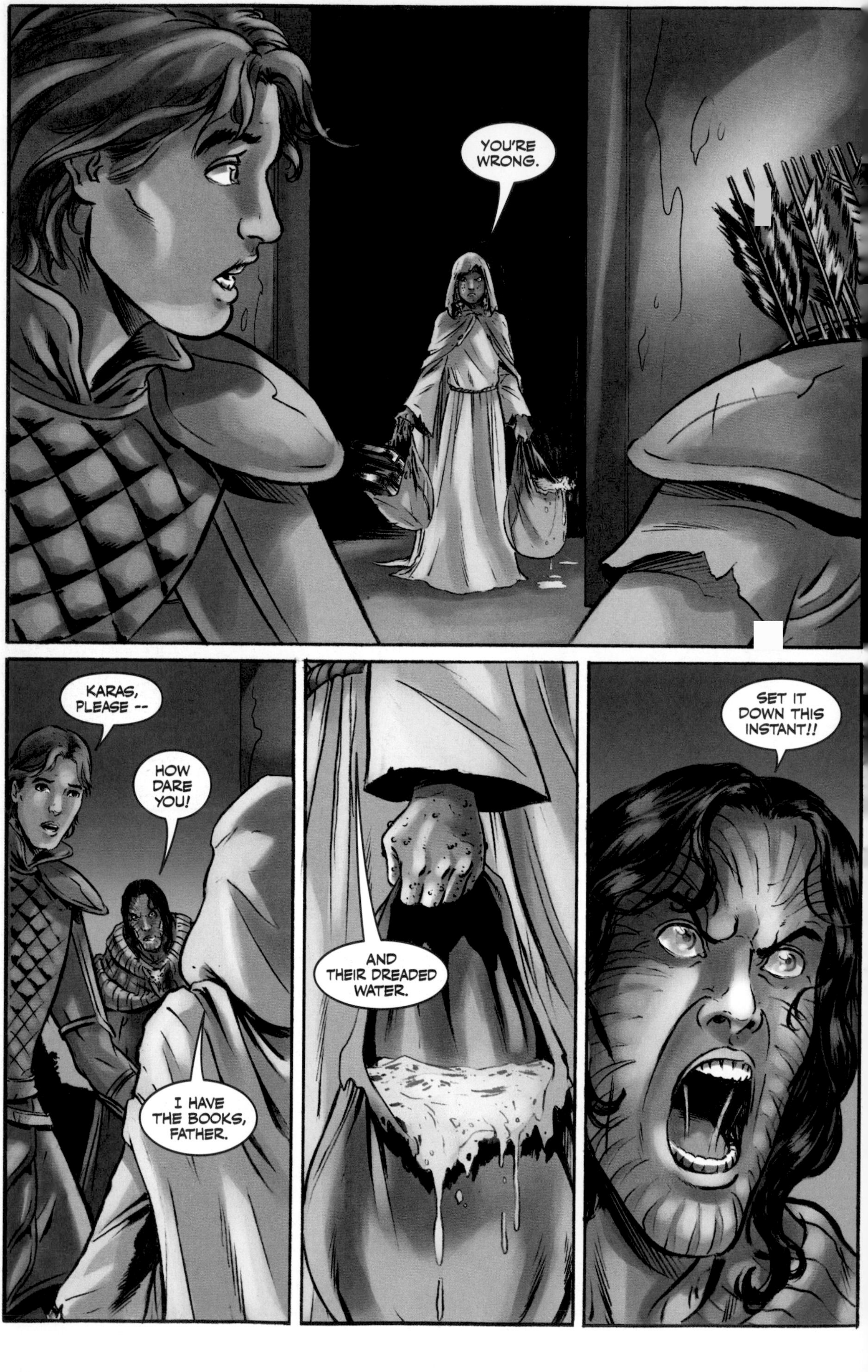
YOU'RE WRONG.
KARAS, PLEASE --
HOW DARE YOU!
I HAVE THE BOOKS, FATHER.
AND THEIR DREADED WATER.
SET IT DOWN THIS INSTANT!!

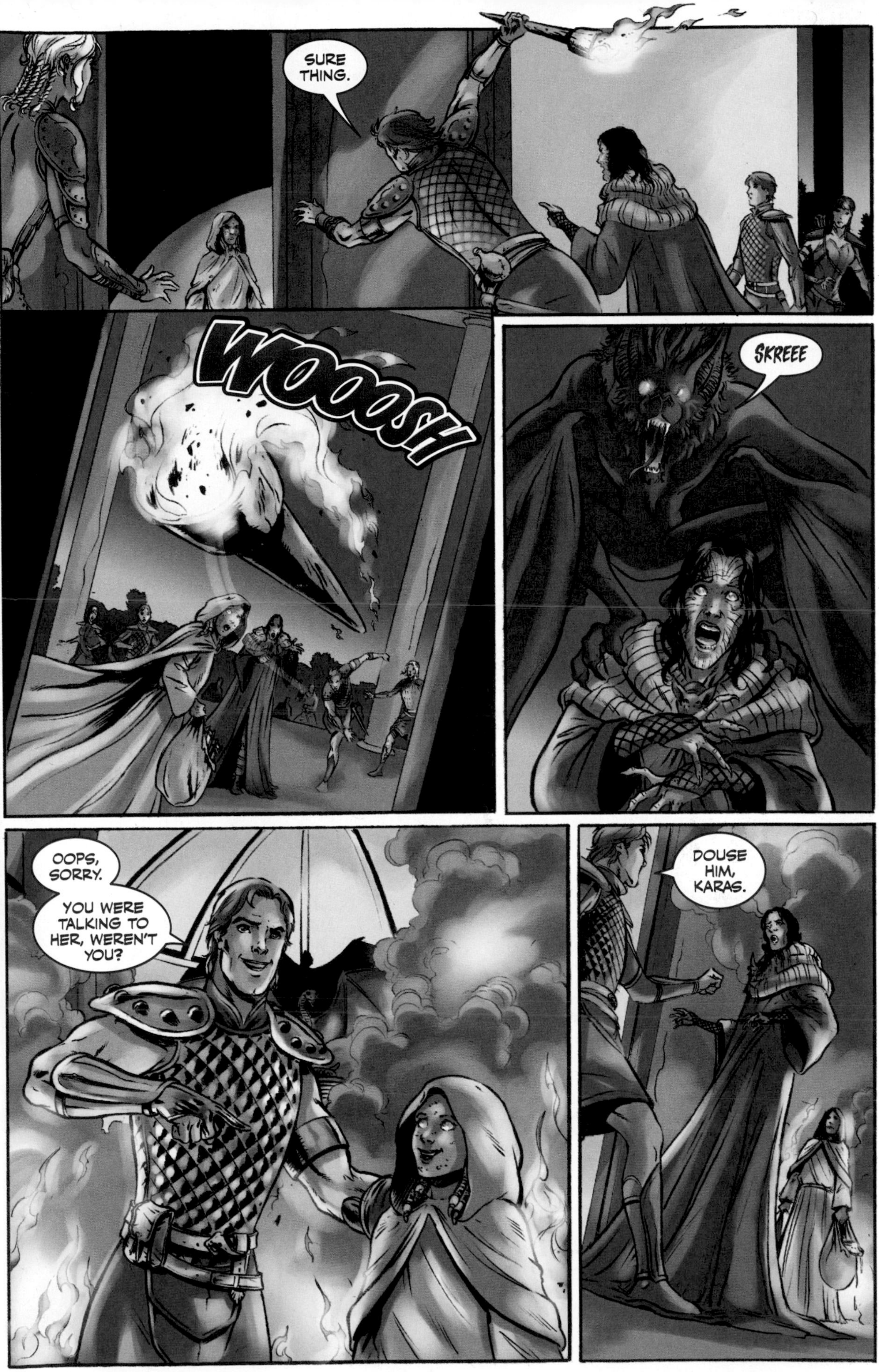
SURE THING.
WOOOSH
SKREEE
OOPS, SORRY.
YOU WERE TALKING TO HER, WEREN'T YOU?
DOUSE HIM, KARAS.

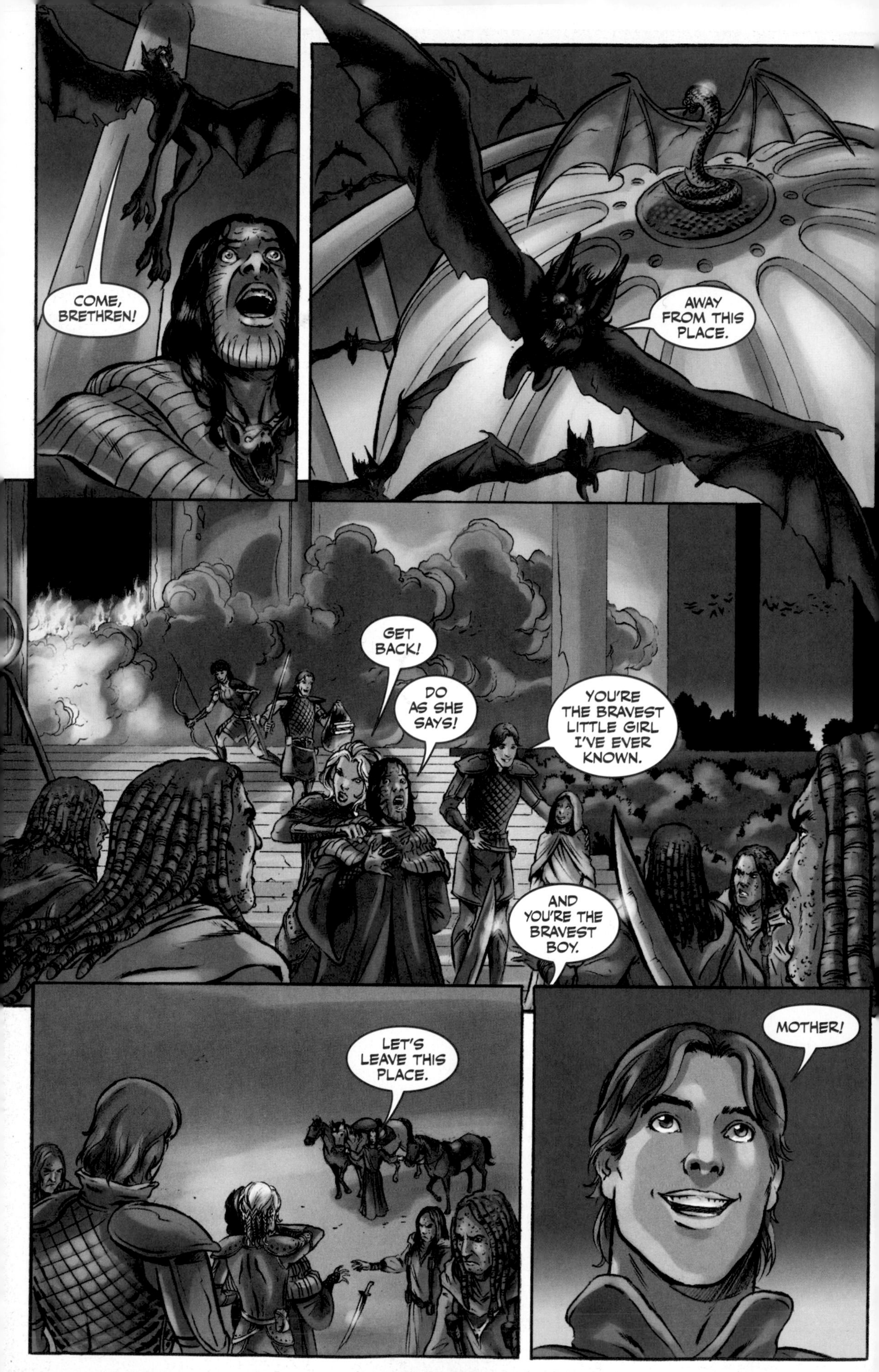
COME, BRETHREN!
AWAY FROM THIS PLACE.
GET BACK!
DO AS SHE SAYS!
YOU'RE THE BRAVEST LITTLE GIRL I'VE EVER KNOWN.
AND YOU'RE THE BRAVEST BOY.
LET'S LEAVE THIS PLACE.
MOTHER!

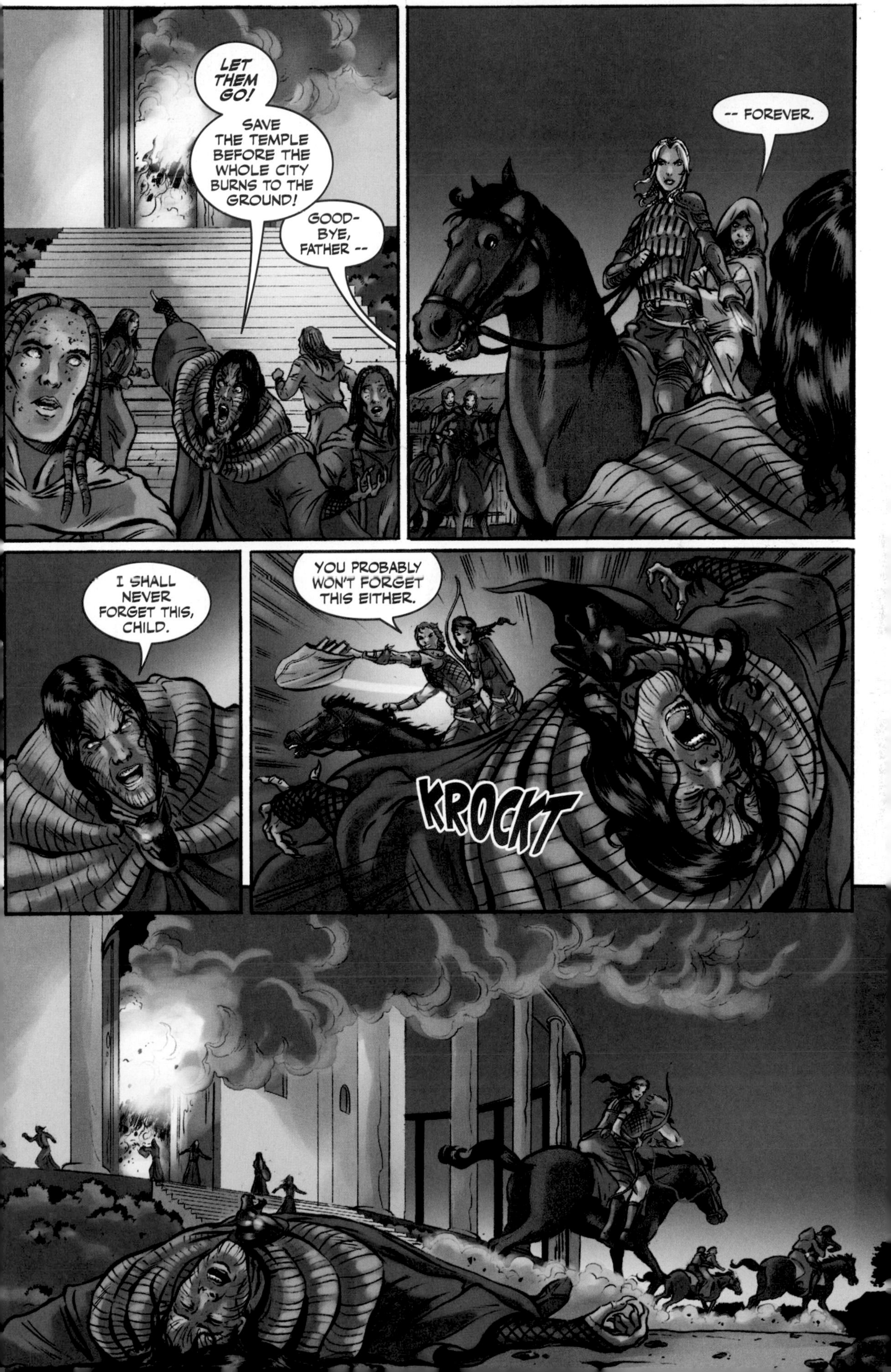
LET THEM GO!
SAVE THE TEMPLE BEFORE THE WHOLE CITY BURNS TO THE GROUND!
GOOD-BYE, FATHER --
-- FOREVER.
I SHALL NEVER FORGET THIS, CHILD.
YOU PROBABLY WON'T FORGET THIS EITHER.
KROCKT

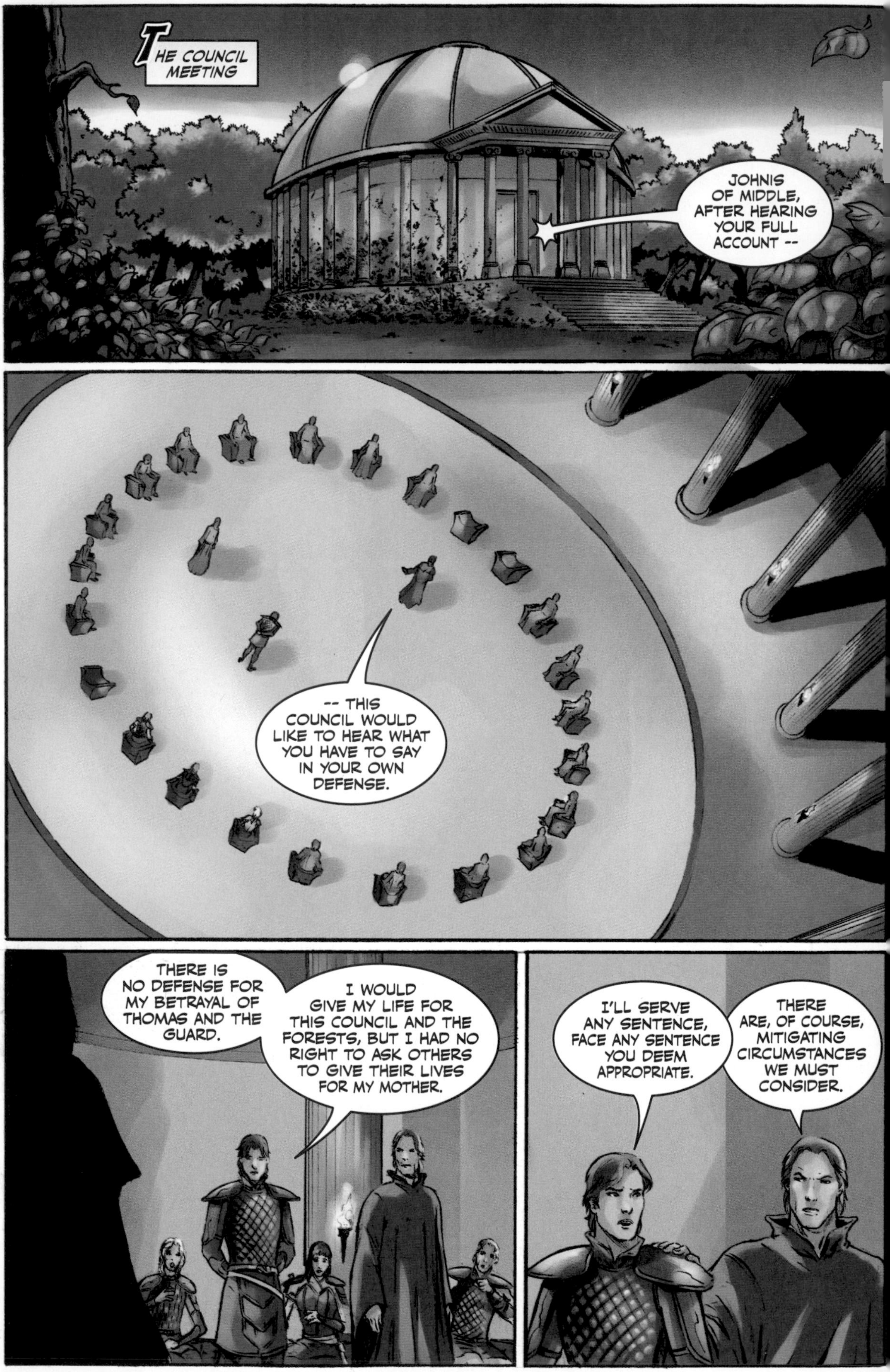
THE COUNCIL MEETING
JOHNIS OF MIDDLE, AFTER HEARING YOUR FULL ACCOUNT --
-- THIS COUNCIL WOULD LIKE TO HEAR WHAT YOU HAVE TO SAY IN YOUR OWN DEFENSE.
THERE IS NO DEFENSE FOR MY BETRAYAL OF THOMAS AND THE GUARD.
I WOULD GIVE MY LIFE FOR THIS COUNCIL AND THE FORESTS, BUT I HAD NO RIGHT TO ASK OTHERS TO GIVE THEIR LIVES FOR MY MOTHER.
I'LL SERVE ANY SENTENCE, FACE ANY SENTENCE YOU DEEM APPROPRIATE.
THERE ARE, OF COURSE, MITIGATING CIRCUMSTANCES WE MUST CONSIDER.

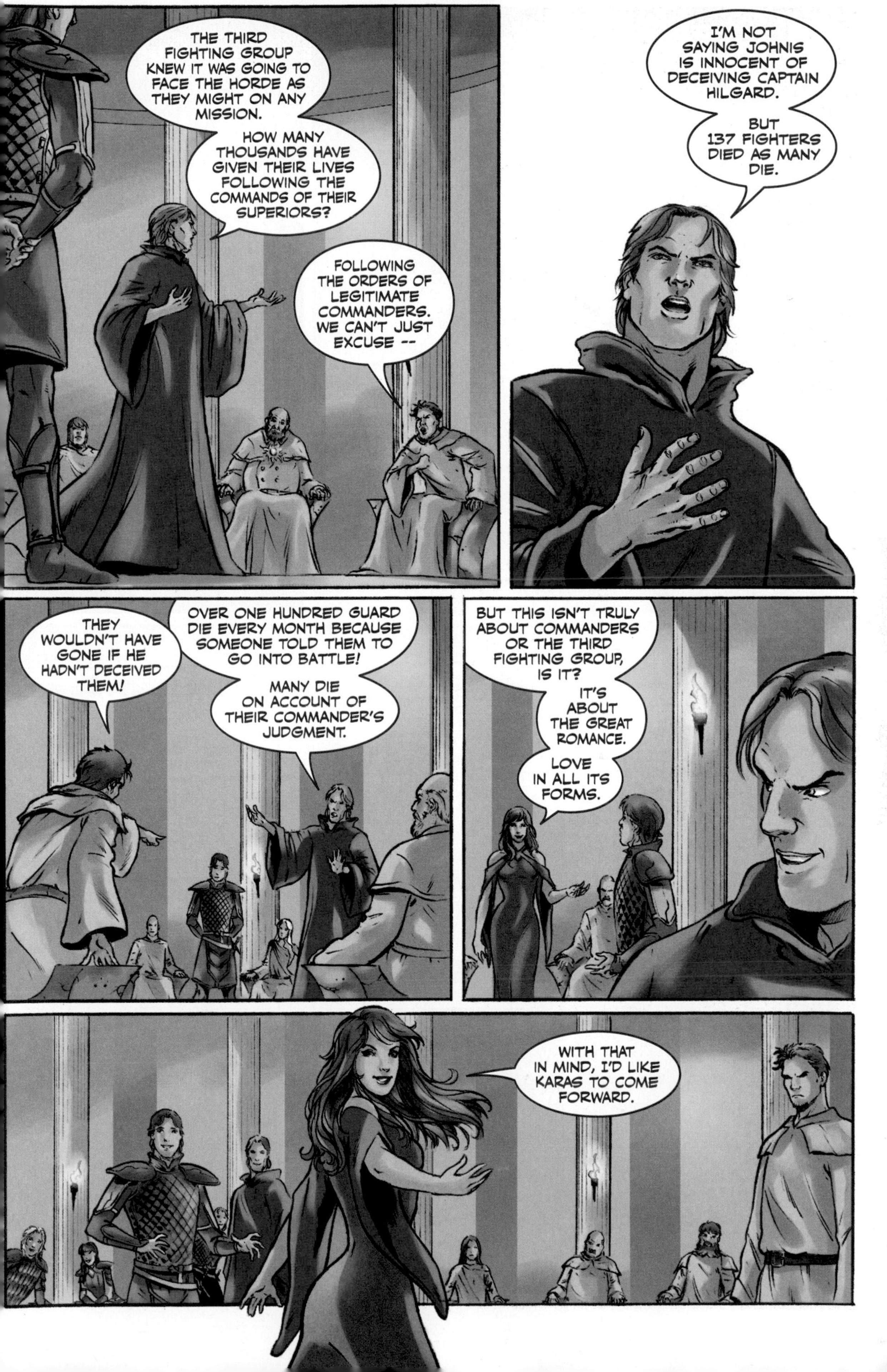
THE THIRD FIGHTING GROUP KNEW IT WAS GOING TO FACE THE HORDE AS THEY MIGHT ON ANY MISSION.
HOW MANY THOUSANDS HAVE GIVEN THEIR LIVES FOLLOWING THE COMMANDS OF THEIR SUPERIORS?
FOLLOWING THE ORDERS OF LEGITIMATE COMMANDERS. WE CAN'T JUST EXCUSE --
I'M NOT SAYING JOHNIS IS INNOCENT OF DECEIVING CAPTAIN HILGARD.
BUT 137 FIGHTERS DIED AS MANY DIE.
THEY WOULDN'T HAVE GONE IF HE HADN'T DECEIVED THEM!
OVER ONE HUNDRED GUARD DIE EVERY MONTH BECAUSE SOMEONE TOLD THEM TO GO INTO BATTLE!
MANY DIE ON ACCOUNT OF THEIR COMMANDER'S JUDGMENT.
BUT THIS ISN'T TRULY ABOUT COMMANDERS OR THE THIRD FIGHTING GROUP, IS IT?
IT'S ABOUT THE GREAT ROMANCE.
LOVE IN ALL ITS FORMS.
WITH THAT IN MIND, I'D LIKE KARAS TO COME FORWARD.

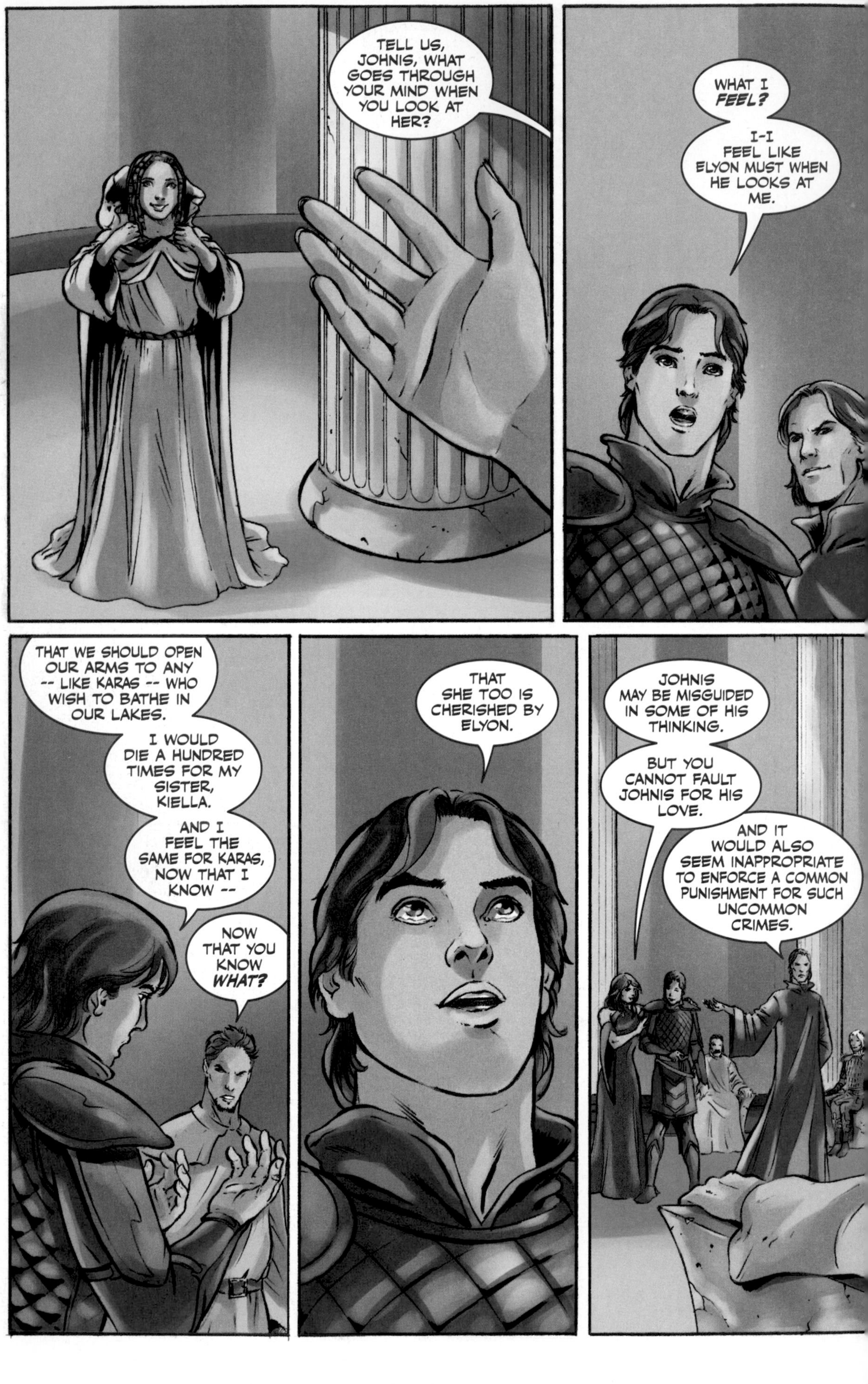
TELL US, JOHNIS, WHAT GOES THROUGH YOUR MIND WHEN YOU LOOK AT HER?
WHAT I *FEEL?*
I-I FEEL LIKE ELYON MUST WHEN HE LOOKS AT ME.
THAT WE SHOULD OPEN OUR ARMS TO ANY -- LIKE KARAS -- WHO WISH TO BATHE IN OUR LAKES.
I WOULD DIE A HUNDRED TIMES FOR MY SISTER, KIELLA.
AND I FEEL THE SAME FOR KARAS, NOW THAT I KNOW --
NOW THAT YOU KNOW *WHAT?*
THAT SHE TOO IS CHERISHED BY ELYON.
JOHNIS MAY BE MISGUIDED IN SOME OF HIS THINKING.
BUT YOU CANNOT FAULT JOHNIS FOR HIS LOVE.
AND IT WOULD ALSO SEEM INAPPROPRIATE TO ENFORCE A COMMON PUNISHMENT FOR SUCH UNCOMMON CRIMES.

AS AN ALTERNATIVE, I PROPOSE HE INSTEAD BE PROMOTED TO THE RANK OF MAJOR.

AS A MAJOR, HE WOULD REPORT DIRECTLY TO ME AND, IN MY JUDGMENT, WOULD ALSO BE REMOVED FROM ACTIVE DUTY --

-- UNTIL WE DEEM HE IS READY TO LEAD IN A BATTLE THAT REQUIRES MORE THAN HIS HEART OR MIND.

BUT THE THIRD FIGHTING GROUP!

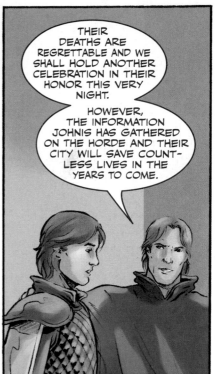

THEIR DEATHS ARE REGRETTABLE AND WE SHALL HOLD ANOTHER CELEBRATION IN THEIR HONOR THIS VERY NIGHT.

HOWEVER, THE INFORMATION JOHNIS HAS GATHERED ON THE HORDE AND THEIR CITY WILL SAVE COUNTLESS LIVES IN THE YEARS TO COME.

NOW THEN --

-- ALL IN FAVOR?

AYE!

AYE!

AYE!

AYE!

AYE!

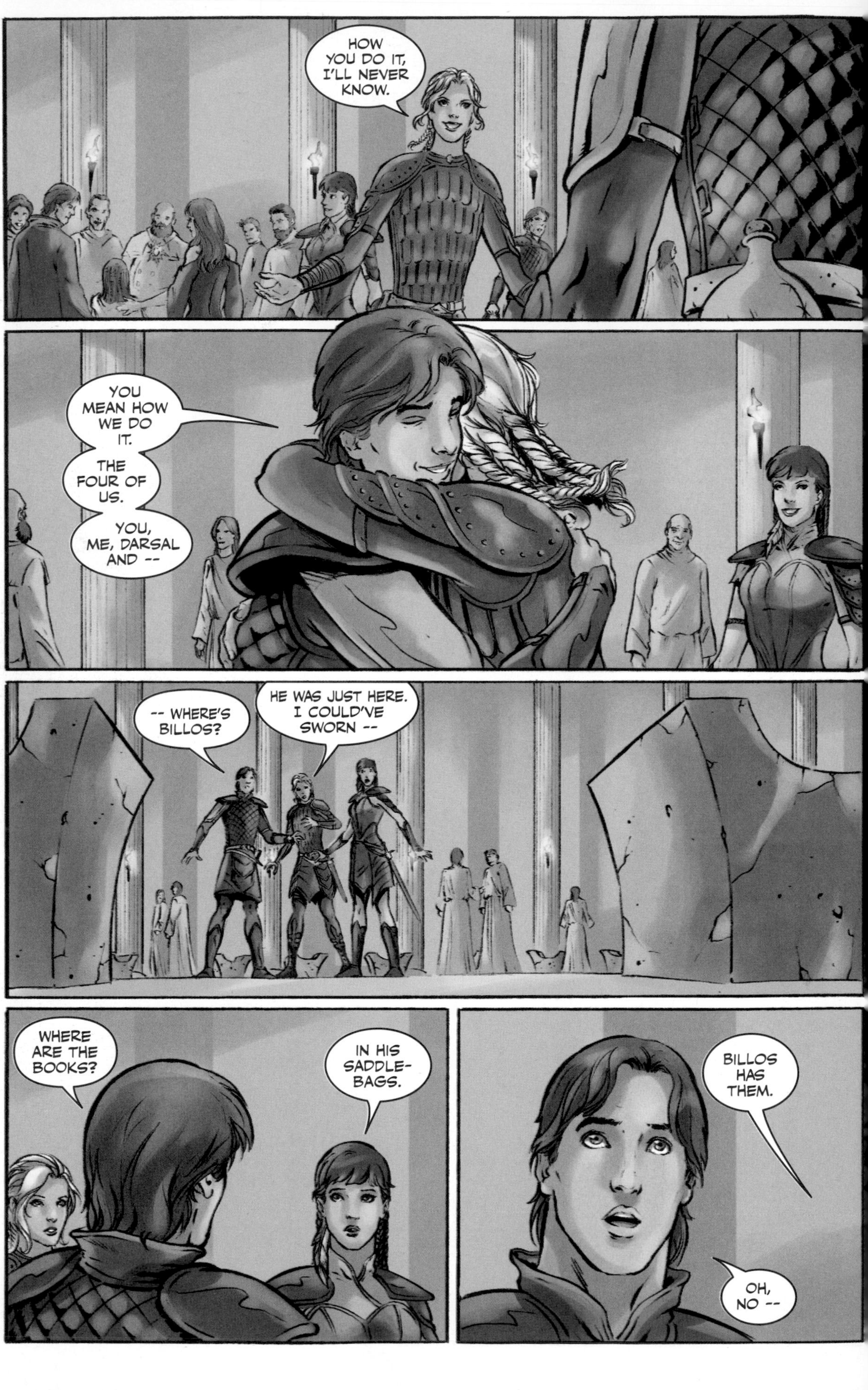
HOW YOU DO IT, I'LL NEVER KNOW.
YOU MEAN HOW WE DO IT.
THE FOUR OF US.
YOU, ME, DARSAL AND --
-- WHERE'S BILLOS?
HE WAS JUST HERE. I COULD'VE SWORN --
WHERE ARE THE BOOKS?
IN HIS SADDLE-BAGS.
BILLOS HAS THEM.
OH, NO --

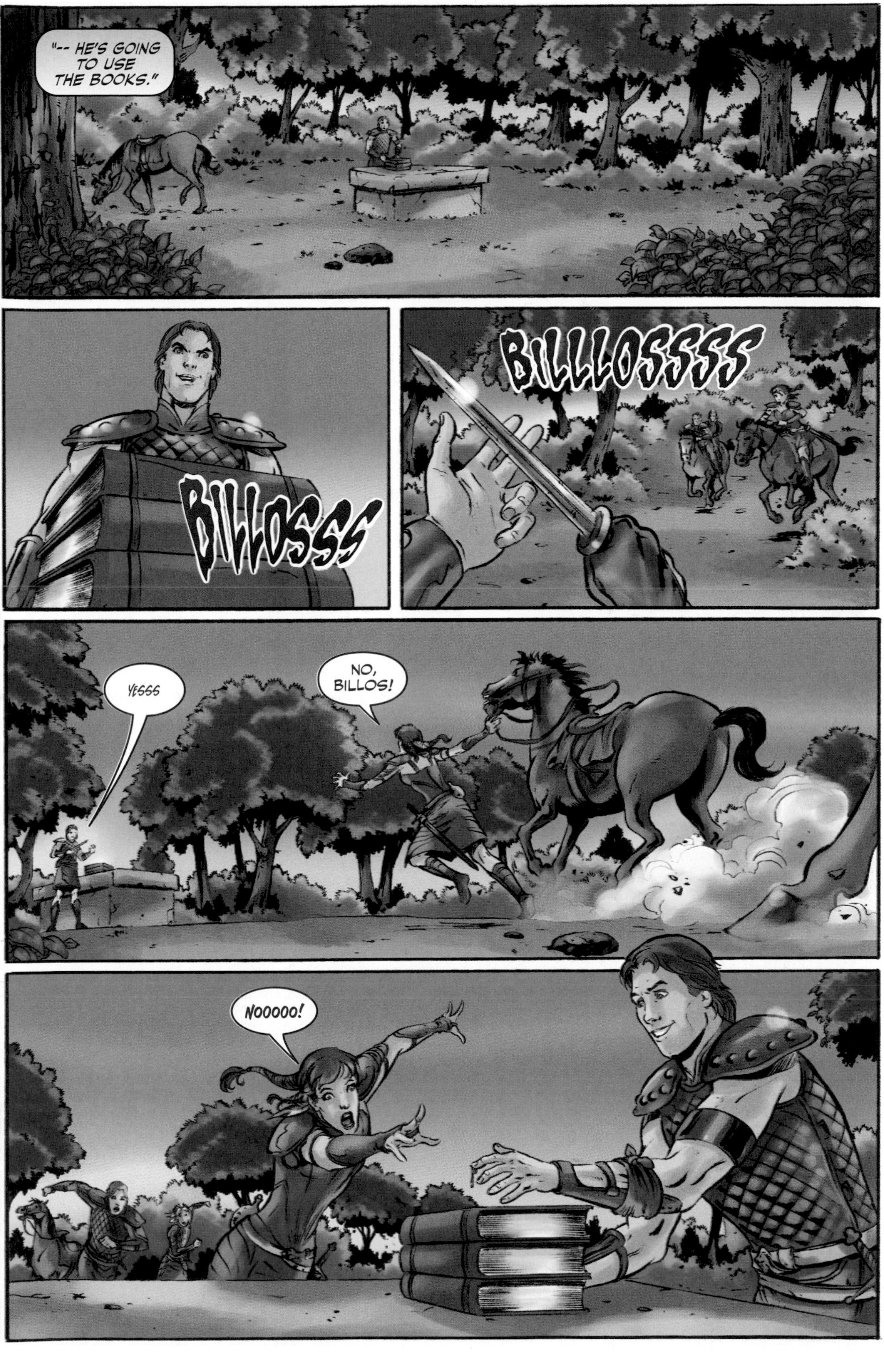
"-- HE'S GOING TO USE THE BOOKS."
BILLOSSS
BILLOSSSSS
YESSS
NO, BILLOS!
NOOOOO!

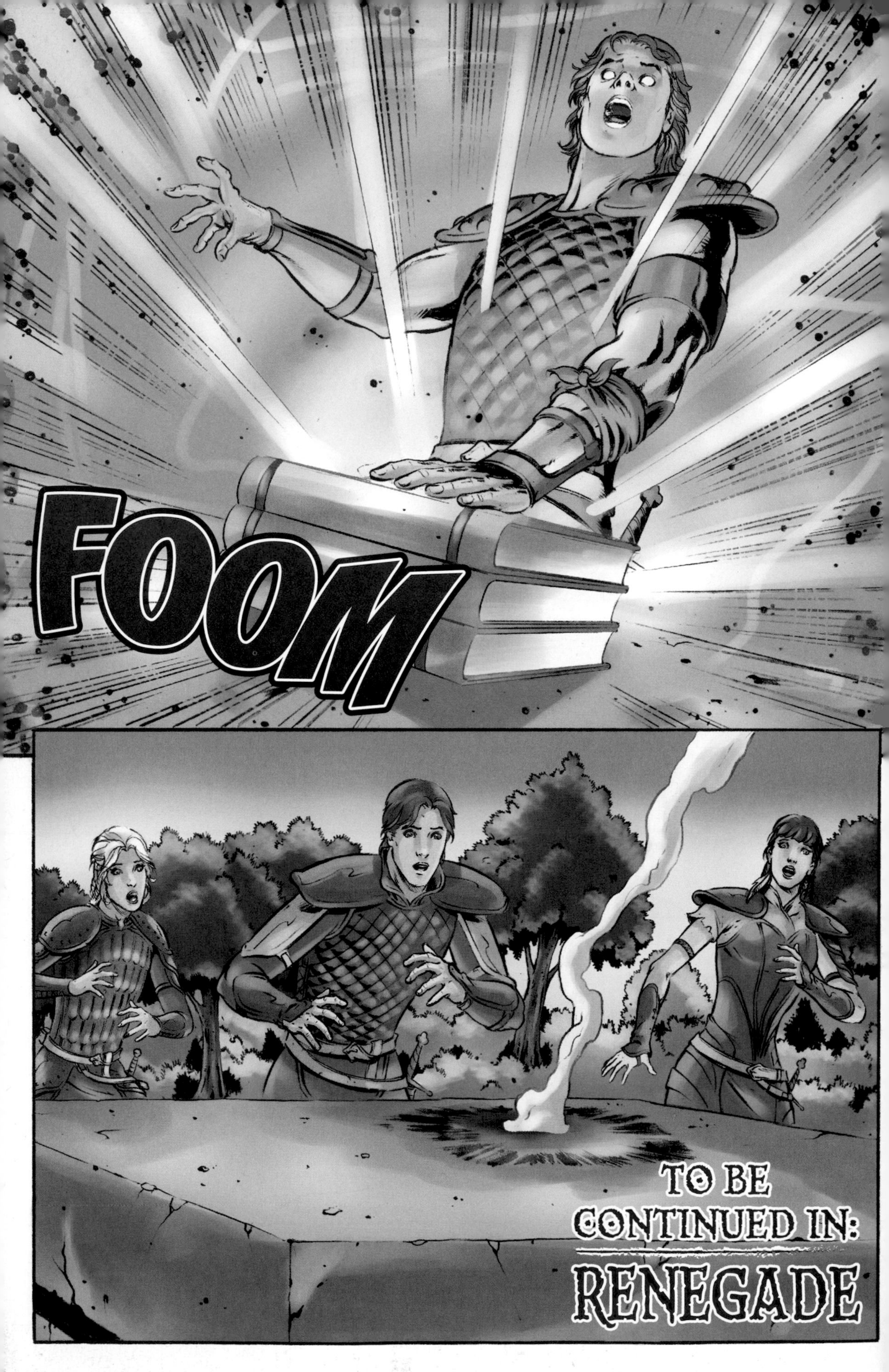
FOOM
TO BE
CONTINUED IN:
RENEGADE

WRITTEN BY TED DEKKER

ADAPTATION BY J.S. EARLS AND KEVIN KAISER

EDITED BY KEVIN KAISER AND JOCELYN BAILEY

ILLUSTRATIONS BY CEZAR RAZEK

COLORS BY ALE STARLING

LETTERED BY ZACH MATHENY

FRONT COVER ART BY EDUARDO PANSICA

PUBLISHED IN NASHVILLE, TENNESSEE, BY THOMAS NELSON. THOMAS NELSON IS A REGISTERED TRADEMARK OF THOMAS NELSON, INC.

THOMAS NELSON, INC. TITLES MAY BE PURCHASED IN BULK FOR EDUCATIONAL, BUSINESS, FUND-RAISING, OR SALES PROMOTIONAL USE. FOR INFORMATION, PLEASE E-MAIL SPECIALMARKETS@THOMASNELSON.COM.

Library of Congress Cataloging in Publication Data

Dekker, Ted, 1962–
    Infidel / by Ted Dekker.
      p. cm. — (The lost books ; bk. 2)
    "Story by Ted Dekker. Adapted by J.S. Earls & Kevin Kaiser"—T.p. verso
    Summary: As Johnis and the other "chosen" recruits of the Forest Guard are pulled into deeper danger to secure the seven lost Books of History, Johnis tries to rescue his mother from enslavement by the Horde, but risks betraying the Forest Dwellers.
    ISBN 978-1-59554-604-3 (softcover)
    1. Graphic novels. [1. Graphic novels. 2. Fantasy. 3. Christian life—Fiction.] I. Title.
PZ7.7.D45In 2008
[Fic]—dc22
                                                    2008036860

Printed in Canada
08 09 10 11 12 QW 5 4 3 2 1

Two Realities One Experience
Enter Anywhere

Keep Reading for an Excerpt from Black Graphic Novel

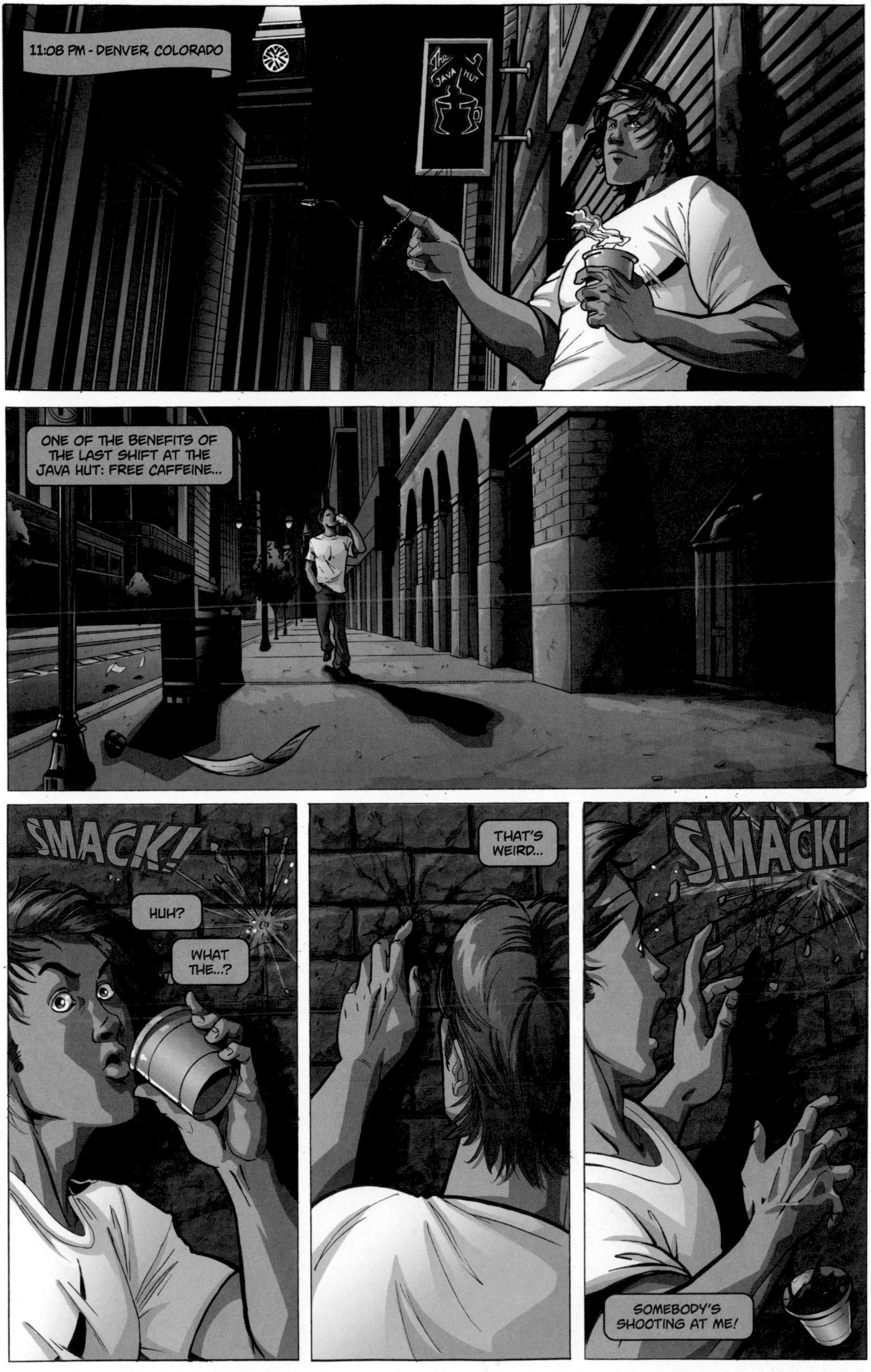
11:08 PM - DENVER, COLORADO
The JAVA HUT
ONE OF THE BENEFITS OF THE LAST SHIFT AT THE JAVA HUT: FREE CAFFEINE...
SMACK!
HUH?
WHAT THE...?
THAT'S WEIRD...
SMACK!
SOMEBODY'S SHOOTING AT ME!

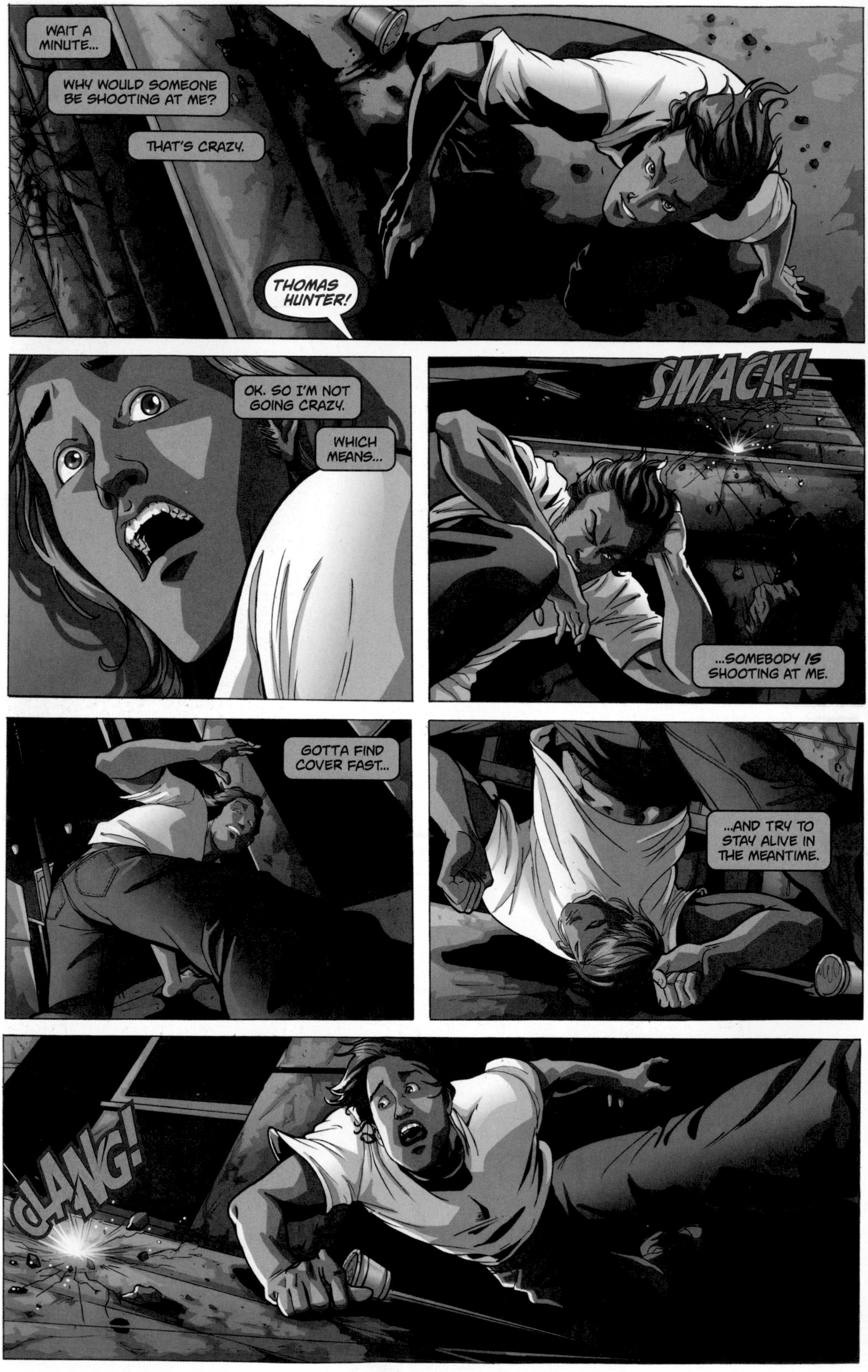
WAIT A MINUTE...
WHY WOULD SOMEONE BE SHOOTING AT ME?
THAT'S CRAZY.
THOMAS HUNTER!
OK. SO I'M NOT GOING CRAZY.
WHICH MEANS...
SMACK!
...SOMEBODY IS SHOOTING AT ME.
GOTTA FIND COVER FAST...
...AND TRY TO STAY ALIVE IN THE MEANTIME.
CLANG!

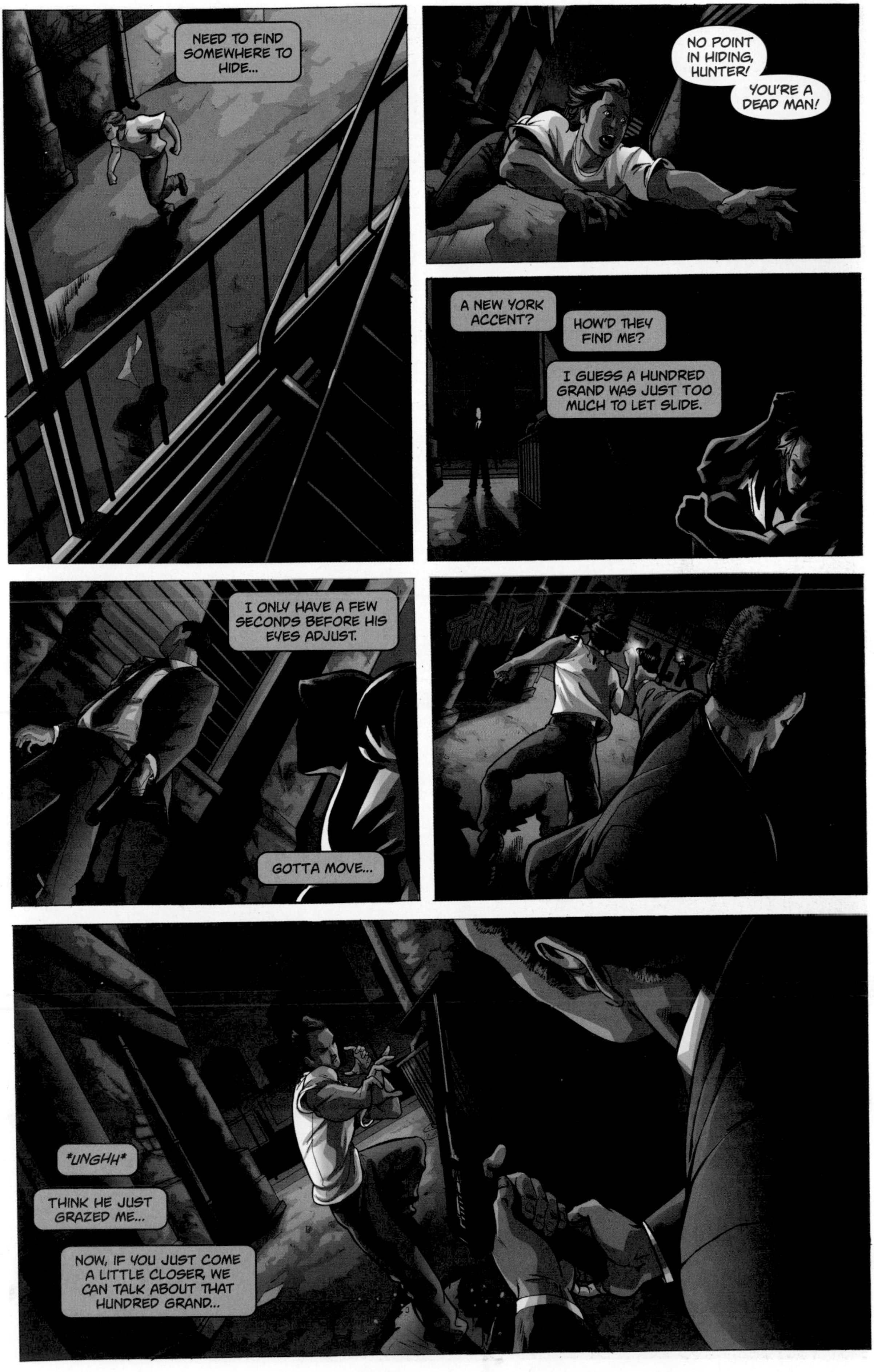
NEED TO FIND SOMEWHERE TO HIDE...
NO POINT IN HIDING, HUNTER!
YOU'RE A DEAD MAN!
A NEW YORK ACCENT?
HOW'D THEY FIND ME?
I GUESS A HUNDRED GRAND WAS JUST TOO MUCH TO LET SLIDE.
I ONLY HAVE A FEW SECONDS BEFORE HIS EYES ADJUST.
GOTTA MOVE...
UNGHH
THINK HE JUST GRAZED ME...
NOW, IF YOU JUST COME A LITTLE CLOSER, WE CAN TALK ABOUT THAT HUNDRED GRAND...

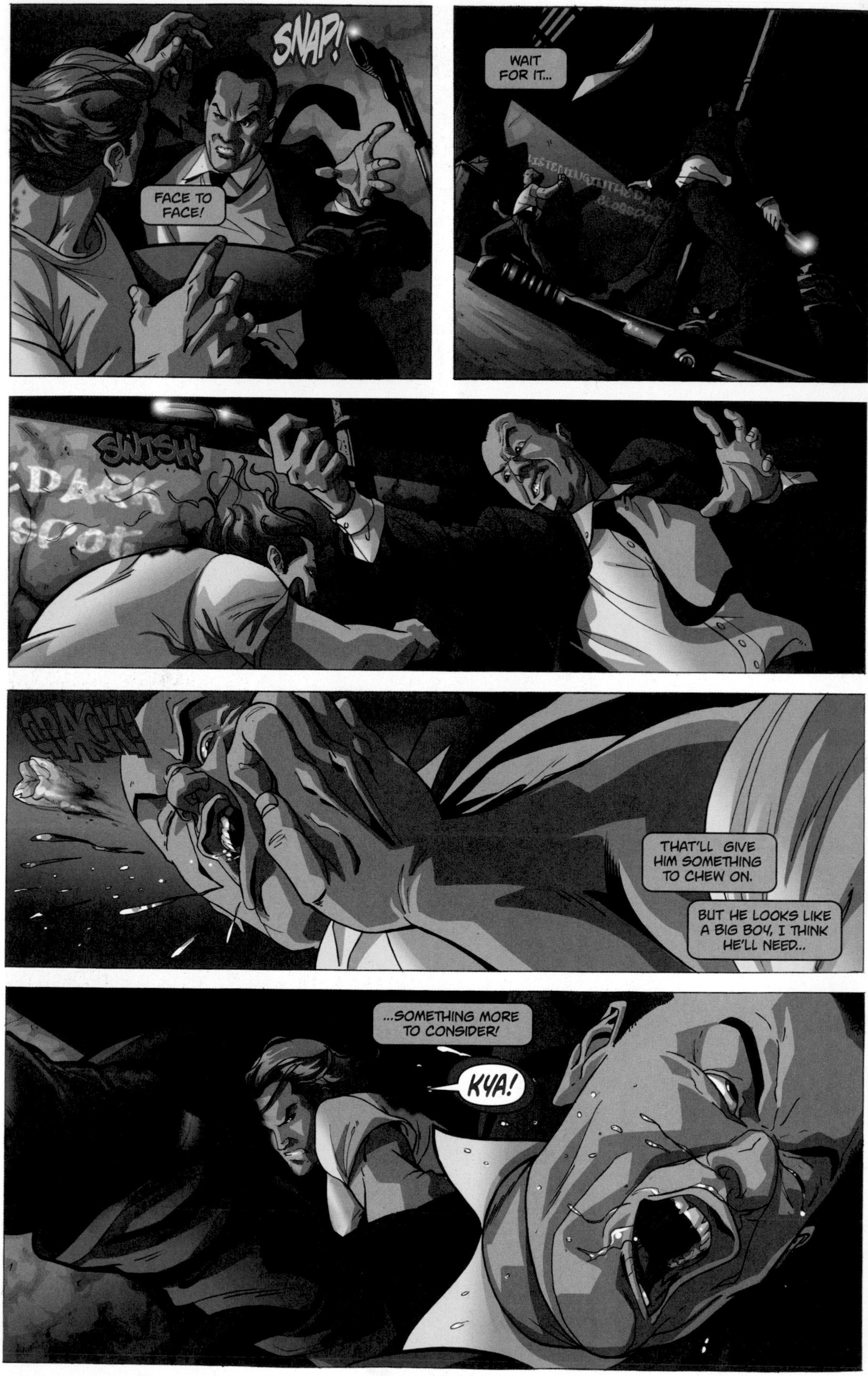
SNAP!
FACE TO FACE!
WAIT FOR IT...
SWISH!
THAT'LL GIVE HIM SOMETHING TO CHEW ON.
BUT HE LOOKS LIKE A BIG BOY, I THINK HE'LL NEED...
...SOMETHING MORE TO CONSIDER!
KYA!

NOT BAD FOR AN OUT OF SHAPE BLUE BELT.

IF THEY FOUND OUT WHERE I WORK THEN THEY KNOW WHERE I LIVE.

UNGHHH

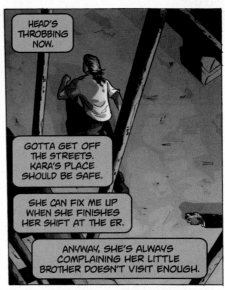

HEAD'S THROBBING NOW.

GOTTA GET OFF THE STREETS. KARA'S PLACE SHOULD BE SAFE.

SHE CAN FIX ME UP WHEN SHE FINISHES HER SHIFT AT THE ER.

ANYWAY, SHE'S ALWAYS COMPLAINING HER LITTLE BROTHER DOESN'T VISIT ENOUGH.

LOOKS ALL CLEAR. THINK I'M SAFE. FOR THE MOMENT AT LEAST.

GOOD THING I KNOW WHERE SHE KEEPS HER SPARE KEY.

MAYBE I SHOULD LIE DOWN... JUST FOR A MINUTE.

KARA WILL BE HOME SOON...

... SHE CAN TELL ME...

...IF IT'S SERIOUS...

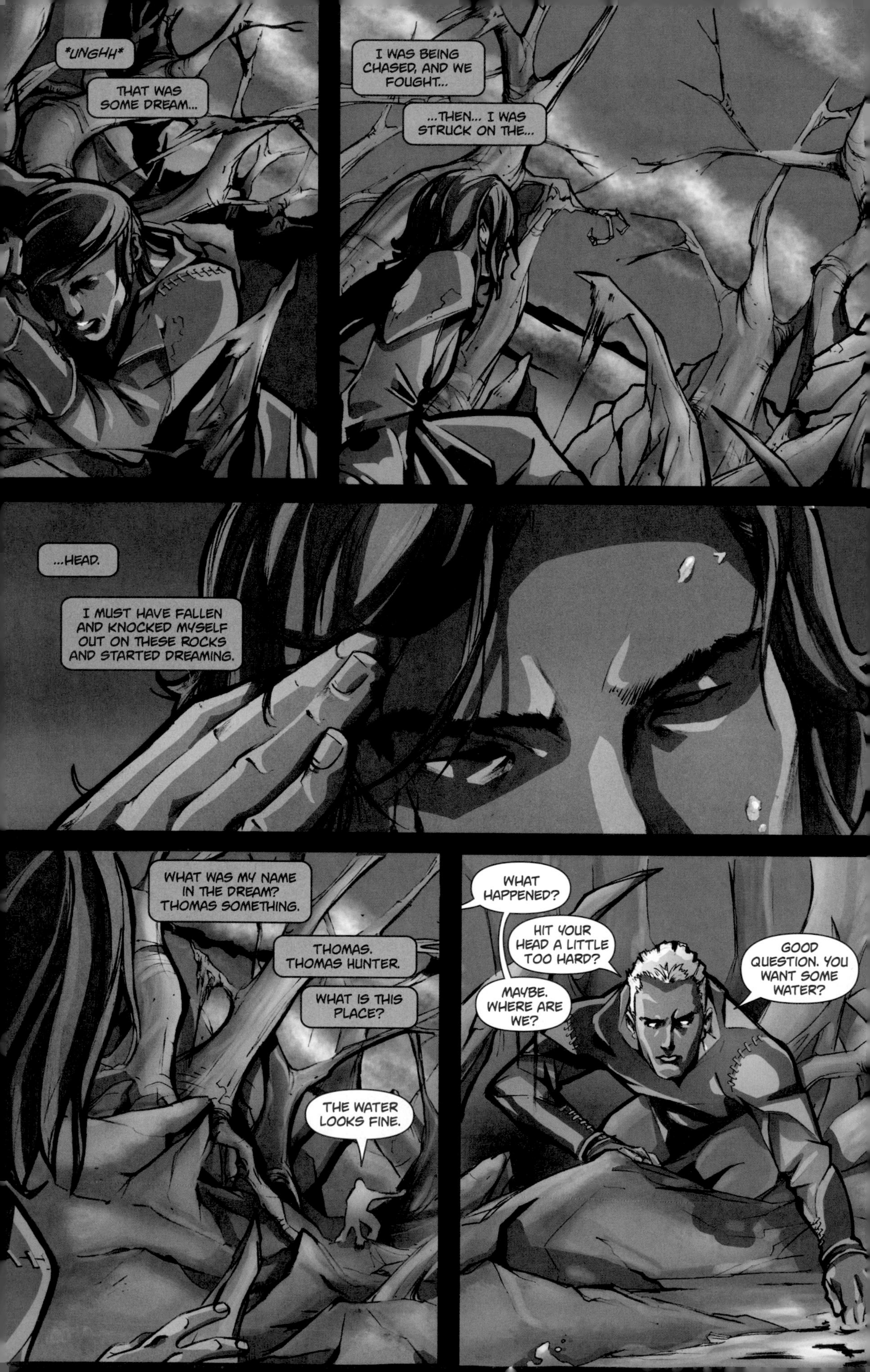
UNGHH
THAT WAS SOME DREAM...
I WAS BEING CHASED, AND WE FOUGHT...
...THEN... I WAS STRUCK ON THE...
...HEAD.
I MUST HAVE FALLEN AND KNOCKED MYSELF OUT ON THESE ROCKS AND STARTED DREAMING.
WHAT WAS MY NAME IN THE DREAM? THOMAS SOMETHING.
THOMAS. THOMAS HUNTER.
WHAT IS THIS PLACE?
THE WATER LOOKS FINE.
WHAT HAPPENED?
HIT YOUR HEAD A LITTLE TOO HARD?
MAYBE. WHERE ARE WE?
GOOD QUESTION. YOU WANT SOME WATER?

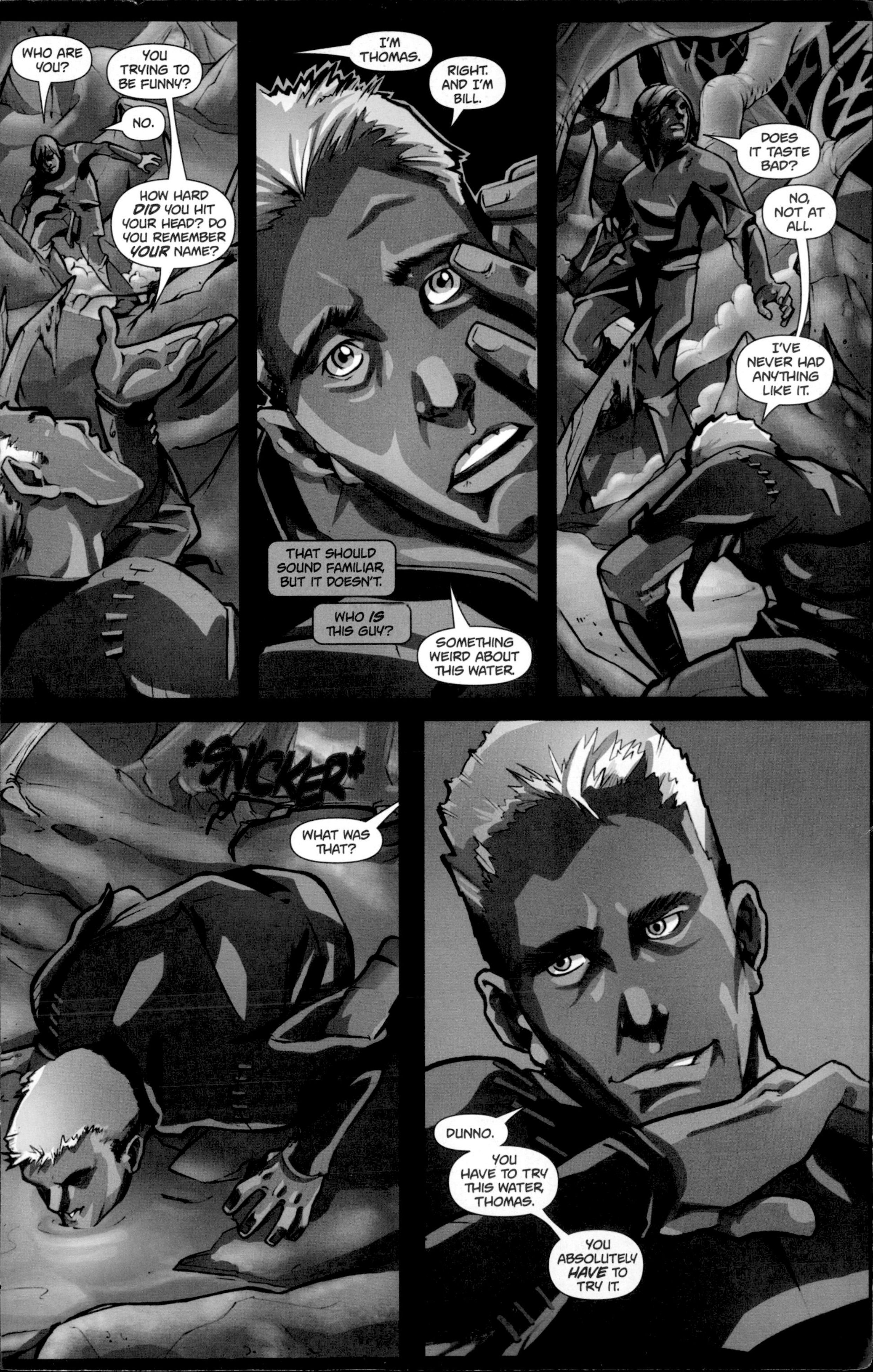
WHO ARE YOU?
YOU TRYING TO BE FUNNY?
NO.
HOW HARD DID YOU HIT YOUR HEAD? DO YOU REMEMBER YOUR NAME?
I'M THOMAS.
RIGHT. AND I'M BILL.
THAT SHOULD SOUND FAMILIAR, BUT IT DOESN'T.
WHO IS THIS GUY?
SOMETHING WEIRD ABOUT THIS WATER.
DOES IT TASTE BAD?
NO, NOT AT ALL.
I'VE NEVER HAD ANYTHING LIKE IT.
SNICKER
WHAT WAS THAT?
DUNNO.
YOU HAVE TO TRY THIS WATER, THOMAS.
YOU ABSOLUTELY HAVE TO TRY IT.

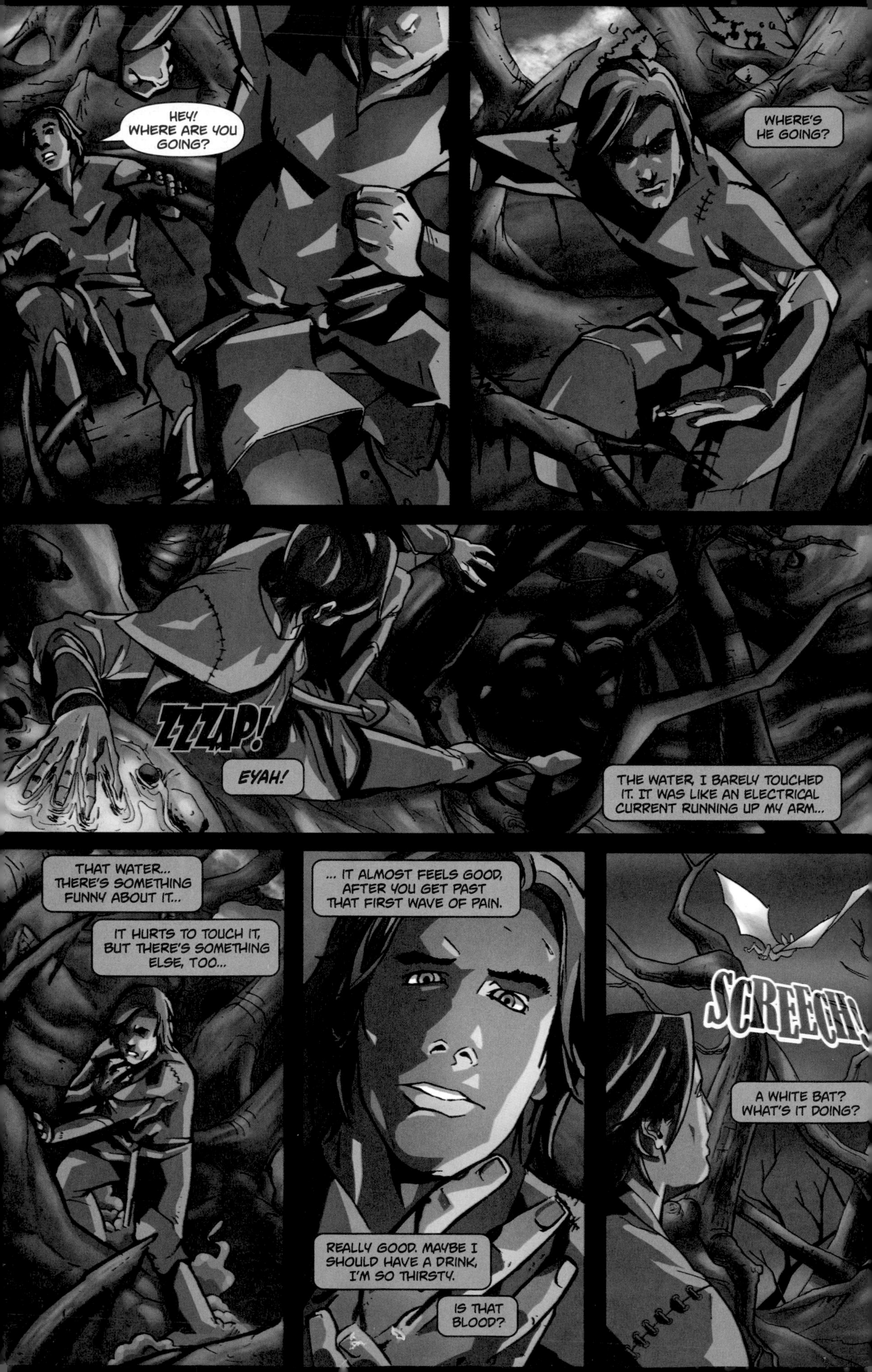
HEY! WHERE ARE YOU GOING?
WHERE'S HE GOING?
ZZZAP!
EYAH!
THE WATER, I BARELY TOUCHED IT. IT WAS LIKE AN ELECTRICAL CURRENT RUNNING UP MY ARM...
THAT WATER... THERE'S SOMETHING FUNNY ABOUT IT...
IT HURTS TO TOUCH IT, BUT THERE'S SOMETHING ELSE, TOO...
... IT ALMOST FEELS GOOD, AFTER YOU GET PAST THAT FIRST WAVE OF PAIN.
REALLY GOOD. MAYBE I SHOULD HAVE A DRINK, I'M SO THIRSTY.
IS THAT BLOOD?
SCREECH!
A WHITE BAT? WHAT'S IT DOING?

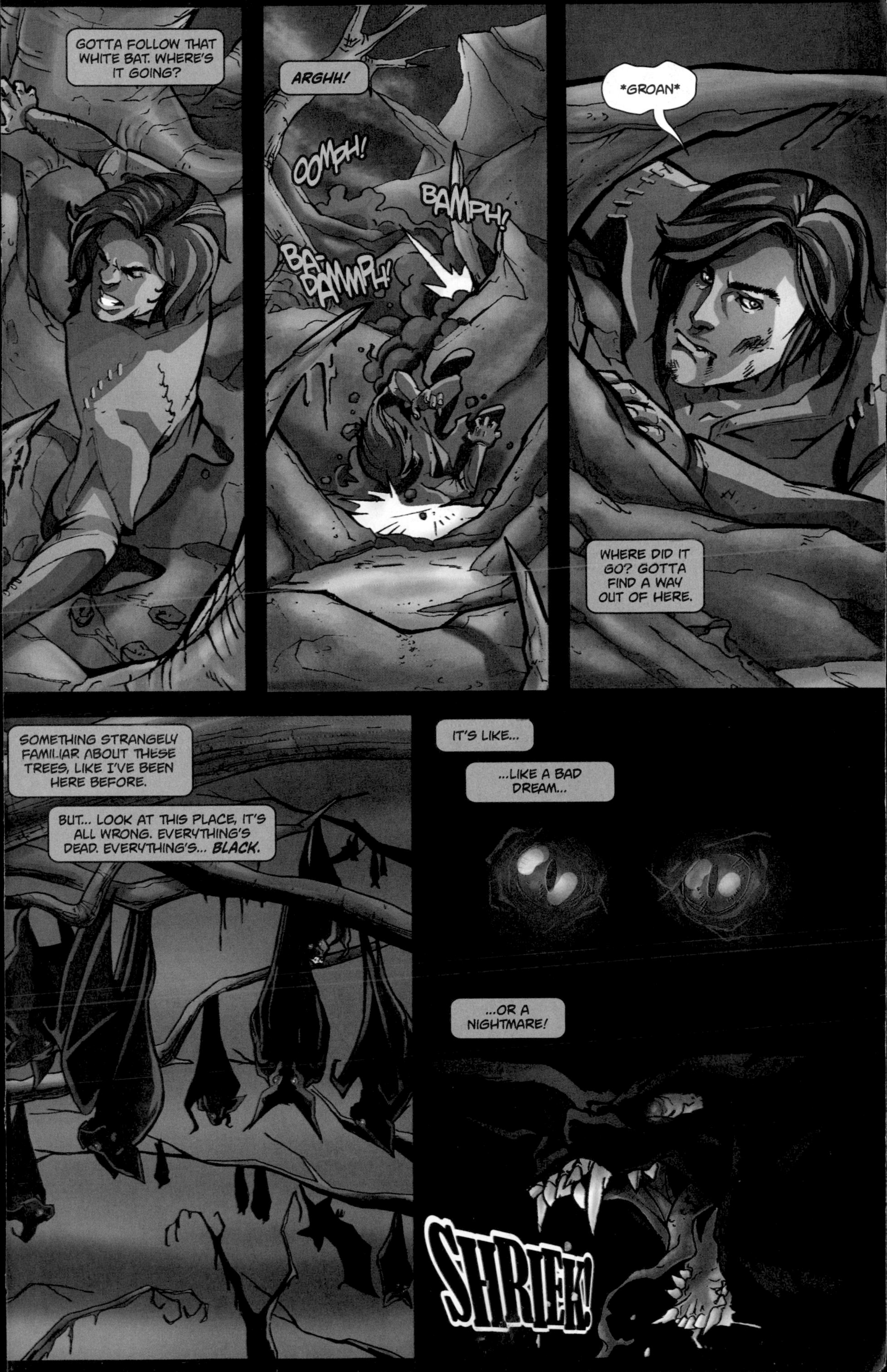
GOTTA FOLLOW THAT WHITE BAT. WHERE'S IT GOING?
ARGHH!
OOMPH!
BAMPH!
BA-DAMMPH!
GROAN
WHERE DID IT GO? GOTTA FIND A WAY OUT OF HERE.
SOMETHING STRANGELY FAMILIAR ABOUT THESE TREES, LIKE I'VE BEEN HERE BEFORE.
BUT... LOOK AT THIS PLACE, IT'S ALL WRONG. EVERYTHING'S DEAD. EVERYTHING'S... BLACK.
IT'S LIKE...
...LIKE A BAD DREAM...
...OR A NIGHTMARE!
SHRIEK!